The Reading for Real Handbook
2nd Edition

The Reading for Real Handbook provides a readable and authoritative account of current theories which underpin reading and the teaching of reading, and offers practical guidance on how to implement these theories.

This new edition has been completely revised to take account of the developments in reading research, and changes in classroom practicalities which have come about as a result of the National Literacy Strategy. The book will help teachers to understand the principles behind the literacy strategy, and how they can make coherent links between the strategy, the learning theories which underpin it, and a continued emphasis on using excellent books across the curriculum. It is essential reading for all teachers in the early and primary years.

Colin Harrison is Professor of Literacy Studies in Education at the University of Nottingham. He is an international expert on reading research and former president of the United Kingdom Reading Association.

Martin Coles is a Reader in Children's Literacy at the University of Nottingham. He was also Co-Director of the *W.H. Smith Children's Reading Choices Project*, the largest investigation into reading habits since the 1970s.

The Reading for Real Handbook
2nd Edition

Edited by Colin Harrison and
Martin Coles

ROUTLEDGE / FALMER
Taylor & Francis Group

London and New York

First edition published 1992 by Routledge
Second edition published 2001 by RoutledgeFalmer
11 New Fetter Lane, London EC4P 4EE

Simultaneously published in the USA and Canada
by RoutledgeFalmer
29 West 35th Street, New York, NY 10001

RoutledgeFalmer is an imprint of the Taylor & Francis Group

Typeset in Goudy by
HWA Text and Data Management, Tunbridge Wells
Printed and bound in Great Britain by
Biddles Ltd, Guildford and King's Lynn

British Library Cataloguing in Publication Data
A catalogue record for this book is available from the
British Library

Library of Congress Cataloging in Publication Data
The reading for real handbook / edited by Colin Harrison
and Martin Coles. – 2nd ed.
    p. cm.
  Includes bibliographical references and index.
  1. Reading–Great Britain. 2. Children–Books and
reading–Great Britain. I. Harrison, Colin, 1945–
II. Coles, Martin, 1952–
LB1050 .R41175 2001
372.4'0942–dc21   2001019930

ISBN 0-415-21995-7

Contents

PART III

How should we encourage children to be readers?

Figures

Contributors

Eric Ashworth was formerly Principal Lecturer in Education at Nottingham Trent University. He has written extensively on children's literacy development, and his book *Language Policy in the Primary School* (1988) was considered seminal in its field. For the past twenty years his writing has emphasised the importance of a coherent, integrated and balanced approach to the teaching of literacy, with reading, writing and spelling taught in a related manner, supplemented by the use of good books which are not just used to teach 'reading', but which are used develop language as a whole.

Margaret Cook has taught throughout the primary and secondary phases in the UK, holding senior management posts in the former. She has also worked as a teacher trainer, a project officer for a family learning programme, and a local inspector for both English and Early Education. She has been actively involved in national testing initiatives in primary education in England for nearly ten years, and is currently a member of both the NFER Key Stage One and Key Stage Two English assessment projects. She is especially interested in the interface between individual assessment and school management.

Martin Coles is a Reader in Children's Literacy at the University of Nottingham, and Academic Manager for The National SCITT (school-centred initial teacher training) in Outstanding Primary Schools. He trained as a primary teacher and taught in Oxfordshire and Zambia. He co-directed the *W H Smith Children's Reading Choices Project*, and is the Series Editor for a new reading programme, *Literacy Land*.

Ros Fisher has taught in primary schools in USA and northwest of England. She is now Reader in Literacy Education at the University of Plymouth working with initial training students and teachers. She has written widely about the teaching of early literacy and is also engaged in research into the implementation of the National Literacy Strategy.

Carol Fox is a Senior Lecturer in Education at the University of Brighton, where she is Subject Area Co-ordinator for English. Most of her teaching and research has focussed on children's literature. She has recently concluded a cross-European project researching the teaching of the children's literature of war and peace, which explored among other themes the issues of bias, national identity, heroism and allegory.

Colin Harrison is a former secondary-school English teacher. Since 1994, he has been Professor of Literacy Studies in Education at the University of Nottingham. He was one of the founding editors of the *Journal of Research in Reading*, and a past President of the United Kingdom Reading Association. He has directed over twenty research projects, mostly in the fields of literacy and information technology.

Tony Martin is head of the Education Development Unit of St. Martin's College, working on in-service projects for teachers and schools in the UK and abroad. These are concerned with teaching and learning and school improvement as well as the specifics of reading and writing. He is a past president of the United Kingdom Reading Association and has published a number of books and articles on different aspects of the teaching of English.

Guy Merchant is Head of the Centre for English in Education at Sheffield Hallam University. His research interests are in the area of literacy development in multilingual contexts. His recent publications include *Co-ordinating Primary Language and Literacy* and *Picture Books for the Literacy Hour*. He was also one of the founding editors of the *Journal of Early Childhood Literacy*.

Jack Ousbey has taught in primary and secondary schools, and in Higher Education. He was an inspector with Nottinghamshire LEA, and a consultant and writer with *Ragdoll*, the children's television company. He now devotes his time to writing, reviewing and running in-service events.

Gervase Phinn is a freelance broadcaster, writer and lecturer, and Visiting Professor of Education at the University of Teesside. He taught in a range of schools for fourteen years before becoming an education adviser and school inspector. He has published many articles, chapters and books about children's literature, as well as collections of his own plays, poems and short stories. He is probably best known for his two best-selling autobiographical novels: *The Other Side of the Dale* and *Over Hill and Dale*, which he read on the BBC 4 programme *Book of the Week*.

Keith J. Topping is director of the Centre for Paired Learning at the University of Dundee, Scotland, working in the interface between education and psychology. He specialises in peer and parent mediated learning, with interests in the promotion of social competence and computer assisted learning and assessment. He works in all sectors of education and many curriculum areas, and has produced nearly two hundred publications, most of which have been in the field of literacy.

Acknowledgements

The editors and publishers wish to express their gratitude for permission to reproduce the following material:

Page 44, quotations from M. Waddell, *Amy Said*, text copyright © 1990 Martin Waddell, illustrated by Charlotte Voake, reproduced by permission of the publisher Walker Books Ltd., London. Page 46, quotations from P. Pearce, 'The Great Sharp Scissors' from *Lion at School and Other Stories*, published by Viking Kestrel, copyright © Phillippa Pearce, 1985. Page 47, quotations from M. Morpurgo, *The Marble Crusher*, published by Egmont. Page 48, quotations from R Swindells, *Hurricane Summer*, published by Egmont Children's Books. Page 76, quotation from *Oxford Children's Encyclopaedia*, 1994 , reprinted by permission of Oxford University Press. Page 78 and Figure 4.4 from A. Royston and G. Hawksley, *My Big Book of the World*, published by Lorenz Books, a division of Anness Publishing Limited. Pages 78 and 85, quotation from J. Barraclough *Jamaica* published by Heinemann, reproduced by permission of Heinemann Educational Publishers, a division of Reed Educational and Professional Publishing Ltd. Page 79, quotation from R. Theodorou and C. Telford, *Polar Bear and Grizzly Bear*, published by Heinemann, reproduced by permission of Heinemann Educational Publishers, a division of Reed Educational and Professional Publishing Ltd. Page 82, quotation from N. Halley, *Eyewitness: Farm* published by Dorling Kindersley. Pages 85 and Figure 4.5, quotations from A.M. Linden, *Emerald Blue*, text copyright © Anne Marie Linden 1994, published by Egmont Children's Books Limited, London. Figure 4.3 from *Factfinders: Countries* by Moira Butterfield, first published in the UK by Franklin Watts in 1993, a division of The Watts Publishing GroupLimited, 96 Leonard Street, London EC2A 4XD. Figure 9.4a 'All About Nicola' from SCAA *Looking at Children's Learning,* London SCAA (page 19 from 'Nicola: "That's my house and that's Daryl's and Sue's"' to 'This is my friend Jessica'). Figure 9.4b Education Department of Western Australia (1997) *First Steps: Reading Developmental Continuum*, Perth Rigby Heinemann.

Phases 1 and 2 from Reading Developmental Chart (Role Play and Experimental Reading). Figure 9.5, Barrs *et al.* Primary Language Record (1988) London ILEA/CLPE, CLPE, Webber St, London SE1 8QW. Figure 9.6, Parent and child records(unpublished) record supplied by the Sefton (UK) Families and School Together Service by kind permission. Figure 9.8, Qualifications and Curriculum Authority, *Target Setting and Assessment in the National Literacy Strategy,* QCA pp 8–9 Uses of assessment (tables only); Figure 9.10 QCA, *Target setting and Assessment in the National Literacy Strategy* p 8 Timescales for assessment (tables only).

Introduction

Colin Harrison and Martin Coles

This is a completely revised edition of the *Reading for Real Handbook*. Current debates about the teaching of reading are at least as vociferous as they were a decade ago, when the first edition was written, and in just about all English-speaking countries, national governments are at least as interventionist in the literacy field as they were a decade ago. What this means is that teachers of reading continue to be vulnerable unless they have not only a clear understanding of what they are doing, but are confident that current research supports their pedagogy. A book published in 1929 by J. Hubert Jagger and entitled *The Sentence Method of Teaching Reading* starts with the words:

> The teaching of reading to little children has been a scholastic battle-ground for generations, a battleground that is strewn with lost causes and exploded delusions.
>
> (Jagger, 1929)

Such controversies still rage on, with teachers very often feeling themselves to be the confused and powerless civilian casualties on the periphery of this battleground.

This book, like its predecessor, attempts to inform teachers and others interested in these issues about the best in current research and practice, but it seeks to avoid taking an adversarial line in the reading debate. We hope it eschews the promotion of any single view and promotes a balanced approach to methodology. We would want to support the point of view taken by those on the Bullock Committee (DES, 1975) which was that

> the difference between good and bad reading teachers is usually not to do with their allegiance to some particular method, but to do with their relationships with children and their sensitivity in matching what they do to each individual child's learning needs.

So this is not a book solely for those who are committed to a storybook approach, nor solely for those who make use of a scheme or schemes. It does, however, try to take account of the fact that we have made progress in our understanding of how children learn to read, and in doing so it attempts to bring together an emphasis on literature, meaning-making and enjoyment in learning to read, together with 'state-of-the-art' thinking and research across an important range of topics: the reading process, the place of 'good' books in a reading programme, hearing children read, the part parents might play, the reading-writing connection, reading across the curriculum, supporting bilingual readers, and providing for children who find learning to read difficult.

Over the past ten years, there have been a series of national enquiries and pronouncements on the teaching of reading in Canada, the USA, Australia, New Zealand, and all of the countries in the UK, and at some point in all these countries there has been additional focusing on the teaching of letter–sound relationships. In this second edition of *Reading for Real Handbook*, therefore, we have given additional attention to the teaching of phonics. We are also aware that the first edition of the *Reading for Real Handbook* was read by teachers all over the English-speaking world. We have attempted, therefore, to make this second edition less Anglo-centric than the first, by avoiding pronouns such as 'here', where 'here' means 'England', and also by providing where necessary a gloss on terms which refer to the English national curriculum or its associated assessment approaches.

This book has two aims. The first is to provide, in a readable and authoritative way, an account of current theories which underpin reading and the teaching of reading. The second is to give practical guidance on how to implement those theories. Rather than simply describing good practice, we aim to offer clear pointers indicating why the practical approaches which are offered for consideration are theoretically sound and can be fully supported by recent advances in theory. Although the book is organised in three parts with the first part putting particular emphasis on theory, each of the authors draws attention to the theoretical underpinning of the practice they are advocating. It is our hope that readers will use the book to reflect on their own classroom practice in teaching reading. As an aid to this reflection there is, at the end of each chapter, a series of questions which are intended as a stimulus to self-reflection and as a potential starting point for staff discussion, as well as an annotated booklist which readers might use to follow up ideas contained in the chapter.

In the opening chapter of Part I, on theories underpinning our overall approach to reading, Colin Harrison offers an overview of our current understanding of the reading process and learning to read. Important though they are, so-called 'psycholinguistic' theories of the reading process can no longer be accepted as fully adequate explanations, and must be integrated into a more complete description, which takes account of new research into processing of information during reading and into how children learn to read. His chapter fully endorses the need for children to have rich, early literacy experiences, but he also suggests, for example, that approaches to teaching reading which ignore the need for children to develop phonemic awareness and an understanding of letter–sound relationships must be inadequate. The major element in these early literary experiences is the texts which children are offered. Jack Ousbey's contribution is a convincing argument that it is impossible to overestimate the importance of good literature. Children can make astonishing progress in reading when their imagination is stimulated by good books. Ousbey argues from first principles that children have a psychological need for such experiences, and that teachers should be encouraged and supported in assisting children to find them through literature. His updated chapter is informed by references to a wide range of books and authors, and some memorable quotations.

An approach which puts increased emphasis on texts chosen by the teacher needs sustaining by careful book choices, and in Part II both chapters address this issue. Gervase Phinn offers advice in the area of children's literature, not only suggesting particular books, but offering ideas about ways teachers can keep themselves informed and updated in relation to this important field. Fiction and poetry are of prime importance, but we are also gradually realising that reading for information and study skills are aspects of the reading curriculum that have been for too long ignored, especially with young children. Such experiences are fundamental to the earliest stages of literacy, and information skills and non-literary texts are now given emphasis in the early stages of all national and state-mandated curricula. Ros Fisher's new chapter explores the ways in which non-narrative texts can be integrated into a real books approach, and she also demonstrates how some story books contain a truer account of other cultures than 'information books'.

In Part III we direct attention to the implementation of good practice in the classroom. In many classrooms the central core of the curriculum for the teaching of reading is the practice of 'hearing children read'. Martin Coles explains how we need to move beyond an 'apprenticeship model', but nevertheless puts an emphasis on the crucial role of the teacher in broadening the reading experiences of children in classrooms. He offers a wide range of suggestions for altering the details of the teacher/child interaction in order to shift the emphasis from a 'read to me' to a 'read with me' approach, in order for the classroom to become a community of readers. A major factor in children's early literacy experiences is the social context in which learning takes place. It is now recognised that instructional practices can offer children unintentional messages about the nature of their learning. Carol Fox's new chapter explores this issue in relation to reading in order that we might ask: 'Do the instructional practices in my classroom give a true picture of what literacy is, what it is for and how it works?'. Early excursions into literacy include attempts at writing as well as reading. We have only recently begun to achieve a satisfactory understanding of the nature of the relationship between early writing and early reading. Eric Ashworth puts this relationship under close scrutiny by discussing the importance of using the child's knowledge of grammar, the relationship between phonemic awareness, learning the alphabet, and early spelling, and he explains how to use current research to ensure that children's first excursions into alphabetic writing are successful. Those who know Eric's work will not be surprised to read his profound reservations about the role of a nationally mandated literacy curriculum in ensuring that children find learning to read an enjoyable and positive experience.

Learning to read does not occur only at school. There is now ample evidence of the significance of parents and other care-givers in the reading development of children. Keith Topping examines evidence of the benefits to children from sympathetic parental involvement in teaching reading. He discusses the differences between parental involvement and parental partnership and outlines recommended practice in this area, updating his chapter with new research evidence into the processes by which partnership approaches come to be effective. Assessment is integral to the teaching process, but there is a variety of ways in which judgements can be made about children's reading, and many ways in which teachers can make use of the information gained. In her new chapter, Margaret Cook discusses how teachers can integrate methods of assessment which are part of a national approach to record-keeping with the need to value the day to day successes that characterise the growth of individual readers.

Are the approaches outlined in the preceding chapters appropriate for children with a reading delay and for those for whom English is not a mother tongue? Award-winning author Tony Martin writes about the ways in which a teacher who wants to use a 'real books' approach can take account of the needs of children who need modified or additional strategies in order to make a good start. Guy Merchant's revised and updated chapter also provides a positive answer. Learning to read and write in more than one language is a significant achievement. There are children in many parts of Great Britain from many different language backgrounds whose bilingualism means they possess a rich and varied knowledge of language, and Guy's chapter explains how teachers can support the multiple literacies of these children in such a way that their confidence in reading English is not built at the expense of other languages in their repertoire.

Anyone brave (or reckless) enough to attempt to write a book on reading owes a number of debts: to the readers from whom they have learned, to the teachers from whom they have learned, and to the scholars from whom they have learned. The editors of this book wish to acknowledge the incalculable debts they owe to their children, students, friends, colleagues and mentors. They are also grateful to readers of the first edition of the *Reading for Real Handbook* for encouraging them to believe that it will continue to be important to support teachers who believe in 'real books', by offering an account of the research which underpins their beliefs and their pedagogy. It is their strong hope that, whatever changes occur in theories of the reading process and the teaching of reading, teachers will never let go of their faith in the power of a book to excite children's minds, and in the value of literacy as one of the most important tools for living.

Bibliography

DES (1975) *A Language for Life*. London: HMSO.
Huey, E. B. (1908) *The Psychology and Pedagogy of Reading*. New York: Macmillan.
Jagger, J. H. (1929) *The Sentence Method of Teaching Reading*. London: Grant Educational.

Part I

What does research tell us about learning to be a reader?

1 The reading process and learning to read

An update

Colin Harrison

A reflection on a confession

In the first edition of this book, I began with the following confession:

> I've thought more about how to begin this chapter than about anything else I've written on reading over the past seventeen years. The reason is that I want to attempt to build a bridge, and I know before I start that the bridge will be a long one, and that my scaffolding and engineering skills may not be up to the task.

On the two islands I wanted to join up were two sets of people: on the first were those whose starting point in looking at the teaching of reading was a belief that learning to read is pointless unless a reader comes to value, enjoy and in some sense possess the books and stories they read. This is the island where (even if they dislike the terms) people believe in 'real books' for 'real readers', and these people are the intended audience for this book. I quoted the work of Margaret Meek (1988) and Liz Waterland (1985), who believe that it is crucial to help children to encounter 'real books', since such children, in Meek's words, 'learn many lessons that are hidden for ever from those who move directly from the reading scheme to the worksheet.'

On the other island were psychologists who have studied and written about the reading process, especially the process of learning to read. I tried to suggest that those who advocate the use of 'real books' are right to place meaning, enjoyment and the stimulation of the imagination at the heart of reading, but that some of their accounts of how children read and come to learn to read have many gaps or inaccuracies, and these may seriously weaken the case for their preferred pedagogy.

Some people were generous enough to tell me that they found what I wrote useful, not only for themselves, but also for others with whom they worked, who were training to be teachers or seeking to upgrade their knowledge. For this reason, I shall retain in this new chapter much of what I wrote in the earlier book. But reading research does not stand still, and over the past ten years, national reading policies have certainly not stood still. In the decade since 1990, governments in most English-speaking countries have chosen to exert greater control over education, and have given particular scrutiny to literacy and to early childhood education. At the same time, while psychologists seem to be in broad agreement about how adults read, there have continued to be fierce debates about how best to teach reading, and these debates have become particularly acrimonious if there is any likelihood of influencing government policy in the literacy field. As I argued in a recent presentation in the USA, 'when research turns to policy, argument gives way to rhetoric' (Harrison, 1999). I want, therefore, before the end of this chapter, to review some of the most recent research, and to bring the threads of argument together around the issue of what should be taught to early readers, and how.

Why do many teachers find the approach of psychologists to describing the reading process unpalatable? Among the reasons why those on the 'real reading' island feel uneasy about communicating with those on the 'cognitive psychology' island is the use made of the term 'skills' in psychology. The title alone of Usha Goswami and Peter Bryant's *Phonological Skills and Learning to Read* (1990) would be enough to convince some people that building a bridge would be an impossibility, since it is to a 'skills' view of reading that they are most opposed. Liz Waterland, for example, felt that most of her unmotivated and unsuccessful readers had been taught too many rather than too few 'skills'. Rejecting the perspectives on the reading process offered by Goswami and Bryant would, however, be very unfortunate, since I would suggest that it is one of the most important books on reading to have been published in recent years. What I must emphasise here is that there is a great difference between a psychologist's defining and giving close attention to one aspect of the reading process, and calling this a 'skill', and it being suggested that this 'skill' should be developed in a decontextualised way. The rationale for the present book is not to boil a 'real books' approach down to a set of 'skills' that can be taught independently of the enjoyment of stories; I am happy to retain the mystery and magic that are in the relationship between a child and a good book. Nevertheless, I feel that it would be immensely valuable for all teachers of reading to have a deeper insight into our current understanding of the psychology of the reading process and of how children learn to read, because this will offer a better theoretical rationale for their pedagogy and will give them a stronger defence for a 'real books' approach. It will also give us better tools for handling those cases in which children do not make a good start.

The reading process: Smith and Goodman were only partly right

Frank Smith and Ken Goodman, by their example and by their writings, enabled many of us to become more knowledgeable about the reading process, and offered legitimacy to many of our own observations of how children read, and of how they learn to read. Ken Goodman's famous dictum that reading is a 'psycho-linguistic guessing game' (Goodman, 1970) became well known and valued by teachers not simply because it seemed to ring true, but because it offered in a pithy phrase a counter-view to another description of reading that some psychologists seemed to be offering. This was the notion that reading was a letter-by-letter decoding operation, in which a person processed text in a manner similar to that in which a computer linked to a speech synthesiser 'reads' information on a disk, proceeding mechanically from letters to sounds, with meaning a low priority, something tacked on at the end of the process. This is clearly not what happens with young children. For them, meaning is paramount, and a book often seems to be not so much a text in which every word needs to be read, but rather a map in which any route is permissible in the journey towards making meaning. Any account of the reading process, or of the process of learning to read, which ignores or denies this fact would be unacceptable to most teachers, since it would contradict the evidence of their professional judgement.

Ken and Yetta Goodman made us aware of the importance of 'miscues' that children make while reading. They taught us how revealing a child's errors in reading can be in enabling us to see the active processes of constructing meaning which go on in the head, and they helped us find ways of monitoring and valuing such information. The Goodmans conducted many interesting studies of children's use of context in their reading strategies. They showed that some children whose word recognition was poor made highly intelligent use of context to help in the search for meaning. And this perspective gave us new respect for the reader as maker of meaning: what the reader brought to the text was just as important as what the text brought to the reader.

Equally, Frank Smith (1971, 1978) did much to make available to a wide audience the results of research into the reading process which emphasised the perspective that 'reading is only incidentally visual', though as Smith always pointed out, this interesting phrase actually came from a paper from another researcher, Paul Kohlers (1968). What Smith stressed was that guessing and hypothesis testing were important aspects of reading. 'Learning to read is not a matter of mastering rules' wrote Smith (1973, p. 184). What teachers needed to start from was the realisation that 'children learn to read by reading'.

However, while much of what Frank Smith and Ken Goodman wrote remains valid, some of what they said is now regarded by psychologists as inaccurate, and there were some crucial omissions. Where they are still thought to be right was in showing how important it is to stress meaning in reading, and that there is no point in the exercise unless it leads to meaning. Smith and Goodman are also held to be correct in stressing the intelligent use of context made by beginning readers to aid word recognition. Where they are now thought to be wrong is to do with the issue of word recognition in the reading process of fluent readers. What I shall argue is that, contrary to some of our long-held beliefs, good readers are *less* reliant on the use of context for word recognition than poor readers.

The most serious omission in the writings of Smith and Goodman is in relation to the detail of how children come to learn to read. Frank Smith wrote: 'children learn to read by reading'. I think that he was correct to say this, but he did not offer details of what precisely children gained from the different stages of learning to behave like a reader. On this crucial issue I shall put emphasis on some concepts which were hardly discussed in the 1970s, but which are too important for us to ignore – and these are *concepts of print, phonemic awareness,* and *analogies in reading.* Each of these topics is important enough to merit detailed treatment. Let me say at the outset, however, that nothing which follows will argue that the teaching of reading should be based on anything other than a child-centred approach, using the best books available.

The reading process: how fluent readers recognise words

Goodman (1970) wrote that reading is 'a selective process. It involves partial use of available minimal language cues selected from perceptual input on the basis of the reader's expectations.' There are two key aspects to the reading process in this account: it is selective, and it is predictive. According to his view, the reader selects graphic cues from the text, which are held briefly in *short-term memory.* The reader then makes tentative decisions about the likely identity of the word or words read, and transfers this information to what Goodman calls *medium-term memory.* Further selective sampling of the text occurs, and the information from this is also transferred to medium-term memory. The tentative accumulated meaning is then checked for its agreement with what is already held in medium-term memory. If it fits in with the prior expectations, in semantic and syntactic terms, the meaning is accepted and transferred into *long-term memory.* If, however, what is encountered next does not match the expected meaning, the reader goes back to the text and scans it again, to pick up further cues, and the cycle continues.

There are all kinds of attractions in Goodman's model. It seems to offer an explanation for the fact that often reading seems a very sloppy process. His suggestion that readers only sample the text very selectively most of the time would appear to explain why, for example, we find it extraordinarily difficult to proofread accurately, and why we not only fail to notice typographical or grammatical errors, but even unconsciously correct them. Equally, Goodman's rich descriptions of how children use context to help build meaning seem to tie in well with his notion of a reader's 'partial sampling of available minimal language cues'. No wonder, therefore, that we tend to follow Goodman in considering the ability to make intelligent use of context to be one of the marks of a fluent reader. On Goodman's view, then, a reader's sampling of the text is 'minimal', but the reader makes maximum use of contextual information in the quest for meaning. Smith's account is very similar to this. He says, 'fluent reading does not normally require the identification of individual words' (1971, p. 105), and at one point goes even further, suggesting that 'the additional stage of word identification involved in mediated comprehension is a snag, a hindrance, not a help to comprehension' (1971, p.207). For this reason, Smith and Goodman are described in the reading research literature as having a 'top–down' model of the reading process. That is, their model relies heavily on prediction and information stored in memory, rather than on information derived from close attention to every word on the page.

In contrast to this view, however, the evidence currently available suggests that for fluent readers the visual processing of text is both fairly complete and very fast, and that most of the time engaging in hypothesis-testing behaviour seems to play a minimal role in the process of word recognition. This may seem surprising, but it is based on evidence collected over thirty years, and by a number of different research groups. This is not to suggest, by the way, that reading is now thought of as a wholly 'bottom–up' process (that is, one in which reading is solely based upon a letter-by-letter analysis of the words on the page, without any input from information stored in memory). The currently accepted view of reading among psychologists is that an *interactive* model of reading best fits the available data, with the reading process largely following a 'bottom–up' model, but with input from 'top–down' processes being used when necessary (an account of all this which is fairly technical, but worth the effort, is the extremely comprehensive book by Rayner and Pollatsek, 1989).

Evidence for the current view comes primarily from eye-movement data, much of which has become available since 1975, the time since which more powerful computers, coupled with new infrared and low-powered laser technology, have permitted much more accurate recording of eye movements than had hitherto been possible (Rayner, 1983; Just and Carpenter, 1985;

Rayner and Pollatsek, 1989). These new and more accurate procedures permit experimenters to know to within a single letter where a reader is fixating (fixing his or her gaze) during reading. We now know that, in normal reading, adults, far from only minimally sampling the graphic information in a text, fixate nearly all words (over 80 per cent of content words, and over 40 per cent of function words, such as *of* or *the)*, and almost never skip over more than two words. Fixations on words generally last from a fifth to a quarter of a second (200–250 milliseconds), and, what is more important, it is now thought that a reader accesses the meaning of a word which is being fixated *before* moving to the next fixation. This *immediacy theory* (Just and Carpenter, 1985) is not fully accepted in every detail by all psychologists, since the theory argues that all processing, including the integration of meaning into the sentence and paragraph, is completed before the eye moves on. Nevertheless, it is broadly accepted, and this has devastating implications for the Smith and Goodman model, since it suggests that under normal conditions word recognition occurs very rapidly, generally in less than a quarter of a second, and – even more importantly – that it occurs automatically, without the reader being dependent on context. Indeed, just as Smith and Goodman (correctly) argued that there isn't enough time for phonemic decoding to take place in the 250 milliseconds of an average fixation, so, it is argued, there is no time for all the hypothesis generating and testing that Goodman's model implies.

The current view, therefore, is that for fluent readers in normal reading, rapid, automatic, context-free word recognition is what occurs most of the time, with fixation duration largely related to the relative word frequency of different words. This model does not deny the use of context as an aid to comprehension, nor is phonemic decoding ruled out, but these are both assumed to be aids to word recognition that are mostly unnecessary for fluent readers. It is in this respect that reading is now regarded as an *interactive-compensatory* process.

The 'interactive-compensatory' model of the reading process

In a celebrated paper, Keith Stanovich (1980) put forward the view that reading should be viewed as an 'interactive-compensatory' process. He suggested that the proportion of time given by any reader to word recognition and to comprehension was not fixed; it was variable, according to the needs of the reader. Stanovich argued that good readers recognised words rapidly because their word recognition was automatic. It was poor readers, by contrast, who needed to make the greatest use of context in order to facilitate word recognition, and they did so at the expense of needing to devote extra time to this part of the process. By 'automatic', researchers mean that the rapid word recognition of a fluent reader is not under conscious control. It therefore takes up very little processing capacity, and this is very important, since this frees processing resources for comprehension. A fluent reader, on the interactive-compensatory model, uses very little processing capacity for word recognition, and is thus able to devote additional mental resources to interpretation. The process is compensatory in that, when necessary, readers compensate by devoting additional resources to the word recognition part of the process.

Stanovich did not, of course, say that it was *bad* to use context in order to help recognise words, only that it took up time and processing capacity. In this respect, one can see why the Smith and Goodman view was so compelling. Frank Smith (1971) made a very similar point to that of Stanovich in his account, when he talked about what he called *mediated meaning identification*, which was his term for word recognition using context or phonemic rules. He wrote:

> Mediated word identification, then, is one way to read for meaning; it is a feasible method, but not the best ... I suggest that mediated word identification is used by any reader, fluent or beginner, only when he has to, and he has to when he finds the passage difficult, when immediate comprehension is not possible.

Smith, however, wrongly believed that letter-by-letter word recognition took up too much time to be feasible in normal reading, and went instead for a model that had the reader moving directly from a light sampling of print to immediate identification of meaning. This was incorrect, but he was on the right lines to search for a model that was rapid, that did not require conscious processing for every word, and which allocated plenty of processing capacity to comprehension. The interactive-compensatory model does this, and in doing so enables us to retain the most important aspect of the Smith and Goodman view, namely that in reading the central goal should always be the quest for meaning. In their descriptions of how beginning readers or poorer readers access meaning their accounts are very close to the 'interactive-compensatory' model.

To sum up, then, where are Smith and Goodman thought to be wrong? The answer is mostly in relation to word recognition in fluent reading. Goodman is now thought to have been wrong in suggesting that in fluent reading only minimal text cues are sampled in the word recognition part of the reading process. Equally, Smith is thought to have been wrong in suggesting that accurate word recognition is 'a hindrance' to fluent reading. What we would now say is that, in fluent reading, word recognition is automatic and rapid. When this is happening, the brain has extra processing capacity available for comprehension. When automatic word recognition is inaccurate or fails, the 'compensatory' mechanisms come into play, and the reader's behaviour approximates more closely to that described by Smith and Goodman. Smith and Goodman were correct in arguing that reading comprehension – for example, in making decisions about what type of text we are reading, or where a story is heading – is a matter of constructing hypotheses which are modified or confirmed. But they were wrong in thinking that word recognition works in this way, except, as we have noted, when the automatic word recognition process fails.

What are the implications of all this? The obvious implication is that accurate, rapid word recognition is really important in fluent reading. It would, however, be unfortunate if such a realisation made some teachers discourage guessing in beginning reading, and revert to a Victorian insistence on accurate, error-free word-attack drills. This would be counterproductive, and the reason is to do with the difference between *being* a fluent reader and *learning to become* a fluent reader. While a child is learning to read, the 'compensatory' part of the reading process is vital. When children are building up confidence, and gradually extending their sight vocabulary, they need to use all the tools available, including intelligent guesswork. Rapid word recognition is important in that it is ultimately one of the facets of good fluent reading. But it is not how we begin, nor is it a goal in its own right. The *purpose* of reading is to gain meaning, not simply to recognise words rapidly. For this reason, it seems wise to add a note on the pedagogical implications of our current view of the reading process, and this is done in the next part of this chapter.

Why we do not need 10,000 flash-cards in a big tin box

At first sight, the realisation that one of the features that distinguishes good readers from poor readers is their ability to use automatic, context-free whole-word recognition would seem to have one inevitable implication – that we should teach children by a 'whole-word' approach. Nothing could be further from the truth. I talked once to a large group of teachers about Stanovich's work, and after my talk, a local English Adviser came up to me and said, 'I'm sure you didn't mean this, but one of my teachers is certain that you've confirmed what she's been wanting to hear since 1960 – that look and say is back! She's ready to make hundreds of new flash-cards!'. Well, the Adviser was correct – I certainly do *not* think that look and say should be revived, and that teachers should now each have a large tin box containing 10,000 words to be used for daily whole-word recognition practice. Having a large vocabulary of rapidly-recognised words is the *result* of being a good reader, not the *cause* of being a good reader, and practising with flash-cards would not necessarily achieve anything except boredom and random guessing for many children. To make the point even more firmly, I would now encourage teachers to accept that what we call 'sight words' (because they are recognised on sight, apparently as wholes) are not processed as 'wholes' at all, but are processed using the same letter-by-letter analysis that takes place in normal fluent reading; it's just that the processing occurs very rapidly (in perhaps a twentieth of a second), and is therefore not apparent to the teacher. What a teacher calls a 'sight word' is also often an exception word in terms of letter–sound relationship (for example *come*, which is not pronounced as in *home* or *tome*), and a child does need to learn such rules. However, having a set of stored pronunciation rules is not incompatible with a letter-by-letter word-recognition process, provided that it works very rapidly.

In the past, whole-word approaches generally stressed some useful aspects of pedagogy – they encouraged children to use picture and context cues, and they often put an emphasis on enjoyment. These approaches are reasonable ones to include as part of the teaching of reading. I cannot imagine any basis, however, on which a decontextualised study of hundreds of flash-cards could be beneficial. If anything, I would sympathise more with the use of flash-cards, on a limited basis, not to teach whole-word recognition but to teach phonics, with, for example, differences between letters and letter groups in individual words being compared. For this very specific purpose, a limited amount of 'decontextualised' analysis of certain words might be defensible. It is worth adding, however, that any 'decontextualised' teaching will be pointless unless it is offered to children in a way that enables them to make connections with what they know and understand already.

How do children learn to be readers? The importance of learning to behave like a reader, and of acquiring four kinds of knowledge

The most fundamental aspect of learning to read is not about skills; it is about learning to behave like a reader. Successful readers pick up books, curl up with them on a bean bag, worry or get excited about what is going to happen to the characters in a story, and later talk spontaneously about what they have been reading to their parents or their friends. As children, many of us became so keen on books that we read under the bedclothes by torchlight, risking the anger or concern of our parents and admonitions that we would ruin our sight. Why does this happen? One answer is that we must have learned that books can give some very special pleasure. Frank

Whitehead (1975) argued that readers have to give more of themselves to a book they are reading than is the case if they are watching television or a film, and that this extra engagement is repaid in our becoming more absorbed, and, ultimately, in our getting closer to the characters about whom we are reading. Put a rather different way by Liz Waterland, reading is more than the sum of its parts; it is like the Tardis – the time machine from the *Dr Who* television series which looked like a 'phone booth from the outside, but a spaceship from the inside. From the outside a book can look relatively innocuous, but once you get inside it, a book can be a time machine, capable of taking you anywhere, and making you a different person from the one who first entered. When Margaret Meek (1988) embarked on her project to teach 'unteachable' children to read, one of her first goals was to enable the young people to obtain some of this sense of enjoyment, of mystery, of commitment to the book they were reading, and to feel that they were doing the things that fluent readers did.

Equally, beginning readers, quite properly, want to feel that they are doing the things that children do when they are successful readers. For this to happen, however, they need to have had certain experiences, and they need to know certain things. They need to have had positive literacy experiences of the sort described in Denny Taylor's *Family Storybook Reading*. These experiences have much in common with those described by Margaret Clark in her book *Young Fluent Readers*. Taylor's book is an ethnographic account of children learning to read and write; Clark's book is written from the point of view of an educational psychologist, and the two books were written 3,000 miles apart, but many of the literacy events described in them are parallel. Taylor writes:

> For Sandy, as with the other children, reading and writing were activities to be shared. They were meaningful, concrete tasks dictated in many ways by the social setting, literate events that occurred as a part of family life, a way of building and maintaining the relational contexts of everyday life.
>
> (Taylor, 1983, p.82)

In the case of Margaret Clark's precocious readers, most had had a good deal of help with reading before the age of four, and this had not been formal tuition; it had been embedded in the social life of the family. Cark writes: 'While half the parents felt the children were helped daily, many stressed that this help was casual rather than systematic, and that it was part of their daily life rather than something separate.'

As well as having experience of a social context in which books are valued, beginning readers need to have at least four other kinds of knowledge:

knowledge of how the world works, knowledge of how language works, knowledge of how stories work, and knowledge of how a book works. This is quite a tall order, but even this isn't the end of the list. If they are to learn to read without much difficulty, they need two more things, which are going to help them cope with the challenge of learning to read in English: one is not directly concerned with print, and the other has everything to do with print. The first is *phonemic awareness*, the second is an ability to learn to recognise new or unfamiliar words by generating *analogies*. Before talking about these final two aspects, let's briefly consider the four knowledge areas. A brief consideration is all that is needed in this chapter, because other chapters in this book will deal with these much more fully.

It may seem trite to mention it, but in order to understand a text, we need knowledge of the world. We are able to generate hypotheses about what's happening in a text because we know things about the world, and how things happen in it. A story which begins, such as Russell Hoban's *A Birthday for Frances*, with a reference to a little sister's birthday can only be understood if the reader or listener knows a good deal about families, and how birthdays tend to be celebrated in Western cultures. This may seem obvious, but of course children from different cultures celebrate birthdays in very different ways. So cultural knowledge and knowledge of social conventions are necessary to understand this book, and to understand the events which happen, such as writing cards and singing *Happy Birthday,* and the tug-of-war in Frances's mind between generosity and selfishness in relation to her sister's present.

The second type of knowledge needed by a reader is of how our language works. A child needs not only a vocabulary but also an understanding of how the language fits together, and a familiarity with many different syntactic structures. Russell Hoban often uses simple vocabulary to express quite complex ideas, but he also often transforms that vocabulary, in ways which make challenging demands on a reader. The linguistic transformations in the story are simple, but unusual, and produce sentences that are complex in structure as well as in terms of its abstract content. The language knowledge needed here is not that of formal linguistic description, of course; what the child needs is a familiarity with the forms the author uses, so that it can recognise and comprehend what is happening in the story.

Knowledge of how stories work is also very important in early reading. Half the fun for children comes from their being able to anticipate what might happen, and from finding that their guess is confirmed, or, better still, finding that what follows is a surprise, albeit an unexpected but satisfying one. This can only happen if the author and the reader share a common 'grammar' of story structure, in which certain events are predictable. A story which begins:

Once upon a time there was a little girl who didn't like going to school. She always set off late. Then she had to hurry, but she never hurried fast enough.

(Pearce, 1976)

is probably going to be a fairy story or a tall story, we would guess, since the phrase 'once upon a time' often signals the opening of a fairy story. The little girl is doing something wrong, in always arriving late at school, so we might guess that she is going to have to resolve some conflict when she does arrive at school in this story. In fact she meets a lion, who asks her to take him to school. Do children expect the lion to eat the little girl? No, even very young children know that this is very unlikely, because the girl has been introduced to us as the main character – so perhaps it's more likely that she will do something heroic involving the lion before the story ends, probably happily. Children's understanding of narrative structure (often very detailed as a result of their watching television) can be very sophisticated. It certainly is one type of knowledge which a reader needs to have, and which nearly all children bring to the classroom when they start school (even if their familiarity with books is low), and upon which the teacher can draw.

The fourth type of knowledge that children need to have in order to begin to read concerns the conventions of print, and familiarity with how a book is put together, Marie Clay's *Concepts of Print* test (Clay, 1979) covers many of these conventions, running from understanding how a book is held and which way up illustrations should be, to much more complex things such as being able to point to speech marks, words, and capital letters. One important point should be made here. Knowledge of the concepts of print is quite a good correlate of early reading competence, but we should beware the causal fallacy – children who are already familiar with books do well at this test, but it would be inappropriate for a teacher to teach these concepts independently of reading good books for enjoyment. Children who have had books read to them are those who become familiar with the concepts of print. For example, a child enjoying the teacher's sharing of *Not Now, Bernard* (McKee, 1980) can readily make an informed guess as to where the word 'ROAR!' is on the page, and can begin to learn to associate speech marks with speech.

It is important for beginning readers to have these four types of knowledge, but let me emphasise once again that we should not wait for a child to acquire them before embarking upon developing that child's literacy. Children gain and develop all four types of knowledge in many social situations, from watching television to going to the shops, but teachers can also develop this knowledge systematically. A teacher who uses a book such as the wonderful *The Lighthouse Keeper's Lunch* (Armitage and Armitage, 1989) will be doing this. *The Lighthouse Keeper's Lunch*, while being a delight to read just as a story, can incidentally develop children's understanding of science, problem-solving, justice, geography, and food. The book also makes fascinating use of quaint vocabulary, and has a story structure which echoes many of Aesop's fables, dealing as it does with the problem of outwitting greedy seagulls. As teachers, one of our most important goals is to help children to become skilled readers, and developing their book-related knowledge is an important part of this. However, unless we also have the goal of helping children to become enthusiastic and self-motivated readers, we may find our efforts ineffectual. Being more aware of the components of knowledge that make up reading can make us more effective teachers, so long as we are aware of the dangers of a utilitarian approach, and we work to avoid teaching the components in a fragmented and incoherent way.

The importance of phonemic awareness and learning by analogy in reading – and why we do not need 'death by phonics'

It is now about thirty years since I plucked up courage and asked Keith Gardner, former UK Reading Association president, what seemed to me at the time to be a very reasonable question: 'Which approach is right? "Look and say" or "phonics"?' In retrospect the question seems embarrassingly naive. I was a seconded comprehensive schoolteacher a few weeks into work on a national reading project (I learned later that the project had been required to take on what one of the team described as 'an airy-fairy English Lit. type' – this was me). Keith Gardner smiled at me: 'Both,' he said, 'but you're asking the wrong question.' He could equally have said that the language experience approach was also 'right', that developing reading through counselling was 'right', and that *Breakthrough to Literacy* was 'right', for each approach has been found to lead to children becoming successful readers, according to various researchers.

The main reason the question is so naive, however, is because it is now generally accepted that children need to be able to develop both a whole-word approach and a phonological approach in recognising words. Automatic, rapid, context-free word-recognition is one of the hallmarks of fluent reading, but a phonological approach to word recognition is necessary for words which are not yet well-enough known to be recognised automatically. As we have seen, children also need to be able to make use of context and all the other types of knowledge they can make available (remember – the fluent reader still makes use of context – but is not dependent upon it for word recognition). So what's the problem? The problem is that 'phonics' and real reading have not been good bedfellows. This is because one of the prime aims of the real books movement has been to stress that reading is *not* about decoding. It is about teaching children to learn to be readers. Liz Waterland argues that conventional practice in schools concentrates on the wrong things. She refers to those who are 'obsessed with teaching decoding' (1985, p. 15), and if her tone seems harsh, we should remember that she is not so much challenging the approach of other professionals as describing her own practice in earlier years.

Very few teachers would disagree with the suggestion that it is valuable for beginning readers to acquire the ability to work out how to recognise words they have not met before. The issue, however, is how this ability is acquired, and this leads us to a conundrum: how is it that some of the poorest readers in our schools are the ones who have had years of teaching of 'phonics'? This problem puzzled me for years, and yet the answer is simple, and comes in two parts. One answer is that the reader may have been taught phonics in a poor or ineffectual way, but the second answer is that no child can profit from the teaching of phonics unless they have *phonemic awareness*. It is very important for us to understand that phonemic awareness is totally different from 'phonics'. Phonemes are the small units of sound which go to make up a word; phonemic awareness is the ability to hear sounds in our head and to categorise them, and is not directly about print. 'Phonics' is about the relationship between sounds and print. Phonemic awareness is what you have if you can play 'I spy'. It is what you have if you can say which of these three words (said aloud) is the odd one out because it does not rhyme: 'fish, dish, *book*'. Unless you have phonemic awareness, therefore, it is impossible to learn 'phonics'.

Many teachers who sympathise with a real books approach are uneasy about whether they should teach 'phonics' systematically. The answer is that in many respects this is the wrong question. What we need to consider is a prior question: how is it that many children come to learn to read without any instruction? What exactly have they learned, and can we help to ensure that what they have picked up without direct instruction is made available to all children? Can we provide the same types of experiences that Denny Taylor's and Margaret Clark's young fluent readers had, so that learning to read does indeed happen 'naturally', but does not happen by chance? I would suggest that we can, but that in making this happen we will be on much stronger ground if we can underpin our pedagogy by research.

We know that children who read early have had the cultural experiences described in the previous section, and that parents who read to their children pass on and develop the four types of knowledge necessary for reading. In recent years, however, we have also come to understand much more about the importance of phonemic awareness, for it is now thought that this is a vital part of the learning-to-read process. Evidence for this comes from a number of sources, but the best known researchers in the field are Lynette Bradley, Usha Goswami and Peter Bryant. Since the early 1980s, these researchers have been developing three arguments through a series of projects. The first is that there is a strong correlational link between knowing nursery rhymes and acquiring phonemic awareness; the second is that there is a strong correlation between acquiring phonemic awareness and learning to read; the third is that these connections are causal ones. As we have already noted, establishing causal connections is very difficult, but Bryant and his co-workers believe that in their longitudinal studies of more than twenty schools they have established such a connection.

The good news for those who support a 'real reading' approach is that these research findings offer tremendous endorsement for the things parents and teachers already do, and indicate the importance of time spent on nursery rhymes, action rhymes and word games as crucial elements in developing literacy. The book by Goswami and Bryant (1990) referred to earlier gives a detailed account of their argument, but the position is also well summarised in a journal article. It is worth quoting from the abstract to this article, since it puts their argument in a nutshell:

> Nursery rhymes are an almost universal part of young English-speaking children's lives. We have already established that there are strong links between children's early knowledge of nursery rhymes at 3;3 and their developing phonological skills over the next year and a quarter. Since such skills are known to be related to children's success in learning to read this result suggests the hypothesis that acquaintance with nursery rhymes might also affect children's reading. We now report longitudinal data from a group of 64 children from the age of 3;4 to 6;3 which support this hypothesis. There is a strong relation between early knowledge of nursery rhymes and success in reading and spelling over the next three years even after differences in social background, I.Q. and the children's phonological skills at the start of the project are taken into account.
>
> (Bryant *et al.*, 1989)

The causal connection is established through a somewhat complex statistical argument which is a little difficult to summarise. It is based on a multiple regression procedure whereby the effects of a number of variables which are correlated with subsequent success in reading and spelling, such as social background, IQ and initial phonological skill, are removed, and at the final stage one is left with a relationship between the two key factors – in this case, nursery rhyme knowledge at age three, and reading and spelling at age six. What Bryant and his co-workers found was that children's knowledge of nursery rhymes did indeed predict success in reading and spelling two to three years later, and, more importantly, that this connection was not the result of differences in the children's intelligence or social background, or even in their initial phonological knowledge, because all these variables were controlled. What Bryant argued was that familiarity with nursery rhymes was what enabled children to become familiar with rhymes, which in turn led to their acquiring phonological awareness, which in turn helped them to succeed in reading.

The next question to consider is precisely *why* phonemic awareness is so important, and to answer it we return to one of Frank Smith's sayings, that we learn to read by reading. What exactly did Frank Smith mean? How is it that simply by reading we come to read more successfully? The answer to this question takes us to our final theoretical concept – the use of analogies in reading. What I want to suggest is that as children practise their reading not only do they develop their knowledge of the world, and widen their knowledge of language, text types, and print conventions, they also use analogies to increase gradually the store of words they can recognise easily and rapidly. This is why reading new books and rereading old favourites are both so important. What are the stages in which this happens?

Initially, as most parents know, children begin by 'reading' books they know off by heart. This is indeed reading, though at an elementary level; children can match the words on the page to the words of a story they know and enjoy. A word is 'read' without any phonemic segmentation, and words are matched by rote association with those in the story. In the first year of formal schooling, if they have not done so before, children begin to be able to 'read' in this way. At the same time, they become more familiar with printed words in a wide range of contexts: as labels, on posters, on displays and in new books. The teacher reads books to and with the children, encourages the learning of letters and sounds through games, stories and poems, and begins to develop early writing activities. But at this first stage a child's reading is very context-dependent. A child can read a book he or she knows, but can't recognise words from it in isolation. Equally, a child can say that a sign says 'STOP' or wrapper says 'Mars', but he or she would not recognise the word if the case of the letters were altered.

Then comes the 'click'. This second stage is in some ways the most exciting for the child, the teacher and the parents. Following models of active meaning-making which the teacher and others have provided, children begin to do three things at once: they begin to use context to make predictions about what is happening in a story, they begin to use semantic and syntactic cues to help make predictions about individual words, and they also begin to make rudimentary analogies in order to help in word recognition. This is when real reading begins, and when the encouragement of intelligent guessing is enormously helpful to the beginning reader, for there must be guessing at this stage. What will make the guessing most valuable will be feedback, discussion and encouragement. Wild guessing can lead to frustration, but if there is a supportive dialogue between the beginning reader and a fluent reader, the beginner can learn from the model of the fluent reader how meaning is built up and how guessing can best be used. The use of analogies is crude at this stage; a child may be able to guess a word using the initial letter as a clue, but little more. The analogy may be no more sophisticated than 'the word *cat* starts with a *c*, so perhaps this new word which begins with *c* is going to begin with the same sound'. Nevertheless, one can appreciate the crucial part played by phonemic awareness in making analogies even at this early stage. However, children can only make this type of simple analogy if they have three things – letter knowledge, letter–sound correspondence knowledge and the ability to hear the sound of the first phoneme in a word so that they can transfer it to another context.

I said earlier that in order to benefit from the teaching of phonics, a child needs to have phonological awareness, but I also emphasised that the teaching of letter–sound relationships needs to be done well, so that a reader can operate independently and benefit from his or her natural ability to generate analogies and thus to recognise new words. This does not need a two-year programme of worksheets, in which learning the letters of the alphabet becomes more important than becoming familiar with Wibbly Pig, Farmer Duck or the Owl Babies. Phonological awareness is crucial for generating analogies, but I would also stress that there is an increasing consensus among experts – including real books advocates – that children will only generate analogies successfully if they also have a basic understanding of letter–sound relationships, i.e. they (i) know the letters of the alphabet and how they are commonly pronounced, and (ii) know how to represent as letters the sounds they hear a word make in their head. I shall return to the issue of how these different types of knowledge are integrated at the end of this chapter.

The use of the term 'stages' may appear to suggest that children's reading development progresses in a fixed and regular pattern. Of course it does not. Children accelerate and regress within a stage, depending on the book they are reading and their mood. But in general this is how progression takes place, and it takes most children a year or more to move to the third stage, in which more complex analogies are made. It is in this third stage that children make tremendous progress in word recognition, using the knowledge that a word can probably be decoded by analogy with other known words. Early analogies are based on rhymes and initial letters, but later children are able to work out how to recognise a word which they have not seen before based upon other sound or spelling patterns, such as recognising *wink* from the analogous word *tank.* Equally, a word with a complex spelling pattern, such as *fight,* may be recognised by analogy with the word *light.* Over a period of perhaps two years, children use their ability to make analogies, together with other sources of information in the text, to assist in word recognition. They gradually increase the number of words they can recognise rapidly, without the need for recourse to the slower processes of using context or decoding by analogy, until they reach the final stage, which is that of the independent reader. For most children, this stage is reached between the ages of 8 and 10. The independent reader can not only analyse words into phonemes when necessary, but he or she can also use 'higher-order' rules to decode difficult words such as *cipher,* in which the *c* is soft because it precedes the letter *i.*

In order for children to become fluent readers it is not enough to be intelligent, to have supportive teaching, to know your letters, and to have phonological awareness. In order to become fluent readers, children have to read, and they have to read widely. It is very valuable for children to reread favourite books, for enjoyment, but also because initially it is unlikely that every word will have been transferred to their rapid sight-vocabulary store. Analogies can only be made by generalising from well-known and retrievable words, so rereading old favourites may have extra value in reinforcing that reservoir of words from which analogies can be made. But to become a fluent reader, a child needs to generate thousands of analogies, and clearly this cannot be done on the basis of just a few books. Here, then, is support from research for the most deeply held belief of 'real reading' teachers – that children learn to read by reading. Put the other way, you can't learn to read *without* reading – there isn't a short-cut. A child who reaches the second stage but who chooses not to read will be likely to remain at that stage, and *become* a poor reader, even if he or she did not start out with any reading problem.

The final point to make in this section is the importance of offering children good books which are valuable in their own right, but which also develop phonological awareness. There are dozens of such books, and in this chapter I shall mention only two. *The Cat in the Hat* and *Each Peach Pear Plum. The Cat in the Hat* is a wonderful example of a book that teaches through fun. It is subversive, dramatic, humorous and simple to read, and children go back to it time and again, often for years, enjoying the cat's scrapes and adventures. It is easy to read because 'Dr Seuss' wrote the book in simple, uncluttered rhymes, with repetition and rhyming never obtrusively dominating the story. In a different way, Janet and Allan Ahlberg's *Each Peach Pear Plum* uses repetition and rhyme in a beautifully controlled manner to lead the reader on a journey in which a gallery of characters eventually meet together when Baby Bunting is rescued and plum pie is enjoyed by everyone. This story is perfect in structure and wonderfully illustrated. Its use of rhyme and repetition is incidental to the story, but was no accident. The story includes rhymes and themes with which many children are familiar from well before they began to learn to read, but this is why so many very young children love the book – it is precisely because of this familiarity that they can read it easily.

Many reading scheme books give special attention to offering repetition and a sequenced development of phonemes and letter clusters, in order that children are faced with a gentle slope of learning. This is entirely reasonable, but what the teacher must decide is whether the book is valuable in its own right, too. There are some delightful books in some reading schemes, and equally there are some awful 'real books'. The important point for the teacher to bear in mind is that, by one route or another, a child will need to read extensively in order to become fluent.

What then needs to be in place in order for a child to learn to read? I have attempted to summarise my answer to this question in Figure 1.1, together with some implications, as I see them, for what the teacher should do in the classroom. The aim in including this table is to demonstrate that the research literature, in this case, a major government-sponsored US review of the research into early reading instruction (Snow *et al.*, 1998), fully supports the approach I am advocating in this chapter, and that there is no theoretical impediment to our arguing for a 'real books' approach, so long as it includes all the appropriate skill development.

It should be clear now why we do not need death by 'phonics'. Instead, teachers' priorities should be on introducing phonemic awareness, through word games, poems, 'rapping' and nursery rhymes. Teachers should also ensure that included on their bookshelves are books that develop phonemic awareness. Next, they should ensure that children have opportunities to move through the four stages of reading described earlier in this section by developing their confidence, extending their enjoyment of books, and widening the number of rapidly-recognised words through using a wide range of reading material. Finally, while all these things are happening, most children will benefit from explicit teaching of letter–sound relationships.

I have included one further table in this chapter. Figure 1.2 offers some suggestions, also derived from research, but this time using a more eclectic perspective, on how the teaching of letter-sound relationships might be approached (see Harrison, 1999, for a fuller rationale for the suggestions). This table puts more emphasis on phonics, and touches areas which are not developed in this chapter, such as the reading-writing-spelling connections,

Effective teaching of letter-sound relationships can only occur if	*Pedagogical implications*
• the teaching of phonics takes place within a programme which forges coherent links between the learning of letter–sound relationships and the fundamental purposes of *reading for meaning* and for personal gratification or development	• make phonics fun. • link phonics to texts which are both worthwhile and fun [eg *The Cat in the Hat*]. • links phonics to texts which have significance for the readers [eg texts they have composed themselves].
• the learning of phonics occurs in parallel with the reader's becoming aware of the nature of books and the concepts of print	• introduce the reading of stories and sharing of big books both before and alongside the teaching of phonics.
• the teaching of phonics takes place within a programme that forges coherent links between the development of *reading, writing and spelling*	• plan the teaching of reading, writing and spelling in a single, coherent programme, and continuously reinforce the relationship between these for the learner
• the learner already has, or is in the process of acquiring, *phonological awareness*	• develop, and continue to develop phonological awareness from the earliest stages of infancy, in the family, and with the emphasis on enjoyment rather than formal attention to the phonemes of English
• the learner has, or is in the process of acquiring, *letter knowledge*, the ability to recognise and discriminate between the letters of the alphabet, both upper and lower case	• encourage children's exposure to informal print-related activities during pre-school years; don't worry too much about possible confusions between case, but try to emphasise lower case and letter sounds in preference to upper case and letter names

• effective reading instruction must also include:
  • extensive *practice* in reading
  • exposure to a *variety* of worthwhile texts
  • continuing to develop the reader's *oral language* and *world knowledge*
	• beginning readers should be offered:
	  • opportunities to reread enjoyable, familiar texts
	  • opportunities to read interesting, worthwhile, unfamiliar texts, including non-fiction and picture books
	  • talk and dramatic play activities

Figure 1.1 What needs to be in place for the teaching of phonics to be effective? (Adapted from Snow (1998), Chapter 6)

which are also enormously important, and in which a real books approach can make learning both enjoyable and effective. Again, the intention is not to burden the teacher or the child with a decontextualised 'skills' approach, but to recognise that there are some aspects of learning to read

Effective teaching of letter–sound relationships	Pedagogical implications
• build on a reader's *phonological awareness*	• develop, or continue to develop this, through verbal play, rhyming activities, clapping or tapping games
• develop *letter knowledge* • *teach spelling* at the same time as you teach reading • *don't worry* about children using invented spelling • *praise* and gently try to emphasise correct spelling from the outset • teach familiarity with the names of *letters of the alphabet after* – not before – teaching letter sounds • do not assume that *environmental print* will of itself induce understanding – it will enhance learning only as a supplement to other more direct instructional methods	• develop familiarity with letters and letter sounds. • help children to recognise a letter's sound wherever they encounter it • encourage children's writing of letters • encourage the child's spelling aloud of such words • discuss 'temporary' spellings • use plastic letters, letter blocks or letter cards, to help children who are just beginning to learn to write • be systematic: make sure that children get help in learning to recognise all basic sounds
• develop *segmentation ability* • help children to segment words into *onset and rime* parts (develop the ability to segment independently of the ability to understand or recognise rhymes) • help children to segment words into *syllables*	• offer teacher-given models of segmenting words into onset and rime in order to sound them out • make use of what we have learned about the staged development of children's ability to use analogies • focus on initial letters and letter groups first • offer teacher-given models of how to segment words into syllables in order to pronounce, recognise and spell them
• *link* the teaching of reading and writing	• teach common spelling conventions; reinforce these in both reading and writing contexts • make use of words grouped by spelling patterns

Figure 1.2 How to teach phonics effectively

which involve skills, and that our teaching is more effective if we are aware of these, and how and why they might best be developed.

How should teachers support children in becoming good readers?

Margaret Clark's young fluent readers were avid readers (1976, p.50). Their parents found it difficult to tell researchers what type of reading their child preferred because they 'devoured anything in print that was available'. These children became in many important respects independent readers before the age of seven. Every one of the children identified in Clark's study had had the good fortune to have been in the presence of 'an interested adult with time to spare to interact in a stimulating, encouraging environment'. Time is always the teacher's enemy, but allies in the form of other adults and older children can assist in offering that 'stimulating, encouraging environment'. In his book on adolescent reading, Frank Whitehead (1975) considered the factors which were associated with avid reading. He found that one factor was more important than any other – and that was the teacher. In Whitehead's study, in every case of a school in which children read many more books than the average, a teacher (and sometimes it was just one in a whole school) was identified as an important provider of encouragement, enthusiasm and resources. A teacher's enthusiasm and encouragement are the greatest gifts they can share with the children they teach, for without them any amount of resources and knowledge may be potentially barren. But knowledge and resources are important, too, and this book attempts to disseminate knowledge and identify some useful resources.

It has been asserted by some that 'real reading' approaches are theoretically corrupt, unstructured and dangerous. On the first point, this chapter has attempted to argue that current research and theory can firmly underpin a 'real books' approach, and in certain respects can offer a more solid, coherent and complete framework for teaching reading than would be possible for some other approaches. On the second point, I would argue that good teaching is never unstructured, and this view is shared by all the authors of the subsequent chapters, whose aim is to help provide that structure, with their own links to current theory ensuring that the foundations of the structure are firm. On the third point I plead guilty – teaching children to read certainly is dangerous, for a child who is an independent reader is a powerful person, and much more likely to have a spirit of independence as a learner. Such a reader is likely to be a challenging critic of what he or she reads, and may well learn from books that both teachers and authors can be wrong. Once we teach children to read, and give them independence, we have a responsibility to help guide their reading, but we cannot teach them how to respond to what they read; we give up that right. Teachers have known for some time what always seems to come as a surprise to politicians: real education *is* dangerous.

Questions for personal reflection or group discussion

1   Has this chapter challenged any of the views you hold? If so, which, and in what ways?

2 How does this account of the reading process tie in with your knowledge of how beginning readers read?

3 Are there any parts of this chapter with which you disagree? What sort of evidence could resolve any such disagreements?

4 What are the implications of this chapter for the teaching of reading in your classroom?

5 What is the difference between 'phonics' and 'phonemic awareness'?

6 What is the difference between teaching 'phonics' and teaching the more extensive use of analogies?

7 How is a wholehearted approach to developing reading through literature compatible with an approach which encourages the development of phonemic awareness, the use of context when necessary, and the use of analogies?

Recommended readings

Goodman, K. (1970) 'Reading: a psycholinguistic guessing game'. In H. Singer and R. B. Ruddell (eds) *Theoretical Models and Processes of Reading.* Newark Delaware; International Reading Association. One of the most important and influential papers on the reading process to appear in the past thirty years. Still more right than wrong.

Goswami, U. and Bryant, P. (1990) *Phonological Skills and Learning to Read.* Hove, East Sussex: Lawrence Eribaum. Quite hard work if you're unfamiliar with the psychological literature, but it tells in detail the story of research into phonological awareness and the formation of analogies.

Snow, C.E., Burns, S. and Griffin, P. (eds.) (1998) *Preventing Reading Difficulties in Young Children.* Washington, DC: National Academy Press. Catherine Snow and her colleagues had a difficult challenge in reviewing the research on this topic in a government-funded initiative, but the consensus view is that they did a good job. Their report is also available over the Internet (at the time of publication of this Second Edition, the report could be located on the Internet via the AmericaReads site or at *http://stills.nap.edu/html/prdyc/*).

Taylor, D. and Strickland, D. (1986) *Family Storybook Reading.* An American account of how to develop literacy in the home. Caring and quietly passionate about the importance of reading.

Bibliography

Armitage, R. and Armitage, D. (1989) *The Lighthouse Keeper's Lunch,* Storytime Giants series. Edinburgh: Oliver &: Boyd.

Bryant, P. E., Bradley, L., MacLean, M. and Crossland, J. (1989) 'Nursery rhymes, phonological skills and reading'. *Journal of Child Language,* 16, 407–28.

Clark, M. M. (1976) *Young Fluent Readers.* London: Heinemann Educational.

Clay, M. M. (1979) *The Early Detection of Reading Difficulties.* Auckland, New Zealand: Heinemann Educational, for Octopus Publishing.

Goodman, K. (1970) 'Reading: a psycholinguistic guessing game'. In H. Singer and R. B. Ruddell (eds.) *Theoretical Models and Processes of Reading*. Newark, DE: International Reading Association.

Goswami, U. and Bryant, P. (1990) *Phonological Skills and Learning to Read*. Hove: Lawrence Erlbaum Associates.

Harrison, C. (1999) 'Is it feasible to attempt to base a national literacy strategy on research evidence?' A report on the implementation of the National Literacy Strategy in England. Presentation given to the National Reading Conference, Orlando, Florida, 1 December 1999.

Hoban, R. (1968) *A Birthday for Frances*. Harmondsworth: Penguin Books.

Just, M. A. and Carpenter, P. A. (1985) *The Psychology of Reading and Language Comprehension*. Newton, MA: Allyn & Bacon.

Kohlers, P. (1968) 'Reading is only incidentally visual'. In K. S. Goodman and J. T. Fleming (eds) *Psycholinguistics and the Teaching of Reading*. Newark, DE: International Reading Association.

McKee, D. (1980) *Not Now, Bernard*. London: Andersen Press.

Meek, M. (1988) *How Texts Teach What Readers Learn*. Stroud: Thimble Press.

Pearce, P. (1976) 'Lion at school'. In D. Jackson and D. Pepper (eds) *The Yellow Storyhouse*. Oxford: Oxford University Press.

Rayner, K. (ed.) (1983) *Eye Movements in Reading: Perceptual and Language Processes*. New York: Academic Press.

Rayner, K. and Pollatsek, A. (1989) *The Psychology of Reading*.
Englewood Cliffs, NJ: Prentice Hall International.

Smith, F. (1971) *Understanding Reading*. New York: Holt, Reinhart Winston.

Smith, F. (1973) *Psycholinguistics and Reading*. New York: Holt, Reinhart Winston.

Smith, F. (1978) *Reading*. Cambridge: Cambridge University Press.

Snow, C.E, Burns, M.S and Griffin, P. (eds) (1998) *Preventing Reading Difficulties in Young Children*. Washington DC: National Academy Press.

Stanovich, K. (1980) 'Toward an interactive-compensatory model of individual differences in the development of reading fluency'. *Reading Research Quarterly*, 16, 32–71.

Taylor, D. (1993 *Family Literacy*. London: Heinemann

Taylor, D. and Strickland, D. (1986) *Family Storybook Reading*. Portsmouth, NH: Heinemann Educational.

Waterland, E. (1985) *Read With Me: An Apprenticeship Approach to Reading*. Stroud: Thimble Press.

Whitehead, F. (1975) *Children's Reading Interests*. London: Evans/ Methuen Educational for the Schools Council.

2 Building a house of fiction

A little, daily miracle

Jack Ousbey

The effortless ease with which young children learn often disguises the range and complexity of their learning. We have always known that the pre-school years are important in terms of intellectual as well as social and physical development, and we are now finding out more about the spectacular changes that occur at this time. We know, for instance, that the structure of the brain changes, not according to a pre-determined plan but by the way it is used, by the information it extracts from the environment, and by the experiences it encounters which arouse interest and curiosity. And the size and quality of this growth are not just a matter of genetic inheritance, they are inextricably and powerfully bound up with the opportunities we provide for the developing brain to hook up with, and share in the consciousness of older and more experienced brains. New meanings, imaginative expansion and greater understanding are nudged into being by such interactions, and the foundations of symbolic thought are laid. By the age of five a child will have set in place more than 50 per cent of its intellectual growth. Consider the first five years of Jenny's life.

Even before she was born, books were part of Jenny's experience. In the last few weeks of pregnancy her mother sang and read to her for a few minutes everyday, believing that the musical sounds of language would help to form a strong bond between parent and child. Jenny had parents, and grandparents, who read regularly to her and in the first few weeks of life, was meeting up with Miffy, Mr Gumpy, Elmer and Rosie, as well as Humpty Dumpty and Little Jack Horner. Long before she could understand words and word clusters she was finding out about the cadences, rhythms and pleasures of stories, whilst, at the same time, she was able to explore the physical fun of touching, grappling with and, occasionally, eating the books which the adults put before her.

Between two and two and a half years of age. Jenny first encountered *Albert and the Green Bottle*. This is a story by Elizabeth and Gerald Rose, of a little man who wishes to make a voyage round the world, and gets his dad to help him build a boat and his mum to provision it. She gives him a bottle of elderberry wine to 'keep out the cold,' and later, when he is shipwrecked, a message which he places in the empty green bottle, leads to his being rescued. Jenny loved this story, asking for it again and again. She examined the pictures closely, asking, and often repeating on the next reading, questions about the events: 'Why aren't those children waving goodbye to Albert?' 'What is that?' (an inky thumbprint on the letter Albert wrote) 'What is that there?' (a picture of a compass) 'Who is that with Albert's daddy?' 'What are they doing with the bottle?' In that part of the story where the storm breaks out and the waves lash around the boat, she always joined in with the phrases, 'Up and over, up and over,' accompanying them with rhythmic movements of her hands, as she rapidly learned the whole of the text of Albert's letter by heart, often 'reading' it at the appropriate moment. It was clear that she relished the final note on the letter – 'P.S. The elderberry wine was lovely' – and pronounced it with an air of complete satisfaction. If, as a reader, Grandpa paused, she would sometimes carry on with the text herself, or maybe urge her partner to 'Keep talking, Grandpa'.

At two and a half, Jenny was aware that books were enjoyable experiences to be shared with people who loved her. She knew much of the language associated with reading – title, pictures, pages, beginning, end, author – and was finding out how books are handled and pages turned. She would sit occasionally, and go through the book rehearsing what she had remembered of the tale. She had extended her knowledge, and vocabulary, to include coastguards, rescues services, desert islands, voyages, expensive items, the Pacific Ocean and palm trees. And when Grandpa had gone back home, she would ask him about Albert on the telephone. 'Bring Albert next time you come to my house. Grandpa'.

A significant feature of these early contacts with story was the easy, effortless way in which the child's understanding grew. She had started out in the Story Club as a raw initiate with no idea of conventions, no experience of the jargon needed to make sense of membership, no mind-store on which to draw. Her membership was valued by her sponsors – the adults in her extended family – and their attitudes to her were positive and encouraging. Most of the early judgements about which books would be read to Jenny were made by the adults, but she was always encouraged to choose the particular story she wanted from a selection of books. Before she could walk, she would crawl across the carpet, look at the books spread out there for her attention, and hold up the one she wanted. She chose the site for the reading too, sometimes an easy chair, sometimes the giant beanbag in her bedroom, occasionally in an improvised blanket house with the reader using a torch for illumination. Clearly these rituals appealed to her. They were creative, involving, and enormous fun.

A year later, when she was about three and a half years of age, books were as much a part of Jenny's waking experiences (and, I dare say, her dreaming world) as eating, talking, playing, getting bathed and dressed, and going out on visits. She had half her library in her toy cupboard under the stairs and the other half in reachable shelves in her bedroom. Some stories she had heard on two or three occasions, other books must have been opened and enjoyed dozens of times. One of the latter, *Three by the Sea*, was a favourite that featured in almost every reading session. As she listened to the story she made observations, asked questions, and often – at moments of high drama – joined in with the reader. At the breakfast table one morning, Grandpa reminded her that the monster in *Three by the Sea* liked to eat children on toast. She proceeded, then, to retell the last part of the story to those people sharing the meal with her.

> One day a monster came out of the sea. He had big yellow eyes. He had sharp green teeth. He had long black claws. And he was really mean. It was time for lunch and he was hungry. On the beach he saw some cheese. 'Blah,' he said, 'I hate cheese,' and he went on by. Soon he came to a rat. The rat was ...

And so the tale unfolded, with much of the expression and intonation, gesture and dramatic emphasis that she had apparently absorbed on the countless readings she had taken part in. This was the first time she had shown, quite so convincingly, the effect stories were having on her. We grabbed the book to check on the accuracy of her recall. As far as we could figure out she had missed out no more than a couple of short phrases from the author's account; it was 176 words long.

At this period in her life Jenny was always ready to take part in any activity which offered her an opportunity to play and pretend, or which introduced her to new experiences. As long as she could sense that what was being proposed would be interesting and enjoyable she was keen to be involved.

'You are the world champion bean-bag diver and toy jumper', said Grandpa, arranging objects on the carpet in the lounge, 'and I am the television commentator. You will line up at the start, run to my chair, climb over my legs, dive onto the giant bean-bag, jump over that line of toys and finish by kicking the blue balloon behind the settee. Ready, steady, go.' And for the next ten minutes Jenny ran and dived and jumped around the lounge to Grandpa's improvised commentary. Eventually his enthusiasm began to wane and she had to press him to continue. 'Again, Grandpa, again. Talk', she would demand. 'Start talking Grandpa.'

It seemed almost as if the dramatic narrative helped her to get around the course, helped her to grow into the role of 'champion bean-bag diver'.

She lost interest when Grandpa finally called time, not wanting to try another circuit without the commentary that he provided and which seemed to bring shape and motivation to the play. Later in the day she was seen trying out the course again, this time introducing her own version of the commentary as she ran and jumped and dived.

How did Jenny recall and rehearse the sequence of events needed to carry out the obstacle race? Where did the language come from when she put her own commentary to the actions? Why is it that each of her commentaries sounded similar to, but was actually different from Grandpa's, and different from each other? And why, when she retold the monster story, was each version identical, almost, to the author's account?

In the first case Jenny seemed able to recreate the obstacle course on her own, because she had actually seen and handled and used the beanbag and toys in the lounge. She was able to 'see' where they should be placed and 'knew' from earlier rehearsals the sequence she had to carry out. The 'seeing' was imaginative and mental, the 'knowing' physical. And when she began to move around the course again the language arose from these 'seeing' and 'knowing' experiences. She had, of course, a speech model (Grandpa) the outline of which she seemed to have internalised but the syntax arose from the ability to generate new and meaningful chunks of language appropriate to this particular context.

In the second case, (and I will quote Seamus Heaney), the language seemed to have 'entered the echo chamber of the head', where, without conscious effort, it was held available in its entirety, alongside, but separate from, all the other units of story language she was accumulating. It would seem very odd indeed, if this fictional store was never raided to enlarge and enrich the child's transactional use of language, and Jenny's ability to frame talk as 'commentary' for instance, must have been influenced by the access to such a store.

It was about this time that Jenny became interested in adding to her stock of songs and rhymes. She enjoyed giving concerts in the back of the car on long journeys, or at night-time in bed. When she heard Grandpa recite, at speed, *Baby's Drinking Song*, she was keen to learn the words, to add the gestures that accompanied the little poem, and to rehearse it until she, too, could say it quickly.

> *Baby's Drinking Song*
> Sip a little
> Sup a little
> From your little
> Cup a little
> Sup a little

Sip a little
Put it to your
Lip a little
   Tip a little
   Tap a little
Not into your
Lap or it'll
   Drip a little
   Drop a little
   On the table
   Top a little

(James Kirkup)

There was a very evident sense of fun in the experience and no mistaking the palpable relish with which she demonstrated her prowess. From a starting point of ignorance to a stage of complete mastery took no more than six or seven minutes.

At first sight this accomplishment may seem commonplace, but think of it this way. The child listens to the unfolding of a story that she has never encountered before and begins to unravel its meaning. Because the sound the language makes is musical and interesting, she is curious about it and anxious to add it to her own language store. She enjoys practising because the art of rehearsal places the control of learning in her own hands, and as she rehearses she cements into place new syntactical patterns, along with the rhythms and rhymes which the poem reveals. Furthermore, she does this in a social setting that invites her to co-operate in imposing order on the activities, and which leads, eventually, to a little performance celebrating her achievement.

I have in front of me two books: the first is a Walker publication called *Polar Bear Cat*, written and illustrated by Nicola Bayley; the second a home-made publication called, the 'Elephant Me Story', by Jenny. Nicola Bayley's story begins, 'If I were a polar bear instead of a cat …' Jenny's story begins, 'If I were an elephant instead of me'. Jenny was about four and a half when she 'wrote' this story. Grandpa suggested she might like to become an author and write a book like Nicola Bayley's. He acted as secretary and helper. The book was made out of one sheet of A4 paper, folded and cut across the middle, then turned into a little, eight-page booklet. Frames were drawn on each page for the illustrations and then Jenny dictated the story and Grandpa wrote it down. Together they checked and re-checked the text and then Jenny made crayon illustrations to complete it. It was a huge success. She read it to everyone who would listen and, when there were no humans available she read it to Godber, her white bear, and the others in her soft-toy family. Not only could she read, she was now an author and illustrator, as well.

So, by the time she was ready to start school Jenny had established the foundations of the house of fiction she was (and still is) building. She knew that books have titles and that each story is written by a writer whose name is on the cover. She knew which way a book is opened and how to turn the pages. She was able to join in with some part of the story and appeared to memorise, without effort, those bits that were funny, or dramatic, or appealed to her. She showed a keen interest in the illustrations, talked about them from time to time, and often expressed in words the ideas she found in the pictures, and; she was developing a well stocked mind, becoming a symbol user herself, and was confident with books and book language. She reacted to stories by linking them to other ideas or experiences or stories she had encountered and she was finding out that messages can be found in print and was keen to have a go at writing herself. She was beginning to read independently.

If we were able to create a Literacy Strategy based on Jenny's experiences and place it in a Nursery/Infants' school, what would it look like? What kind of environment? What sort of context? What activities and pursuits would the children follow?

First of all, there would be books available in abundance, not just in the library area, but in every teaching space, plus the corridors, the hall and the entrance area. Many of the books would be open, to show the marvellous illustrations by people like Korky Paul, Debi Gliori, Quentin Blake, David McKee, Mick Inkpen, Ruth Brown and John Burningham. Most of the books would be fiction, with a good number of poetry anthologies, nursery rhymes, fairy stories, alphabet and counting books. There would be a special magic 'Story Room' with coloured lights, black-out curtains, cushions, murals, a mobile blanket house, hats and clothes of all kinds with a story-teller's lantern and throne. There would be a poetry dais in each room where children (and adults) could present their own stories and poems, or ones that they had learnt by heart.

The adults in the school would be book enthusiasts. Each teacher would read and recommend a children's book each week to the other staff. Once every half-term the library service would mount a display of new fiction and recommend, in turn, titles they had enjoyed. There would be a regular team of parents joining in with these activities. Visitors to the school would be expected, from time to time, to read with small groups, or simply talk about books in an informal way.

Every day, every child in the school would perform a 'little, daily miracle' by learning a poem, or rhyme, or an interesting piece of text, by heart.

Occasionally, some groups would present a batch of their 'miracles' to an audience and listen, in turn, to the audience presenting theirs. There would be, in the school, a Publishing Room where materials for making books would be available and, at certain times, parents who would help edit and make books, and advise about presentation. The teachers would demonstrate how books, like *Dear Zoo* and *The Polar Bear Cat*, can be used as models for the children's own stories. Autobiographies, with photographs, would feature in the work – 'My Book about Me', written by Me – and authors would visit. Instead of giving additional diagnostic tests, exercises, drills, flash-cards and phonic practice to those children experiencing some difficulty in cracking the reading code, each one would have a large, wooden treasure chest, with a lock and key and their name on the lid. The chest would contain twenty books specially selected for that child. Several times a week they would open the chest, choose a book and share it with a teacher or parent. They would be encouraged to talk about the pictures, ask questions, and re-tell the story. The adult would act as secretary, to copy out the re-telling and help make it into a book. Together they would rehearse a reading of the new version. There would be no tests, no marks, no pressure, and no anxiety – just interest, application and fun.

And, of course, the very best adult readers would hold regular sessions with target groups where specially selected, challenging stories would be read aloud, with opportunities, also, for old favourites to be heard again and again. As children developed in confidence and understanding, the habit of individual, silent reading would have a daily slot of at least twenty minutes. (Some years ago a UNESCO world study felt able to assert that a reader needs to have read a million words in order to be literate, a target impossible to achieve solely by the group-reading of an enlarged text.)

The head-teacher of this school would encourage her staff in their search for strategies which interest children and help them to learn well. She would provide her parents with a simple outline of the school's philosophy, listing also the ways in which their children were being helped to become vigorous language users. She would stress that literacy events occur at all times, in all activities that they involve listening, talking, thinking and writing, as well as reading, and that the least successful way of teaching is to resort to 'bits' – bits of phonics, bits of look-and-say, bits of grammar, bits of punctuation, all taught from 'bits' of texts. Recent research sponsored by the Teacher Training Agency has confirmed that coherence, making connections between literacy and other learning activities, is a distinctive characteristic of effective teachers of literacy (TTA, 1999).

This head-teacher would see that one of the best ways to help children to understand how texts work at a transactional level is to employ modern technology. Using the right software, texts can be scrolled on to a large screen to be explored and investigated. Words and phrases can be underlined, boxed, highlighted, deleted, amended and edited, easily and effectively. What better way, for instance, to show how speech marks are used, than to highlight, first, the words that are actually spoken (say in yellow), and then demonstrate how the speech marks are opened and closed (say in red). And, as many of these texts would be ones produced by the children and teachers themselves, they would have an immediate relevance, a recognisable importance to the authors.

Jenny is now fourteen. She has just finished reading Ted Hughes's *Birthday Letters*, and *Letters Home*, by Sylvia Plath. In the last few months she has read teenage books by Janni Howker, Sylvia Waugh, Jean Ure, Robert Cormier, Robert Swindells, Nicholas Fisk, James Watson and Ian Stachan ('too many of his to remember'), as well as *Brave New World*, *The Clockwork Orange*, *1984*, *The Wasp Factory*, *The Leopard*, *Romeo and Juliet*, *Animal Farm*, and Barry Unsworth's *After Hannibal*. Several of Michael Rosen's wonderfully comic poems she has committed to memory and, when pressed by her friends, presents them for their amusement. And all of this has happened outside of school, without the advice or guidance of teachers.

'I read', she says, 'because I get carried away with a good story. I go deep into a book, experiencing different emotions and meeting people who are totally different from the people I know. It is entertainment, I suppose, but you have to work at it a bit harder. It's a sort of escapism. It calms me down after a row. Don't ask me why I enjoy reading – I read because I love books.'

Jenny has learned well because she has had experiences that reveal rather than structures that explain; because literacy has been an infinitely larger affair than learning to read and write step by step; because she positively enjoyed learning and sensed, early on, that this was a world she wanted to enter. All the unfashionable words appeared in her lexicon of learning – fun, delight, celebration, novelty, magic, creativity, love, imagination – sitting easily alongside their more respectable neighbours – application, achievement, perseverance, absorption and single-mindedness.

Unfortunately, the English National Literacy Strategy has nothing to say about the context in which learning activities take place; nothing to say about the relationships between teacher and pupil; no advice to give about the different backgrounds, talents and rates of growth of individual children; ignores the enormous potential for learning which nestles inside the word 'fun'. I wonder how many of the children who work through the designated sequences of the Strategy – hour by hour, day by day, term by term, year by year – will end up saying: 'Don't ask me why I enjoy reading – I just love books.'

Questions for personal reflection or group discussion

1 Do you share the writer's views about the centrality and importance of good stories in the teaching of reading?

2 Should schools which are involved in early reading work have an agreed, articulated policy for book selection? What kind of criteria would form the basis for such a selection?

3 Is it possible to list ways in which teachers of young children can develop their understanding of children's literature?

4 What specific activities and initiatives would help to bring children and books together before statutory schooling begins?

5 What steps can a school take to ensure a positive reading environment?

6 What can be done in the classroom to help children know about books and authors?

7 How did Jenny learn to read fluently and well, when she had little or no explicit teaching of blending, sounding out, or building up. Is she unusual?

Recommended reading

Butler, D. (1979) *Cushla and her Books,* London: Hodder & Stoughton. An astonishing, inspirational account of the power of story to sustain and nourish a severely handicapped baby.

Fox, G. et al (1976) *Writers' Critics and Children,* London: Heinemann. This excellent collection of views and insights into children's literature includes the seminal essay by Ted Hughes, 'Myth and education'.

Iser, W. (1974) *The Implied Reader.* London: John Hopkins University. The final chapter of this classic text, 'The Reading Process' offers a clear and comprehensive picture of what happens when a reader makes contact with a good story.

Also five good children's books:

Just Dog, Hiawyn Oram, ill. Lisa Flather, Orchard Picturebooks:London, 1998 .

Frog and the Birdsong, Max Velthuis, Red Fox, London, 1991.

Courtney, John Burningham, Jonathan Cape, London, 1994.

Twice My Size, Adrian Mitchell, ill. Daniel Pudles, Bloomsbury, London, 1998.

The Wonky Donkey, Jonathan Long, ill. Korky Paul, Bodley Head, London 1999.

Bibliography

Nicola Bayley (1984) *The Polar Bear Cat,* London: Walker Books.

Rod Campbell (1982) *Dear Zoo,* London: Picture Puffins.

Edward Marshall, ill. James Marshall (1982) *Three by the Sea*, London: Bodley Head.

Elizabeth and Gerald Rose (1972) *Albert and The Green Bottle*, London: Faber and Faber.

TTA (1999) *Effective Teachers of Literacy*, London: Teacher Training Agency.

Part II

Which books should we use?

3 Choosing books for young readers

Gervase Phinn

> The people who want higher literacy standards most are primary teachers. They know more than anyone the joy of watching a child grasp the skills of reading, of seeing a child find out about the real world and many imaginary ones too, through books.
>
> (Barber, 1997)

'Are you here to hear me read?' The speaker was Helen, a small, healthy-looking little girl of six with long golden plaits, wide unblinking eyes and a face as speckled as a thrush's egg. I met her when I was listening to children read in a small village primary school some years ago.

'That's right,' I replied, 'Here to hear you read.'
'I'm a very good reader you know.'
'Really?'
'I use expression.'
'You probably use dramatic pause as well,' I said smiling and staring into the large pale eyes.
'I don't know what it is,' she said pertly, 'but I probably do.'

Helen did, in fact, read with great fluency, expression and confidence. She paused dramatically in her reading.

'I am a good reader, aren't I?'
'No,' I said mischievously. 'You're not.'
'I am,' she said firmly.
'You are the best reader I think I have ever heard,' I told her.
'I'm very good at writing as well,' she commented casually when she snapped the book shut.
'Really?'

'Would you care to see my writing?'
'I would love to,' I said.
'Poetry or prose?'
'Poetry please.'
'I have my poems in a portfolio.'
'I guessed you would,' I replied, chuckling.

Helen's writing was as confident and as clear as her reading.

'And why are you such a good reader?' I asked.
'Because I read a lot,' she said simply. 'And I love books.'

Helen then told me about her favourite authors and poets and how, from the earliest age, the adults in her life – mummy, daddy, granny and grampa – had sat her on their knees, read to her, told her stories, talked about books, taken her to the library and to the bookshop, bought her books for Christmas and her birthday and helped her build up her own little collection of books in her bedroom. In the evening there was a quiet time when everyone in the house read. Of course, it should come as no surprise that Helen was a highly competent, confident and keen reader. She had been raised in that rich, motivating reading environment where books are important and valued, an environment which produces the lifelong reader. This, of course, is the key to reading. As Jane Shilling (1999) wrote in her excellent article: 'If a child is to learn to love reading, it needs to be presented as a natural, essential pleasure, not as a duty.' She continues to describe the environment in which her own son, a voracious little reader, is reared – an environment, like Helen's, 'entirely permeated with narrative':

> I certainly did not set out to create a precocious reader. There are in our house no early reader systems designed to inveigle unwary toddlers into premature literacy, not even those little board books containing emasculated versions of more complex texts. What I did was to read to him, nightly, from the moment he came home from hospital, aged three days. I read the books I liked as a child – 'Beatrix Potter', '*Orlando, the Marmalade Cat*', '*The Wind in the Willows*', Ralph Caldecott's books of poetry, and so on.

She concludes her article with some sensible advice for parents:

> Surround a child with books from birth, make them an ordinary part of his life as knives and forks and plates, present reading as an activity as natural and essential as breathing, and at seven years or so, you will

have your reward – the singular semi-silence broken only by heavy breathing, an occasional half laugh, and the regular swish of a turning page that is the sound of your child setting off to explore new worlds whose only boundaries are the covers of his book.

It has, of course, been ever thus.

> I read every book that came my way without distinction – and my father was very fond of me, and used to take me on his knee, and hold long conversations with me. I remember, that at eight years old, I walked with him one winter evening from a farmer's house, a mile from Ottery – and he told me the names of the stars – and how Jupiter was a thousand times larger than our world and that the other twinkling stars were suns that had worlds rolling around them – and when I came home, he shewed me how they rolled round. I heard him with profound delight and admiration; but without the least mixture of wonder or incredulity. For from my early reading of Faery Tales, and Genii etc. etc. – my mind had been habituated to the Vast.
>
> (Holmes, 1990 quoted from Coleridge's Letters 1, 1780)

This is what teachers should be about – habituating children to the vastness of literature. Schools should be for all children, and particularly those in homes where there are few, if any books and little if any importance placed on reading, what the home is for the most fortunate children like Helen. They should provide an environment for reading where children are exposed to reading material that arouses their interest in, and develops a love of reading. They should be cheerful, optimistic, welcoming places where children are surrounded with language and presented with a rich and stimulating variety of stories, poems, plays and non-fiction material which will make them smile and laugh, be captivated and curious, sometimes feel sad and a little scared and which will encourage them to want more and more and more. From the very start, books should have a real literary quality, with the power to engage the child's active interest.

Choosing books for children

What are needed are beginning texts that fascinate children and convince them that reading is delightful and helps one to gain a better understanding of oneself and others – in short, of the world we live in and how to live in it. To achieve this, primary texts should stimulate and enrich the child's imagination, as fairy tales do, and should develop the child's literary sensitivities, as good poems are apt to do. The texts should also present the child with literary images of the world, of nature and of man, as these have been created by great writers.

(Bettelheim, 1982)

There cannot be a teacher in the country who would not subscribe to this view or who would dispute the recommendations contained in *The National Curriculum* and in *The National Literacy Strategy* which endorse it:

Teaching should cover a range of rich and stimulating texts and should ensure that pupils regularly hear stories, told or read aloud, and hear and share poetry read by the teacher and each other ... Reading should include picture books, nursery rhymes, poems, folk tales, myths, legends and other literature. Both boys and girls should experience a wide range of children's literature.

(English in the National Curriculum, Programme of Study for Reading, Key Stage 1, Paras 6 and 7, 1989)

In the early stages, pupils should have a carefully balanced programme of guided reading from books of graded difficulty, matched to their independent reading levels. These guided reading books should have a cumulative vocabulary, sensible grammatical structure and a lively and interesting content. Through shared reading, pupils should also be given a rich experience of more challenging texts.

(The National Literacy Strategy: Framework for Teaching, 1998)

Teachers know that to become as successful a reader as Helen, children are familiar with and use a range of strategies to understand the text and need the support and encouragement of sensitive and enthusiastic adults to develop the love of books. They also know that the provision of a wide range of good quality texts is essential. These principles are at the heart of *The National Curriculum* and *The National Literacy Strategy* and have formed the basis for the successful teaching and encouragement of reading for many years. But where does the teacher start? What books in particular should be presented to children? Which material is appropriate? What are the qualities of 'a good book'?

Before selecting books for the young reader there are a number of questions one should ask:

- Is the book visually appealing and eye-catching? Picture books with bright, colourful and beautifully illustrated covers demand to be picked up and read.

- Is the subject appropriate to the children in terms of age and maturity? Does it avoid being moralistic, overly sentimental and patronising? Does it portray class, gender and culture in a non- stereotypical way?
- Is the story worth telling? Does it read well aloud and bear a re-reading? Is it entertaining and challenging? Does it contain some excitement and suspense? Does it kindle curiosity and imagination? C. S. Lewis argued vehemently that :

> No book is really worth reading at the age of ten that is not equally worth reading at the age of fifty – except of course information books. The only imaginative works we ought to grow out of are those which it would be better not to have read at all.
>
> (C. S. Lewis, quoted in Meek, M. *et al.*, 1977)

- Is the language appropriate, natural and meaningful? Does it encourage children to predict what will happen, to anticipate and become involved in the narrative? Is there a richness in the expression and an imaginative use of words? Does the writer make some demands on his or her readers in terms of language? Good books expose a child to language in its most complex and varied forms, presenting the thoughts, emotions and experiences of others in a vivid and dramatic way.

> Aesthetic properties of language are to be found more than anywhere in literature. Literature is nothing if not language formed in highly deliberate ways. From the earliest pre-school stages of development, children are interested in forms of language. Wide reading, and as great an experience as possible of the best imaginative literature, are essential to the full development of an ear for language.
>
> (The Report of the Committee of Inquiry into the Teaching of English Language, 1988, Chapter 2, Para 21)

- Is the dialogue appropriate to the characters? Is it clear, authentic and understandable? Does it capture the rhythms of speech? Does it reflect the speech patterns of those for whom it is intended?
- Do the illustrations enhance the story, adding meaning to the words rather than detracting from them? Do the pictures link closely to the text?

> All early reading material should be attractive not only in presentation but also in content. The words and pictures should complement each other in such a way that the child needs to examine both with equal care.
>
> (A Language for Life: The Bullock Report, 1979)

- Is the print clear, well spaced and of an appropriate size?
- Are the characters rounded and convincing? Do they live and breath on the page, develop and grow in the reader's mind? Can children readily identify with the characters and enter into their lives?
- Is the story by a real writer, not merely a book especially written to teach children to read?

> Authors who genuinely want to write for children do not count the words in a sentence. They know instinctively where phrases start and stop because they shape narratives and incidents.
>
> (Meek, 1982)

- Is the story of real interest to the teacher? Does she enjoy reading and re-reading it, presenting it and discussing it with her children?

FOUR GOOD STORIES

John Masefield described a good story as having 'a remarkable opening, proper pauses and notable climaxes'. Here are four good stories.

Amy Said by Martin Waddell, illustrated by Charlotte Voake
(Reception/Year 1)

Martin Waddell has written many fine books for younger readers and all have enormous appeal. His stories are wonderfully warm and sympathetic and capture the imagination of children as well as enhancing their linguistic abilities.

Amy Said is an original and compelling short story: funny, bright and full of happy life and movement. It has a lively rhythm, lots of repetition and a robust little character whose actions delight young children. Big sister Amy is an expert about what to do at Gran's house and she gets her little brother into a whole lot of bother.

> When Amy and I stayed with Gran,
> I wanted to bounce on my bed
> and Amy said I could.
>
> I bounced a bit,
> then a bit more,
> then bit more.
> Then I fell off the bed. And Amy said ...

There follows a series of lively escapades: swinging on Gran's curtains, painting Gran's walls green, picking Gran's flowers, making a bike track in Gran's garden, ending up with Amy falling SPLOSH in the mud. The story ends on a happy note.

> Gran never gets cross!
> She put us both in the bath and
> the water was lovely and warm.
>
> We splashed just a bit, but the bit
> splashed out on Gran's floor.
>
> And Gran said …
> NO MORE!
> Then she helped us get dry and she said
> we should try to be good.
>
> And Amy said …
> that we would
> because we love our Gran …
>
> And we want to come back
> again and again and again.[1]

Martin Waddell is an artist with a keen ear for the spoken word and his use of language is unparalleled. This story is guaranteed to make young children become completely absorbed and chuckle with delight. It is:

> A story that makes us laugh without malice is to be treasured …Comic writing both reflects and experiments with the familiar world and represents our reality; and comedy for children tends to be most effective when it is robust, springing from characters whose actions upset and embarrass convention and power. Children laugh most readily at comic writing which evokes a picture and sound, bringing antics and collisions alive in the theatre of the imagination.
>
> (Jones and Buttrey, 1970)

The Great Sharp Scissors by Philippa Pearce, from *Lion at School and Other Stories*, Puffin (Years 2 and 3)

The Great Sharp Scissors by Philippa Pearce contains a fast moving plot, rounded characters, a spareness in the prose and sharp, clear dialogue. The twelve-page story is full of wit, wisdom and suspense and will captivate a young audience. It begins:

> Once there was a boy called Tim who was often naughty. Then his mother used to say 'Tim!' and his father shouted 'Tim!' But his granny said, 'Tim's a good boy, really.'

The reader's interest is immediately aroused. Tim resents being left alone while his mother visits his poorly Granny.

> He scowled and stamped his foot. He was very angry.

Tim's mother warns him not to let anyone into the house but when a strange man calls and offers to sell him a most remarkable pair of great sharp scissors that will cut anything, Tim cannot resist. :

> 'I'll have them,' said Tim.

With the great sharp scissors in his hand, he now has the opportunity to give vent to his feelings. He snip snaps the buttons off his father's coat, he cuts the carpet into hundreds of little pieces, he chops the legs off the tables and chairs and the clashing blades slice though the clock on the mantelpiece.

> By now Tim knew that the great sharp scissors would cut anything. They would cut through all the wooden doors and floors. They would cut through all the bricks of all the walls, until nothing was left. Nothing. Tim went and sat at the bottom step of the stairs and cried.

Fortunately, his second visitor, a strange woman who smiles kindly at him, exchanges the scissors for some special magic glue. When Tim's mother arrives back from Granny's, Tim has repaired everything and the house is back to normal. The story ends on the ironic but immensely warm and re-assuring note that is never missed by the little listeners.

> 'Granny's much better, and sends her love. I see you've been a good boy, Tim. Everything neat and tidy ...' She made a pot of tea, and she and Tim had tea and bread and butter and raspberry jam. In the middle of it, Tim's father came home, and he had some of the raspberry jam too.

The Marble Crusher by Michael Morpurgo, Mammoth,
illustrated by Linda Birch (Years 3 & 4)

There is real sincerity in Michael Morpurgo's writing. His plots are both
exciting and thought provoking and combine humour with a deep
understanding of children's thoughts and feelings.

Albert is ten years old – 'a quiet, gentle sort of boy with a thatch of stiff
hair that he twiddled when he was nervous'. And Albert gets really, really
nervous when he starts his new school, a 'school which was noisy and full
of strange faces'. He is teased because the gentle, smiling, good-natured boy
is easy to tease and he believes anything people tell him.

> 'My dad,' said Sid Creedy, 'he played Centre Forward for Liverpool.
> Did for years. Then they asked him to play for England, but he didn't
> want to – he didn't like the colour of the shirt.'

Albert believes all the tall stories Sid tells him – that the balding Mr. Cooper
is not a teacher at all but 'an escaped monk', that Mr. Manners has six
wives like Henry the Eighth and twenty-two children and that the
headteacher has a monstrous marble-crushing machine. There is the gripping
scene when Albert is discovered playing marbles, a game which have been
banned in school.

> He was crouching under the teacher's table, taking careful aim, when
> Mr. Manners came in behind him silently. 'Albert,' he said. 'Albert,
> are you playing marbles?' 'Oh … Yes sir,' and Albert remembered at
> once – he remembered the punishment too and began to twiddle his
> hair. 'They will have to go, all of them mind,' said Mr. Manners. 'Empty
> your pockets, lad,' and he held out his big chalky hand. 'I'm surprised
> at you, Albert, and disappointed – very disappointed.'

There is no sentimentality or condescension in this story; it is full of gusto,
lively authentic dialogue, immediacy and wit. In *The Literacy Hour* it is
suggested that the teacher demonstrates reading strategies using a shared
text, focusing on the writer's intention. There is a high level of interaction
in this activity, where pupils are encouraged to respond to the teacher's
questions through offering suggestions, referring to the text to support
personal opinions, linking with their own personal experiences, examining
how a text is constructed and exploring the features of the language used.
The Marble Crusher is a short story ideal for this kind of study of narrative
structure, setting, character, use of dialogue, significant detail and the
effective use of language

Hurricane Summer by Robert Swindells, Mammoth. (Years 5 & 6)

Robert Swindell's skill as a storyteller is second to none. His novels and short stories, which frequently deal with issues fundamental to children growing up and learning how to cope, are invariably funny, sad, exciting and totally compelling. *Hurricane Summer*, set at the time of the Second World War, has a challenging and fast-moving plot centring on Jim, who worships the brave, dashing, dare-devil fighter pilot, Cocky, who lodges at his house. Words are used sparingly but to great effect, characterisation is strong and Swindell weaves a gripping story guaranteed to captivate older juniors. The opening of the novel immediately hooks the reader:

> Funny things friendships. They tend to come and go, but most people have a special friend who stands out among all the others. I'm lucky. I've got two. One of them's been dead a long time now, but it doesn't matter – he'll always be my friend. As for the other ... well as I said, friendships are funny. Best thing I can do is tell you about them.

Jim is bullied at school by Clive Simcox, a large, unpleasant, lonely boy who ambushes his victim on the way from school. Jim is really frightened of Simcox and tries to keep out of his way but with little success.

> He used to wait for me in the mornings too, and trip me as I ran past. I'd arrive at school with grazed knees and dirt on my blazer and red eyes from crying and everybody would know Clive had had another go at me.

What makes Jim feel worse is that he is constantly reminded of his cowardice when he sees Cocky, the fearless fighter pilot with the infectious grin – 'a big gangly schoolboy for whom the War was nothing but a rippling adventure'. Then one day Jim learns the truth, the truth that Cocky lives in constant fear.

> He turned his head to look at me. 'And you think we're fearless Jim? You think I'm not afraid?' He snorted. 'I'll tell you this Jim. If I could – if I dared – I'd get up right now and start running, and I wouldn't stop till I was somewhere they'd never find me. And that's true of all fighter pilots.'

The novel moves to an exciting and poignant climax where Jim, knowing that he is not the only one in the world to feel frightened and lonely, faces the bully. *Hurricane Summer* is an ideal text for reading aloud and for discussing themes and motives. It can be used successfully for 'guided reading' as part of *The Literacy Hour*. Children could explore the author's point of view, identify and discuss explicit and implicit meanings, analyse characters and examine the language and structure.

Amy Said, The Great Sharp Scissors, The Marble Crusher and *Hurricane Summer* have all the qualities which are important when thinking about the books to present to young people. The powerful and carefully crafted language has an immediate appeal. Children enjoy reading and hearing about those very much like themselves. They love tales about boys and girls like Amy and Tim, Albert and Jim, who have moods and get angry as they do, who sometimes feel lonely and afraid, who are sometimes naughty and get into trouble but who, in the end, receive the reassurance of being loved and wanted. They enjoy sharing the experiences and emotions that a well-written story triggers and willingly project into it their own feelings of fear, insecurity anger, joy and relief.

Good writers, like Waddell, Pearce, Morpurgo and Swindells, never patronise their young readers. They know that children are curious, eager, sharply observant and that they love stories that absorb their attention and which make demands upon them. Such stories are important in developing children's language but are more important in their emotional development. Many psychologists now argue for a notion of learning that includes emotional knowledge. I believe that books like the ones described above make a significant contribution to emotional literacy. Stories, like the four described, explore ideas of right and wrong, jealousy, friendship, disappointment, fear and happiness, being accepted and rejected, moral dilemmas and the making of choices, in which the characters ultimately find security, comfort and love. They go to the very heart of children's joys and anxieties.

The reading teacher

Before recommending a range of other good quality books, I need to state the obvious: teachers must be reading teachers if they hope to promote the reading of the children they teach. They need to enthuse about books, recommend titles and authors, read extracts to whet the appetite, regularly ask children about what they are reading and have enjoyed and let children see that they themselves gain great satisfaction and pleasure from reading. Teachers must be readers themselves. There is no short cut, no easy answer, and no definitive book list. Teachers need to have read the books they present to children, they need to select them with care and knowledge and be skilled in judging when and how to use them. Keeping up with the plethora of material is time-consuming and demanding but it is also highly enjoyable and rewarding.

Teachers might keep up with their reading in a number of ways:

- By having close and regular contact with *The Schools Library Service*. The librarians advise on and recommend titles, organise courses and conferences, workshops and book reviewing groups and produce fiction, poetry and non-fiction lists. Teachers might try to visit *The School Library Service H.Q.* on a regular basis and depart with a small collection of books for reading: a couple of picture books, a poetry collection, a short story anthology, some recently published non-fiction texts, perhaps a controversial children's story about which the librarian wants an opinion and one or two books the librarian feels they might enjoy.
- By keeping in close and regular contact with a good bookshop. Suppliers who specialise in children's literature, such as The Children's Bookshop, 37–39 Lidget Street, Lindley, Huddersfield HD3 3JF and Madeleine Lindley Ltd in Oldham, select books with knowledge and care. They will send material, recommend titles, tell their customers what new publications have come on the market and which are the most popular with children. They also will attend teachers' courses and parents' evenings to mount displays and sell books. The Country Bookstore, Hassop Station, Near Bakewell in Derbyshire (E-mail: *mail@countrybookstore.co.uk*) is an on-line bookstore with over 15,000 titles in stock and with 1.5 million titles listed. Teachers can search by title, author or key word, browse numerous categories, including author information, and place orders on-line for titles in print not only in the United Kingdom but those published in the United States. The store can also do a search for out-of-print titles.
- By reading the reviews. Over the school holidays teachers might catch up on the new books reviewed in such journals and booklets as those produced by *The Thimble Press* and *The School Library Association*. The bookseller, Waterstones, produces an excellent *Guide to Children's Books*, an annotated booklist in which the very best of classic and contemporary fiction books for children is reviewed. *The Good Book Guide to Children's Books*, published by Penguin Books, is also a must.
- By listening to children and finding out what they enjoy reading. Some writers like Helen Cresswell, Gene Kemp and Dick King-Smith have a universal appeal, others, like Margaret Mahy, Diana Wynne Jones and William Mayne, are an acquired taste and some, like Ivan Southall, Penelope Lively and Meindert Dejong, they learn to like given time. The stories children enjoy depend on a number of factors: age and maturity, ability, environment, experience and interests, even the mood they are in at a particular time. Like adults, children have preferences and a story which one child will read avidly might have little impact on another.

Title:	The Hodgeheg
Author:	Dick King-Smith
Author Information:	Farmer, teacher, freelance writer
	Writes original, unsentimental, entertaining
	which appeal to all childrenstories
Genre:	Amusing animal adventure story

Plot: The hedgehogs at Number 5A dream of reaching the Park. Max sets out to solve the problem of how to get them across the busy main road

Language :	Very accessible, lively, sometimes poetic

Related texts: *Ace, Daggie Dogfoot, Dodos are Forever, Emily's Leg, The Fox Busters, Friends and Brothers, George Speaks, Harry's Mad, Magnus Powermouse, Martins' Mice, Noah's Brother, Paddy's Pot of Gold, The Queen's Nose, Saddlebottom, The Sheep-Pig, Sophie's Snail.*

Age Range :	6 – 10 years

Figure 3.1 Story record

Some teachers find it useful to keep a record of what they have read with brief notes about the book for future reference. A simple and easy to complete example is shown in Figure 3.1.

Some recommended texts

The National Literacy Framework for Teaching sets out clearly the teaching objectives for Reception to Year 6 and outlines the kinds of stories, poems, plays and non-fiction texts children should encounter as they progress through the primary years. Central to the *Framework* is *The Literacy Hour*, a dedicated time each day where the teacher develops children's reading skills through instruction, questioning, eliciting responses and refining and extending children's contributions. *The Literacy Hour* is not, however, about going through a minimum of texts in maximum, pleasure destroying detail, interrogating the writing in such a way that children are turned off books and reading. As David Blunkett states: 'The Literacy Hour enables children to learn poetry, prose and creative writing, with access to more texts than ever before.' (The Times, Friday, 23rd July,1999). It is about developing in children a love of reading by using a wide range of really interesting and challenging books and dealing with these books in a sensitive way. This material should include :

Prose

Nursery Tales	Folk Tales	Traditional Stories
Wonder Tales	Fairy Tales	Stories with Familiar Settings
Tall Stories	Anecdotes	Family History Stories
Jokes	Tongue-Twisters	Puns
Word Puzzles	Warning Tales	Fables
Myths	Legends	Sagas
Parables	Dilemma Stories	Stories from Different Cultures
School Stories	Historical Stories	Science Fiction
Ghost Stories	Mystery Stories	Humorous Stories
Fantasy Stories	Monologues	Adventure Stories

Poetry

Playground Chants	*Nursery Rhymes*	*Miniature Poems*
Simple Counting Rhymes	Action Verse	Syllabic Poetry
Songs and Lyrics	Rhythmic Verse	Haiku
Rhyming Couplets	Clerihews	Tanka
Patterned Poems	Kennings	Cinquains
Humorous Verse	Free Verse	Performance Poetry
Tongue-Twisters	Prayers	Conversation Poems
Alphabet Poems	Riddles	Narrative Poetry
Limericks	Shape/Concrete Poems	Ballads
Choral Verse	Acrostics	Epitaphs

Non-fiction

Simple Non-fiction Texts	Simple Instructions	Information Texts
Signs	Simple Dictionaries	Glossaries
Labels	Recounts of Events	Indexes
Captions	Recounts of Visits	Thesauruses
Lists	Non-Chronological Reports	Explanations
Letters	Encyclopaedias	Articles
Newspapers	Magazines	Advertisements

Circulars	Flyers	Discussion Texts
Debates	Editorials	Leaflets
Rules	Recipes	Directions
Commentaries	Diaries	Journals
Biography	Autobiography	Anecdotes
Reference Texts	Discussion Texts	Public Documents

The range of texts described below, offers teachers suggestions for stories and poems to use in *The Literacy Hour* and reflects the recommendations contained in *The Literacy Strategy*. It also satisfies *The National Curriculum* requirements for wide reading. The list is very selective and contains only a very small number of the 90,000 or so children's books in print. Last year over 7,000 new titles were published. The books recommended are those which many children have read and enjoyed, which fulfil the criteria outlined earlier in this chapter, and in some measure represent the great variety of reading material now available. The selection is simply illustrative of the many books which will appeal to children, and offer excellent opportunities for word, sentence and text-level work. The stories, poems and non-fiction material can be also used for 'shared' and for 'guided' reading and also for independent reading outside *The Literacy Hour* of course.

THREE PICTURE BOOKS

There is now a vast range of picture books, varied in design, story and illustration. Good picture books, like the ones described, foster the skills of reading, stimulating and supporting the early reader as she or he struggles to decode print.

They also have a great emotional impact. The picture books of John Burningham and Shirley Hughes, for instance, with their themes of mums and dads, friends, neighbours, gardens, shopping, pets, babies and everyday family life have a massive appeal. They are warm, funny, entertaining, re-assuring books and children recognise the situations and identify with the wonderfully rounded characters who, like real children, get angry, fearful and frustrated and who are sometimes naughty.

Alfie Gets in First by Shirley Hughes, Bodley Head

All Shirley Hughes books are heart-warming, appealing, cleverly written and illustrated with witty panache. Children deserve to hear them read aloud and have access to them on the library shelves. In this good-natured story, Alfie locks his mum and the baby outside with amusing results. In *The Snow Lady* (6–9 year olds), Samantha, Sam for short, loves playing in the street with her dog and her friend Barney but her next-door neighbour, Mrs. Mean, is always complaining. Other books by Shirley Hughes include : *Another Helping of Chips*, (6–9 year olds), *Chips and Jessie* (6–9 year olds), *Here Comes Charlie Moon* (6–9 year olds), *Hiding* (6–9 year olds), and *It's Too Frightening for Me* (7–9 year olds). *Dogger*, (3–8 year olds) is another delightful portrait of a minor family crisis when Dave loses his favourite toy.

Whatever Next! by Jill Murphy, Macmillan

> 'Can I go to the moon?' asked Baby Bear.
> 'No you can't,' said Mrs. Bear. 'It's bathtime.'

Whatever Next ! is a cleverly written and captivating story with lively, colourful and humorously detailed illustrations. Other splendid stories by Jill Murphy include : *The Worst Witch* (7–9 year olds), *A Bad Spell for the Worst Witch* (7–9 year olds) and *The Worst Witch Strikes Again* (7–9 year olds). Her novel *World's Apart*, which is suitable for older readers (11-year olds) is a poignant account about a young girl growing up knowing nothing about her father who left home when she was a baby. When she is eleven Susan learns about her father and determines to find him.

Monsters by Russell Hoban, Gollancz

Monsters ! Monsters ! Monsters ! John just cannot stop drawing them. His obsession leads to strange and disturbing events. *Bread and Jam for Frances, Bedtime for Frances* and *Best Friends for Frances,* by the same author, with pencil drawings by Lillian Hoban, are three other captivating and sympathetic tales for younger readers. Hoban's novel *A Mouse and his Child,* which is suitable for 10–11 year olds, is an exciting and poignant adventure story about the clockwork mice who search for their lost home.

THREE NOVELTY AND POP-UP BOOKS

Despite the frowning experts, children are delighted and fascinated by many pop-up books ; they love the cleverness and originality and enjoy the element of surprise. The worst kind of pop-up books are mass-produced and fall apart after just a few readings. The prose is mechanical and the illustrations garish. The very best pop-up books are sturdy with well-written texts – they are masterpieces of paper engineering, designed to stimulate and support the beginning reader through lively narrative, lyrical repetition of language, verbal jokes and bright original illustrations. The most comprehensive and unusual selection of pop-up books, die-cut reading books, flap books and novelty books with puppets, squeakers and moving parts, is produced by *Child's Play International*. The early reader is encouraged to touch, listen, watch, act out, sing, join in, as well as read the lively text. Children who do not, as yet, have the necessary reading skills, are encouraged to communicate through the spoken word and through rhyme and rhythms, to experience the language. The range includes :

Phone Book by Jan Pienkowski, Orchard Books

Push the little red button on the front and the telephone will ring, but the whole menagerie of pop-up animals are just too busy to answer it. Jan Pienkowski has written and constructed dozens of delightfully inventive and beautifully finished pop-up books. *Dinnertime, Gossip, Toilet Book* ('don't forget to flush it !'), *Little Monsters* and *Small Talk* (4–6 year olds) are but a few. *Haunted House* (5–8 year olds) has monsters, ghosts, ghouls and things that go bump in the night and which jump from the page. In *Fancy That* (4–6 year olds), the story of the old woman who swallowed the fly is here in pop-up form.

Maisy Goes to Bed by Lucy Cousins, Walker Books

Maisy Goes to Bed and *Maisy Goes to Playschool* are warm, original and interactive stories for very young children with bold, bright pictures and sturdy construction. Little fingers love to pull tabs and lift flaps as they help Maisy, the little mouse, to get ready for bed.

Ruth's Loose Tooth by Nicholas A. Kerna, Child's Play
International

Ruth is a great brown cow with an old wiggly tooth. Everyone tries to help her pull it out. The mouse and the goat, the fish and the crow and a variety of other helpful animals and birds tug and toil through the text, each of them heaving on a long piece of string that stretches from page to page. This clever little book is part of the *Child's Play Action Books Series*. Others include *Curious Kittens*, *The Peek-o-Boo Riddle Book* and *Hide and Seek* (4–7 year olds).

THREE FOLK AND FAIRY-TALE COLLECTIONS

The familiarity of the fairy tale and the folk tale, the magic and fantasy, the wild, wonderful and exaggerated characters, the fast action and terrible events, the constant repetitions and finally the happy ending where good triumphs over evil, all combine to create a powerful and fascinating story which captures the child's imagination and remains with him or her long after it has been heard. Characters like *Cinderella*, *Rapunzel*, *Red Riding Hood*, *Jack and the Beanstalk* and *Snow White* will appear in different guises throughout fairy-tale literature. The stories are sometimes about kings and castles, brave princes and archetypal evil witches, giants and trolls, wicked stepmothers and fairy godmothers, but can also be about ordinary people, their hopes, dreams, shrewdness and heroism. There are many traditional and modern folk and fairy tale anthologies, and teachers need to explore collections from all over the world which offer insights into other cultures and into other times. Here are just a few:

Classic Fairy Tales, Puffin

There is a wealth of English, Irish, Scottish and Welsh folk and fairy tales in this attractive volume, some well-known, others less familiar, but all rattling good reads.

British and Irish Folk Tales by Kevin Crossley-Holland, Orchard Books

This splendid collection contains the most popular of traditional stories, all told in clear, accessible language and with great verve and lively description. Kevin Crossley-Holland has produced many volumes of fairy and folk tales including: *The Dead Moon and Other Tales from East Anglia and the Fen Country*, (9–11 year olds) and *The Faber Book of Northern Folk Tales* (9–11 year olds).

The Faber Book of Favourite Fairy Tales by Sara and Stephen Corrin, Faber & Faber

Sara and Stephen Corrin have spent a lifetime collecting the most entertaining and unusual folk and fairy tales. Over the years they have compiled a whole range of modern and traditional story collections intended for particular age groups: *Stories for the Under Fives*, *Stories for Six Year Olds and Other Young Readers*, *Stories for Seven Year Olds* and so on. Each collection is based on a theme, for example there are heroes and heroines for the eight year olds and humour for the nine year olds.

THREE BIG BOOKS

The use of 'big books' or enlarged texts is a feature of *The Literacy Strategy*. Sharing stories, poems and non-fiction material with the whole group in the first part of *The Literacy Hour*, the teacher actively involves the children with the text, demonstrating how the 'black and white marks upon a page' carry meaning. She may work from the same 'big book' over five days with a combination of reading and linked writing activities. In this period children will be encouraged to listen attentively, think about the story or poem, talk about the situations and the characters, join in the reading, offer their views, interpret the pictures, anticipate and predict, point out significant words and phrases, use their knowledge of context and sentence structure in their 'quest for meaning'. There is a plethora of big books for both Key Stages on the market but the ones listed below have been tried and tested.

The Big Hungry Bear by Don and Audrey Wood, Child's Play International

There is only one way in the whole, wide world to save the ripe, red strawberry from the big hungry Bear ... This bright, beautifully-illustrated book has an immediate appeal and children will be intrigued and excited by the simple, entertaining story. They will enjoy talking over the reading and using the various clues to guess the outcome. There is a bright red story sack containing the mouse, strawberry and wooden knife to use alongside the reading and discussing and a *Little Mouse Sequence Game*, where children are encouraged to match words and pictures and undertake a whole range of simple language-based tasks. An audiotape version of the story, read by Patrick Macnee and enriched by music and a catchy song, is also available.

Mrs. Honey's Hat, written and illustrated by Pam Adams, Child's Play International

When Mrs. Honey wears her hat little does she know that it will be transformed by a whole menagerie of animals. A delightful text for sharing and exploring, with humorous illustrations and big, bold, well-spaced type. This lively story is ideal for use in *The Literacy Hour* with very early readers. Children will be able to join the reading when they feel confident enough, make predictions about what might happen next to Mrs. Honey's hat, participate in discussion about the main points of the narrative, re-tell the story in correct sequence and represent the story in drawings, storyboards, collages and murals. Child's Play International has produced a doll to accompany the story and 12 Velcro hat decorations to attach to Mrs. Honey's hat. The teacher shares out the hat pieces, tells the story and the children pass the doll along adding the various items.

A World War Two Anthology selected by Wendy Body, Pelican Big Books

For use with older primary children, this intriguing collection of words written both at the time of war and later, cleverly juxtaposes fiction and fact, drawings and photographs. There is a whole range of different forms of writing : poems, accounts, journal extracts, skipping rhymes, pieces of dialogue, extracts from novels, telegrams and letters. The selection contains a superbly poignant and optimistic poem by Richard Eburne, aged twelve. It is a very useful resource for use when studying longer texts which take place at the time of *The Second World War*, novels such as *Carrie's War* (Nina Bawden), *Goodnight Mr. Tom* (Michelle Magorian), *Hurricane Summer* (Robert Swindells), *Conrad's War* (Andrew Davies) and *Dolphin Crossing* (Jill Paton Walsh).

THREE STORY BOOKS FOR YOUNGER READERS

The range of story books is vast : fantasy, ghosts, science fiction and animal stories, adventure, mystery, family and school stories, cartoons, nature, evolution, hobbies, sport, history – the list is endless. As teachers, it is our responsibility to bring children and books together and give them a range worth their time and attention. The following small selection might be the core of a classroom library for early readers :

It Shouldn't Happen to a Frog and Other Stories by Catherine Storr, Piccolo

These warm-hearted and satisfying stories are about Lisa, a modern girl caught up in the traditional fairy tales of *The Frog Prince*, *The Three Bears*, *Bluebeard* and *Cinderella*. They give a modern twist to the favourite children's tales and are lively, inventive and great fun to read aloud. They offer excellent models for children to write their own 'alternative' fairy tales and on which to base drama activities.

Stories From Around the World, Federation of Children's Book Groups, Hodder and Stoughton

Over twenty-one thousand children from all over the world took part in the testing of these stories. The aim of the collection is 'for families and teachers to share these stories with children in the hope that it will bring our love of storytelling to others'. The fifteen stories range from the affectionate and humorous to the sad and touching and they are written by such accomplished writers as : Anita Desai, Grace Hallworth, Edna O'Brien, Alf Proysen, Joan Aiken and Virginia Hamilton. This collection is ideal for 'guided reading' sessions, offering excellent opportunities for more able children to deepen and widen their understanding of different texts, develop the skills required to read increasingly demanding material, learn about aspects of short story structure, character, description and dialogue and engage in reading strategies such as predicting, locating, checking, confirming and self correcting.

A *Necklace of Raindrops and Other Stories* by Joan Aiken, Puffin

These eight enthralling, ingenious and magical stories all told with economy and poetic intensity by a masterful storyteller. They are best used in the 'shared reading' sessions where the teacher can lift the text off the page, explain, interpret, draw out meanings and encourage discussion of storyline and character. The more able reader will enjoy the challenge of the lively and imaginative text.

THREE COLLECTIONS OF MYTHS AND LEGENDS

Myths are usually ancient traditional stories of gods and heroes concerned with the origins of life and death. The story of Persephone, the daughter of Zeus, for example, is a Greek myth as is the tale of Prometheus. Persephone spent half the year on Earth and six months in the Underworld. Prometheus made men from the clay in the ground, taught them many arts and gave them fire that he stole from heaven.

A legend usually tells of the making of a nation through the exploits of its heroes. Legends like those of Robin Hood, King Arthur and Beowulf are said to be based on truth but have been exaggerated over the years. They are tales of daring deeds, fast action, and strong emotion and are peopled by larger-than-life characters who show great courage, perseverance in the face of adversity and a nobility of spirit.

The *Dreamfighter* by Ted Hughes, Faber & Faber

Ted Hughes is better known for his poetry but he can tell a captivating tale as those who have read *The Iron Man* and *The Iron Woman* will know. In this colourful collection of creation stories we are introduced to a clever, scheming and sometimes mischievous God, working hard to fashion his creatures and breathe life into them. He has some wonderful successes but sometimes there are a few mistakes. *How the Whale Became and Other Stories* is another carefully-written and inventive collection of creation myths. Here, Hughes tells how each of the animals became as we know them today. Long ago when the world was new all the creatures were alike but with a little practice they became altogether different. In *Tales of the Early World*, God appears as a brilliant artist who is sometimes a little surprised by the creatures he makes. 'Some things take an awful lot of work,' He sighs. 'But others – they just seem to turn up.' The stories offer superb models for children's own creation myths.

The Puffin Classic Myths and Legends by Roger Lancelyn-Green, Puffin

Beautifully and concisely re-told, the stories of the Trojan Wars are brought to life with all the excitement, intrigue and drama. Tales of epic heroism like that of King Arthur are simply and poetically told and the text is enhanced by the superb woodcuts. This is a useful text for teaching children to recognise the elements of myths and legends and identify and describe characters and their relationships. The collection offers an excellent stimulus for a range of written, artistic and dramatic activities.

The Orchard Book of Creation Stories by Margaret Mayo, Orchard Books

A fascinating collection of inventive tales from around the world, each one drawn from a different culture. There are West African, North American Indian, Polynesian, Eskimo, Aborigine, Scandinavian, Egyptian and Central American tales, which explain just how things happen and why. Discover how the first man popped out of a pea-pod in Alaska, why the Central American monkeys look like human beings, how fire, in the North American Indian story, was hidden in the trees and why, in the Scandinavian story, the sea is so salty. Children will enjoy inventing their own creation myths, illustrating them and presenting them to the class.

THREE CLASSSIC NOVELS FOR OLDER READERS

The Adventures of Tom Sawyer by Mark Twain, Viking

Tom Sawyer, first published in 1876, is the enduringly popular tale of the irrepressible small-town boy growing up in the South at the time of the American Civil War. The novel is filled with memorable scenes: Tom tricking his pals to whitewash the fence, his friendship with the unconventional Huck Finn, his courtship of the pretty Becky Thatcher, his pursuit by the evil 'Injun Joe' and the exciting discovery of the hidden treasure. This is a story full of action and suspense and wonderfully-drawn, memorable characters. Simplified versions and guided readers never succeed in capturing the linguistic richness of the original story. This edition is the complete and unabridged text but the reader is helped through the story by the generous annotations, captions and explanations of history, poplar culture, geography and customs. It is lavishly-illustrated with drawings, diagrams, maps and paintings. Other classic novels published in this series, and which would be valuable additions to any school book stock, include *Around the World in Eighty Days*, *The Call of the Wild*, *Heidi*, *The Jungle Book* and *Treasure Island*.

Swallow and Amazons by Arthur Ransome, Red Fox

Set in the Lake District, this stirring tale of adventure is the first in a series about two families: The Walkers and the Blackets. The four children in the novel are independent and resourceful and spend their summers camping on Wild Cat Island playing pirates and sailing. When they challenge the town children to prove their seamanship, the real adventure begins. There are strong story lines, a great deal of humour, many rounded characters and careful descriptions in Arthur Ransome's novels and they offer excellent texts for using in *The Literacy Hour* to examine with children the language and structure of a carefully-crafted story and for investigating the author's point of view.

Moonfleet by J. M. Faulkner, Puffin

Moonfleet has all the ingredients of a rollicking adventure story: smugglers, buried treasure, hidden passages, shipwrecks, exciting chases along the beach and a dreadful curse. This is a compelling story of fast action and chilling menace and is full of the atmosphere of eighteenth-century England. The novel is inaccessible for the less fluent reader because of the detailed and sometimes complex language, but it is worth reading aloud or using extracts to show children how a master storyteller weaves a fast-moving and gripping story.

THREE SHORT STORY COLLECTIONS FOR OLDER READERS

Short stories, by their very brevity and spareness of build are often more suitable for discussion than novels are. In stories you will find many details that deserve to be looked at closely. These details – crucial words and sentences, pivotal incidents, speeches and motives can be related to theme intention, attitude, criticism of life to show how these abstractions are embodied in the story.

(Barnes and Egford, 1973)

The Ceremony and Other Stories by Martyn Copus, Fontana Lions

Seven very funny stories, full of verbal wit, true-to-life characters, amusing escapades and clever surprises and which are guaranteed to keep the reader's attention. The stories centre on Terry, who is forever using his imagination and finding himself up to his neck in trouble. Of course, Tony, his best friend, is always there to suggest new ideas and adventures. The first story in which Terry, to be one of the gang, has to pass the dreaded initiation ceremony, will make the reader laugh out loud. Simply written, gripping and hilariously funny and with clever twists at the end, these stories will ensure a lot of laughs. This is an excellent collection which will appeal to boys in particular and is ideal for demonstrating how good-quality, short-story writing is constructed.

A Northern Childhood by George Layton, Longman

A Northern Childhood is a warm and funny collection written in a lively, conversational style. The stories are based on the writer's own childhood experiences in Bradford where he grew up in the 1950s. Amusing storylines, strongly drawn characters, authenticity and humour characterise these very funny, often touching and always optimistic stories about boys growing up in a northern city.

The Turning Tide and Other Stories, edited by Gervase Phinn, Nelson

A wide selection of lively writing by well-known writers. Included in this anthology are stories by Joan Aiken, Gene Kemp, Berlie Doherty, Christine Bentley, David Harmer and Marjorie Kinnan Rawlings. There are funny, sad, contemplative, poignant and challenging stories that show the whole range of styles and structures. Imaginative follow-up activities are written at the back of the collection to encourage pupils to respond to the material and develop *The National Curriculum* requirements of reading, writing, listening and speaking. The ideas for writing offer individual, pair and group work ideal for *The Literacy Hour* activities.

NOVELS FOR OLDER READERS IN DIFFERENT GENRES

There is no doubt at all in our minds that one of the most important tasks facing the teacher of older juniors is to increase the amount and range of their reading. We believe that there is a strong association between this and reading attainment.

(A Language for Life : The Bullock Report, HMSO, Para 9.4.)

Ghost Story: *The Ghost of Thomas Kemp* by Penelope Lively, Penguin

Strange things start happening in James's house. In trying to get to the bottom of the mysterious happenings he discovers a rather unusual ghost. Penelope Lively has written a number of novels where the past comes back to haunt the present – *The House in Norham Gardens, Astercote, The Driftway, The Revenge of Samuel Stokes* – and always succeeds in engaging the reader's interest.

Fantasy: *Wings* by Terry Pratchett, Doubleday

Like all Terry Pratchett's novels, this is one that boys in particular just cannot put down. It is a compelling fantasy story about a group of gnomes who live beneath a large department store soon to be razed to the ground. This is the tale of their epic journey to the Outside and the dangers that they meet.

Mystery: *The Dark Behind the Curtain* by Gillian Cross, Hippo Books

Things are not going too well at the rehearsals for the school play. There are mysterious goings on and the children are convinced that there is something sinister lurking behind the curtains. This is gripping read with a strong storyline, wonderfully drawn characters and plenty of surprises, suspense and thrills.

Science Fiction: *Space Hostages* by Nicholas Fisk, Puffin

This novel has all the ingredients for an exciting and original story : strong plot, well-drawn characters, lively dialogue and plenty of suspense. A crazed and dying pilot, nine children and a top secret spacecraft and all of them out of control find themselves lost in space. Who will take charge ? Brylo is the clever one but Tony is the strongest – and nobody argues with Tony. This is a very readable and thought-provoking story, written by the prolific and very popular children's writer.

Humour: *The Turbulent Term of Tyke Tyler* by Gene Kemp,
Penguin

Children love Gene Kemp's books. Her stories are easy to read, original, full of amusing incidents and packed with lively characters who get up to all sorts of adventures and antics. The last term at primary school is a fraught time for the teachers, particularly when a certain class contains the notorious Tyke Tyler. This is an excellent novel to read out loud and serialise over a few sessions.

Adventure: *The White Horse Gang* by Nina Bawden, Penguin

Nina Bawden is a fine author who writes with a deep understanding of children. Her books have gripping plots and wonderfully-drawn characters and contain a richness of language well worth studying. In this novel a group of lively children who need money for a good cause, kidnap the son from a very wealthy family and demand a ransom. Things do not work out quite as they expected and there is a thrilling development of the story and an exciting climax. This is an excellent text to demonstrate to children how a good writer uses a range of techniques to build up tension. It is also a useful novel to show young writers how to use significant detail in writing and draw rounded realistic characters.

Historical Story: *The Eagle of the Ninth* by Rosemary Sutcliff,
Puffin

Rosemary Sutcliff is a writer of enormously powerful stories who introduces children to demanding and complex subjects and stirs up deep feelings. In this beautifully-written novel, Roman Britain comes alive. A soldier begins his dangerous lonely journey North to find out what happened to the lost legion and bring back the standard of the Eagle. This is another text useful for showing children how to build up suspense in a story, create believable characters and use vivid detail and description.

Sport Story: *Tiger of the Track* by Michael Hardcastle, Magnet

This is the sequel to another very readable short novel, *Roar to Victory*. Lee has to face a new challenge when his elder brother says he is a weakling. Determined to prove his brother wrong, he decides to ride on the toughest motorcycle circuit in Britain. Michael Hardcastle is a prolific writer of sports stories that will appeal to reluctant boy readers in particular. The pace is fast, the plots action-packed and the language very accessible.

School Story: *Dear Mr. Henshaw* by Beverly Cleary, Penguin

One of the finest American writers for children, Beverly Cleary writes with verve and imagination and creates warm-hearted, original stories and memorable characters. In this novel, written in the form of a series of letters, Leigh writes to a favourite author and soon they are corresponding regularly. This is an interesting text to use as a model for children's own writing and offers lots of possibilities for oral and drama work.

War Story: *Goodnight Mr. Tom* by Michelle Magorian, Kestrel

An extraordinary book full of superb characters, crackling dialogue and a fascinating plot. Tom, evacuated from London, is billeted on the strong-minded, bad-tempered, and humourless Mr. Tom. The lonely child and the crusty old man develop a warm, gentle relationship that brings tears to the eye. This is a beautifully written novel and ideal for studying in some detail over a period of time.

THREE POETRY ANTHOLOGIES

Island of the Children, an Anthology of New Poems, compiled by Angela Huth, decorations by Jane Ray, Orchard Books

The poems in this collection vary in style and subject and are all previously unpublished. Angela Huth wrote to over a hundred poets and published their responses in this splendidly rich and original collection. There are poems of different lengths, moods and subjects, by well-known poets and unknown writers, each one generously printed and beautifully illustrated.

Lizard over Ice, edited by Gervase Phinn, Nelson

This anthology contains over 150 exciting and largely unfamiliar poems including haiku, jokes, chants and charms, epitaphs, ballads, acrostics, concrete poems and riddles. Poems modern and traditional come from Europe and Africa, the Caribbean, America and the Far East. Some of the poems have been written by children.

The Kingfisher Book of Children's Poetry, selected by Michael Rosen, Kingfisher Books

A comprehensive collection of sad, funny, moving and powerful poems, produced in clear print with bold, bright illustrations. There are traditional favourites, ballads, lyrics, patterned poems, riddles and nonsense verse and many more. 'What you have in this book,' writes Michael Rosen, 'are hundreds of thoughts, dreams and ideas trapped in words for you to read, say or sing.' The companion volume, *The Kingfisher Book of Comic Verse*, edited by Roger McGough, incorporates all kinds of verse from the witty to the bizarre, the subtly amusing to the hilarious.

THREE INDIVIDUAL POETRY COLLECTIONS

Ask a Silly Question by Irene Rawnsley, Methuen

Brimming with laughter and fun, this delightfully-inventive collection is full of sparkling language and shrewd insight. Written around four themes: *Me and My Family*, *In School*, *In the Playground and Out and About*, this collection is a must for the primary classroom. Teachers will smile as they recognise children like Tracey Johnson, the *Teacher's Pet* and Jonathan, the *Copycat*, and children will laugh loudly at *A Nut up my Nose* and *Changing Places*.

Thawing Frozen Frogs by Brian Patten, Viking

An imaginative and varied sequel to *Gargling With Jelly*, this collection is excellent for introducing children to the whole range of poetry: sad and serious verse like *Aphasia* sits alongside manic and hilarious poems like *The Utter Butter Nutter*. Children love the sound, speed, action and humour of Brian Patten's poetry.

Classroom Creatures by Gervase Phinn, Roselea Publications

Meet *The Little Chatterbox* who has a particular way with words, join mum and dad on *Parents' Evening*, go along on the *School Trip* to Scarborough, eavesdrop on the *Interrogation on the Nursery*, read the *Letter to the Headteacher* and meet a whole collection of children, parents, teachers and the dreaded school inspectors. All those involved in the education of the young will recognise the delights and disasters of everyday life in school. Illustrated with panache by Matthew Phinn.

THREE NON-FICTION BOOKS

There is a massive range of non-fiction books now available, written specifically with children in mind. There are comprehensive guides to history, geography, art, music and the world of science, and also engrossing and very readable texts on more esoteric subjects like philosophy and astronomy. There are books on every conceivable subject from incredible insects to dangerous dinosaurs. The following reference books are all 'un-stuffy', brightly-illustrated, innovative and bring the information to life in a clear, concise and entertaining way.

Keeping Clean: A Very Peculiar History by Daisy Kerr, Watts Books

This is the third book in a fascinating series that includes *Mummies*, *Underwear* and *Vanity*. In this superbly-illustrated and clearly written volume, the author gives a very public account of a very private subject. From Ancient Roman sponge sticks to Viking ear-wax removers from medieval bath houses to the 264 commodes of Versailles, from the monks' multi-seater lavatory to the astronauts space funnels – we learn all about ablutions through the ages.

Anne Frank: Beyond the Diary by Rudd van der Rol and Rian Verhoeven, Puffin

The Diary of Anne Frank is a must for all older children and this companion volume, with superb photographs and clear, simple text, helps the young reader to understand about Anne's life and the frightening world in which she lived. Another book by these fine writers is *Dear Anne Frank*, a series of letters written to Anne by children today. The letters are moving, perceptive and thoughtful and can lead to some lively discussions about Anne's world compared to the world as it is today.

Incredible Cross-Sections by Stephen Biesty, Dorling Kindersley

Children will spend hours looking though this fascinating book and studying the highly-detailed cross sections of building and machines that range from a mediaeval cathedral to a Spanish galleon. It is full of remarkable facts and figures and is guaranteed to intrigue. All the Dorling Kindersley books contain superb designs and stunning photographs that bring the world of non-fiction to life. Other books worth adding to the library collection are: *The Children's Encyclopaedia, The Eyewitness Atlas of the World, The Child's Book of Art* and *The Illustrated History of the World*.

Conclusion

The National Curriculum and The National Literacy Strategy both stress the vital importance of providing rich and stimulating texts – fiction, poetry, playscripts and non-fiction material. All pupils are entitled to hear, read and discuss picture books, nursery rhymes, folk tales, legends and other stories in different genres, to be exposed to literature which will challenge and excite them and to learn, through lively discussion and sensitive analysis of the texts, just how language works. Children should :

> Encounter an environment in which they are surrounded by books and other reading material, presented in an attractive and inviting way. Activities should ensure that pupils hear books, stories and poems read aloud … as well as rhymes, poems, songs and familiar stories (including traditional stories from a variety of cultures).
>
> (English in the National Curriculum, Programmes of Study, Key Stage 1, 1989)

If we provide children with this variety of stimulating texts, with stories and poems that fascinate, excite, intrigue and amuse, that give them fresh insights, that open their minds and imaginations and that introduce them to the wonderful richness and range of language, then we produce avid, enthusiastic and discriminatory readers and offer them the very best models for their own writing. This is no new philosophy. It has been a fundamental belief of all those who have attempted to open the wonderful world of literature and language to the young. As Goethe said: 'Everything has been thought of before. Our challenge is to think of it again.'

Questions for personal reflection and group discussion

1 In more schools, heads need to develop clear, well-formulated policies which are subscribed to by the whole staff and which form the basis of a planned programme of reading.
(From *The Teaching and Learning of Reading in Primary Schools: A Report by HMI, Para 80,* Department of Education and Science, 1990)
Few schools have consistent policies which ensure that children receive a suitably broad and balanced experience of good literature, including poetry, from year to year.
From *Aspects of Primary Education: The Teaching and Learning of Language and Literacy, an Inspectorate Review by HMI, Para 21,* Department of Education and Science, 1990)

As a staff, examine your school's English Policy Document. Does it include an agreed plan for reading development? Are there clear and well-understood aims and a description of the methods for achieving them? Is there a book selection policy? Are there procedures for assessing and recording progress?

2 In the HMI report, *The Teaching and Learning of Reading in Primary Schools*, certain characteristics were listed of those schools which achieved high standards of reading. One characteristic was that the schools *had a wide variety of appropriate books and other materials, effectively organised and matched to individual needs* (Para 6, xii). The report concluded that: *Good standards of reading cannot be achieved without adequate and suitable resources* (Para 86).

   How do you as a staff decide what is adequate and suitable for the pupils in your school? How do you keep up to date with children's literature? For example, does each member of staff review books and report back to colleagues? Discuss and write down the ways in which you could keep yourselves better informed about children's literature.

3 Look at the book corner in your classroom. Is it attractive and inviting? What are the weaknesses in the stock of books? Does it contain a full range of reading material including:

   - books without words
   - big books
   - poetry
   - non-fiction and reference material
   - books suitable for the struggling reader
   - books suitable for the gifted reader?

4 Devise an annotated booklist for parents which includes advice on the selection of books.

5 Devise a set of guidelines for children about the selection of suitable books.

6 Conduct a small-scale survey of the children in your class to discover what they read and the factors which influence their choice of books. You might consider such areas as:

   - book jacket
   - subject matter
   - illustrations
   - familiarity with author
   - print layout
   - paperbacks v. hardbacks
   - teacher influence

- parental influence
- influence of television (adaptations etc.)

Recommended readings

Bennett, Jill (1975) *Learning to Read with Picture Books*. Stroud: Thimble Press. This short book has become a standard source of ideas about and inspiration for changes in the way young children are helped to become readers. It focuses on books themselves supplying a comprehensive annotated selection of real books for beginning readers which is updated as new editions are printed. There are a number of useful journals which will help you to increase your knowledge of children's books and keep you in touch with the world of children's books.

Books for Keeps, six times a year. Feature articles and short reviews.

Books for Your Children, three times a year. A lively journal aimed at parents.

Dragon's Teeth, four times a year. The anti-racist children's book magazine with features and reviews, mainly on multicultural books.

Language and Learning, three times a year. Contains articles from teachers on the work in the classroom they are doing in the field of language.

Language Matters, three times a year. Contains articles on language and literacy teaching in school.

Signal, three times a year. Reflective articles on various aspects of children's literature.

Also: Book Trust Touring Exhibitions provide a focus of interest, offering children and parents the opportunity to look at, handle and read carefully selected children's books, e.g. *Children's Books of the Year* – an annual exhibition of over 300 titles for children of all ages (Book Trust, Book House, 45 East Hill, London SW18 2QZ

Bibliography

Barber, M. (1997) 'Transforming Standards of Literacy' in McClelland, N. (ed) *Building a Literate Nation*, London: Trentham Books

Barnes, D.R. and Egford, R.F. (1973) *Twentieth Century Short Stories*, London : Harrap

Bettleheim, B. and Zelan, K. (1982) *On Learning to Read : The Child's Fascination with Meaning*, London : Thames and Hudson

DES (1979) *A Language for Life: The Bullock Report*, Dept of Education and Science, London: HMSO

DES (1988) *The Report of the Committee of Inquiry into the Teaching of English Language: The Kingman Report*, Dept. of Education and Science, London: HMSO

DES (1989) *English in the National Curriculum, Programme of Study for Reading, Key Stage 1*, Dept. of Education and Science, London: HMSO

DfEE (1998) *The National Literacy Strategy: Framework for Teaching*, Dept. for Education and Employment, London: HMSO

Holmes, R. (1990) *Coleridge: Early Visions*, London: Hodder & Stoughton
Jones, A. and Buttrey, J. (1970) *Children and Stories*, Oxford: Basil Blackwell
Meek, M. *et al.* (1977) *The Cool Web*, London, The Bodley Head
Meek, M. (1982) *Learning to Read*, London, The Bodley Head
Shilling, J. (1999) 'Creating an Appetite for Adventure', *The Daily Telegraph*,
    24.7.99

4 Reading is more than words and sentences

Ros Fisher

Reading to learn and learning to read

Twenty five years ago the Bullock Report stated,

> The primary teacher ... has it in his power to establish a language policy across the curriculum. Whether or not he is taking that opportunity will depend upon the extent to which the various uses of language permeate all the other learning activities, or to which, on the other hand, language learning is regarded as a separate activity. The distinction is a crucial one, and a great deal follows from it. For language to play its full role as a means of learning, the teacher must create in the classroom an environment which encourages a wide range of language uses.
>
> (DES, 1975:12.3)

This notion of language across the curriculum became established in most schools and to a large degree planning for English recognised the interlocking of language development and learning. The idea of reading to learn alongside learning to read is reinforced in the National Curriculum. Authors such as Mallett (1991), Neate (1992) have explored ways of helping children to use text to locate information. Others have examined the use of different text types in the primary classroom Littlefair (1992), and Wray and Lewis (1997).

The introduction of the National Literacy Strategy, or any teaching programme where the emphasis is exclusively on teaching literacy skills aside from content, could be seen to imply that literacy is a separate skill and that literacy is best taught in separate lessons and outside of 'content'. Indeed there is a great deal of knowledge about the language itself and how it works that is best learned in an English lesson. However our own experience and evidence from children's reading preferences show that neat objectives do not cover all that reading encompasses. Reading is a useful tool in school across a range of subjects to locate, investigate and evaluate information and in everyday life for many different purposes. Reading is to be enjoyed. It entertains, it provides us with ways of escape it gives us vicarious experiences. It is not only fiction or narrative that does this but non-fiction: information books can also be a source of enjoyment, read for no other purpose than recreation. Rosenblatt (1991) points out that we read for different purposes and that these do not always fit neatly into categories of 'for information' or 'for pleasure'. She says,

> reading is not all of one piece. We read for information, but we are conscious of emotions about it and feel pleasure when the words we call up arouse vivid images and are rhythmic to the inner ear. Or we experience a poem but are conscious of acquiring some information about, say, Greek warfare (p445).

You only have to watch two children sharing an information book together to see the truth of this.

I shall start this chapter by looking at the types of text children will encounter in school and at home and consider what there is to learn about these in order to help children to use them confidently and effectively. Then I shall explore ways in which the teacher can teach children to use a range of texts to learn about literacy at home as well as at school, and about other aspects of the curriculum. I shall also consider how this can be done both inside and outside specific literacy lessons and without losing the important notion that literacy is both what we learn and a means whereby we learn about our world.

Range of text types

The National Literacy Strategy (NLS) Framework for Teaching (DfEE, 1998) splits the framework of objectives into 'fiction and poetry' and 'non-fiction'. The framework recognises six main non-fiction text types: recount, instructions, non-chronological reports, explanations, persuasive or discussion text and alphabetically ordered text. Within each general text type NLS suggests a range of occasions when these types of text might be used, see Figure 4.1.

Purposes

One of the first things to recognise about the different kinds of text children will encounter is that the purpose of the text will influence the way the

Recount	Recounts of observations
	Recounts of visits
	Recounts of events
	News reports
	Autobiography
	Diary entries
Instructions	Rules
	Recipes
	How to construct ...
	Plans
	Timetables
Non-chronological reports	Report of information from own experience
	Report of information from own research
	Reports to describe and classify
	Linked to work in other subjects
Explanations	Flow charts
	Diagrams
	Explain a process
	Answer a question
	Linked to other subjects
Persuasive writing/ discussion	Letters from newspapers
	Articles from newspapers/books
	Advertisements
Alphabetic	Dictionaries
	Thesauruses
	Glossaries
	Indexes
	Encyclopaedias
	Atlases

Figure 4.1 Non-fiction text types

text is laid out and the language that is used. The NLS framework (DfEE, 1998) is quite explicit about this and explains the features of each text type. See Figure 4.2. It is important to notice that these summary descriptions of the text type do not come until relatively late in the primary years. Earlier work concentrates on familiarising children with the language and structure of the text through both reading and writing. They are only expected to know the particular features of the text by the term given in brackets in the figure below. Even the youngest children in school enjoy looking at and talking about a whole range of texts.

These are not hard and fast rules. In fact books will often contain more than one text type: an information book could easily include non-chronological reports, explanations and instructions. However, familiarity

Recount	Introduction to orientate reader Chronological sequence Supporting illustrations Degree of formality adopted Use of connectives e.g. first … next … once (Y5T1T21)
Instructions	Noting intended outcome at beginning Listing materials or ingredients Clearly set out sequential stages Language of commands, e.g. imperative verbs (Y4T1T22)
Non-chronological reports	Introduction to orientate reader Use of generalisations to categorise Language to describe and differentiate Impersonal language Mostly present tense (Y6T1T13)
Explanations	Impersonal style e.g. complex sentences: use of passive voice Technical vocabulary Hypothetical language (*if…then, might when the* …) Use of words/phrases to make sequential, causal logical connections, e.g. *while during, after, because, due to, only, when, so* (Y5T2T15)
Persuasive/ discussion text	Use of language to gain attention, respect etc. Use of persuasive devices and definitions Use of rhetorical questions Deliberate ambiguities Sequence of points Provision of examples, illustrations, evidence etc. (Adapted from Y5T3T12 and Y6T2T15)
Alphabetically ordered text	Alphabetical order Use of definitions and explanations etc.

Figure 4.2 Features of main text types

with the language and structure of the different text types can provide useful insights for children that will help their expectations when reading and their control over their own writing. It is also important to recognise that purpose affects not only how the author organises the text, but how we read that text. As Rosenblatt proposed we do not always go to a text with the same purpose as the author intended. The reader may bring different purposes to the reading of the same text at different occasions. For example,

I may browse through a recipe book on a winter's evening or I may go to it with the purpose of baking my Christmas cake. At each occasion my way of reading will be different.

For children it is also important that they see the different types of texts they meet in school as being part of the world and not just books from shelves at school. For example, they may read a recount text about Shakespeare at school but should recognise that is the type of text they meet when they read about their favourite footballer in a Fanzine.

Compare these two examples of information text:

> William Shakespeare was the eldest child of the bailiff (mayor) of Stratford on Avon. In 1582 Shakespeare married Anne Hathaway. Their first child Suzannah, was born the following year and twins, Hamnet and Judith followed in 1585. Hamnet died when he was 11. Nobody knows what Shakespeare was doing for a living in his early twenties, but by 1592 he was earning money as an actor and playwright in London while his wife and family remained in Stratford.
>
> (*Oxford Children's Encyclopaedia*, 1994 p300)

and

> Daniele (pronounced Danny-ellie) Dichio was born on the 19th October, 1974 in Hammersmith, London. He and his girlfriend, Claire, have a new-born son, Luca. The six foot three striker started his career at QPR, the team he supports, scoring 20 in 75 games, before his dream move to Italy and Sampdoria. Troubled with injury, however, he was sent on loan to Lecce before chucking it all in and coming up to Sunderland.
>
> (A Love Supreme, 1998 p16)

Each of these examples of recount, telling about a particular person, adopt some (but not all) of the features described in Figure 4.2. The introductory sentence orientates the reader to the subject. The sequence of the text is chronological. Sentence structure is complex containing a lot of information in a few lines. Including texts from children's own lives gives a powerful message that reading is not only a school based practice but has a relevance throughout our lives.

Audience

In addition to the purpose of the text, the author has had to make a decision about the audience. This also influences the decisions that are made about the language and words that are chosen. Consider the following passages based on the kind of information texts that are written for children. Here, although the content of the text is similar the language is used with different degrees of formality.

> Rodents' teeth are made for gnawing. The front teeth, or incisors, keep on growing. Animals such as guinea pigs need hard food to wear their teeth down. A guinea pig has short ears, short legs and no tail.

and

> Some silly people say that if you hold a guinea pig up by its tail its eyes will fall out. Well that's rubbish, and anyway you can't do that, because guinea pigs don't have tails. Guinea pigs have really good front teeth which are brilliant for gnawing things. These teeth go on and on growing all through the animal's life, and are self sharpening – imagine that!

In each of these the writer's view of their audience is different. In the latter language is used in a conversational way to entertain as well as inform. In the former a more formal style is adopted and more technical language is used. This does not imply that one text is better than the other, rather that the author's intentions and view of their reader are different. Children can compare and evaluate the two styles: as with us there will be those who prefer one to the other. This is personal taste and is also related to the reader's purpose at the time of reading.

Subject

Different subjects have different types of text that are used more than others. The type of information that is to be included requires different types of texts. To take the example of Geography, the kind of text types which children may encounter include: non-chronological reports as in information books about places; explanations, as in 'how to make a rain gauge'; recounts as found in autobiography, diaries, letters etc.; persuasive writing, as found, for example, in some information about the environment. To these can be added maps, charts, and diagrams which each require a particular kind of reading.

If children can come to these texts with familiarity they are more likely to be able to locate, evaluate and use the information found therein. Equally, using a wide range of text types increases the understanding that children gain from their reading around a topic. There does not have to be a straight split between fiction and non-fiction; for pleasure and for information. Consider the way in which study of the second World War can be enriched by use of information books on the war, the reading of a novel such as

Goodnight Mr Tom by Michelle Magorian (1981) and poems by poets of the time. Consider also how children's writing using their experience of a range of different genres and text types can increase their understanding of the issues and knowledge of the facts.

Another look at purpose

Finally we need to help children understand that writing and reading are not neutral activities. The author has his/her own viewpoint which affects the choice of vocabulary, language and even what information is contained in the text. Compare these two reports from information books on the Caribbean:

> Central America is a bridge of land between North and South America. Thick rainforest covers the sides of the mountains. Most people are farmers. They grow coffee, sugar and fruit. Tropical fruits, sugar and spices also grow well on the beautiful islands of the Caribbean. Tourists come here to enjoy the hot sunshine, the sea and happy Caribbean music.
>
> (Royston and Hawsley, 1995)

> Rich people and poor people in Jamaica have very different lives. A small number of very rich families own most of the land and can buy whatever they want or need to be comfortable. But for many people life is hard. One third of Jamaicans live in poverty. They struggle to afford decent housing, healthy food or medicine when they fall ill.
>
> (Barraclough 1995)

Here, although both extracts are factually correct, the author's choice of information and perspective has given a different picture of the same subject. Critical literacy perspectives encourage teachers to help readers look beyond what is written to the underlying cultural context. Luke (as cited in Jongsma, 1991) states,

> our aim is to get students to construct and to challenge texts, to see how texts provide selective versions of the world ... with an eye towards transforming social, economic and cultural conditions (p518)

The close analysis of texts specified in the NLS teaching objectives and the rewriting of texts for different audiences helps children explore their understanding of the text as more than a neutral artefact.

Learning to read

Let us now look at how we might use this knowledge to teach children to read. Look at the following extract and say what sort of book it comes from and who is the intended audience:

> Polar bears are the largest of all bears. They are three times heavier than a male lion!
>
> They have long thick coats to keep them warm. They also have a thick layer of fat under the skin for extra warmth. Their skin is black, but their fur is white. In the snow their prey can't see them coming very easily.
>
> Polar bears have sharper teeth than grizzly bears, because they eat more meat. Their claws are sharp too, to help them grip slippery seals. Polar bears are excellent swimmers. They swim with their front paws and steer with their back legs. Underwater they keep their eyes open, but can close their nostrils.
>
> (Theodorou and Telford, 1996)

With your knowledge of text you can easily tell that this is from an information book written for children. You recognise the way the text is structured with an opening introduction to orientate the reader followed by description of the subject, here polar bears. You know that the polar bears referred to here are polar bears in general and not a particular family of bears as would be the case were the text narrative. The language features are also typical of this type of text and helped in your recognition. Language is used to describe and differentiate e.g. 'They are three times heavier than a male lion'. The present tense is used throughout. The language is impersonal and simple technical terms are used such as, claws, fur, prey, nostrils. This is a good example of how you as an experienced reader have implicit knowledge of the information that I have just made explicit for you. In the same way we can make use of children's experience of text and help them to recognise the features of which they already have some implicit knowledge. Beverley Derewianka from Australia has written usefully about the different text types and explains clearly the structure and features of several types of text (See Derewianka 1996).

The literacy strategy provides us with opportunities to look closely at texts in order to examine their language and structure. Using texts on a range of topics we can consider alongside children how a text fulfils the writer's purpose and how effective this is for the reader. We can look at the way in which authors use language in different ways for different audiences. We can take texts that are useful in other curriculum areas and help children to become familiar with the way they are written and organised. We can encourage children to look critically at the texts they use and consider what opinions the author is betraying and whether this is helpful or not to our purpose as a reader.

The close scrutiny of texts is an interesting and revealing study. However, we do have to be wary that deconstruction does not become destruction. If texts are only ever picked to pieces we can easily lose our purpose in the activity. Deconstruction of text is not a worthwhile academic study in its own right, it is a means of helping readers gain greater control over reading and writing so they can use this for their own purposes. It is very important that texts are enjoyed and used as well as being studied. There is time in literacy lessons to read the whole or extracts of text or to take texts that are already familiar from other contexts. There is opportunity outside these lessons to read novels or poems at greater length and to use reference material as part of work on other subjects.

There is evidence that even very young children have a sensitivity to different types of text and can from a very early age make use of this knowledge in their retelling (Pappas 1991, Fisher 1997). Clearly, having a familiarity with the various text types they are likely to encounter will help with fluency in reading as they use their knowledge to confirm expectations. This will also help with their writing for a range of purposes as they are able to choose the most appropriate language and text structure for their particular purpose and to be aware of how their choices are influenced by their own experience and how this may affect the reader.

It is equally important that teachers themselves are familiar with different text types and confident in their use. There is time in literacy lessons to *demonstrate* how and when particular texts can be used. These demonstrations can be linked to work in school such as using a dictionary to find out how to spell a word. Or linked to the world outside school as when a teacher might choose to look at a particular information book perhaps because of a news item.

Shared reading and writing gives teachers the chance to *model* how texts work and how authors choose the language they use with their own purposes in mind. Here the close relationship between reading and writing is most apparent when the teacher can model the authors' decisions in shared writing – a useful reading lesson. Here the teacher is *scaffolding* the learning, helping all children (regardless of decoding ability) to learn about the language and structure of the texts they meet. We are very good at modelling the reading of narrative, emphasising how enjoyable stories are and how we can predict what may happen and so on. We are not so good at modelling to young readers how we read information books, not always starting at the beginning and judging what we read in relation to our own information.

With the youngest children teachers can model how we use an information book and show how questions can be posed to which the book may yield an answer (Fisher 1999).

In addition, shared reading and writing provides the opportunity for metacognitive modelling in which the teacher models the thought processes of the experienced reader or writer. For example, in the earlier example from the two books on Jamaica, the teacher might reflect out loud 'I wonder why these two books make Jamaica sound like two different places. I wonder who wrote them. Perhaps I'll look in another book to see what it says'. Metacognitive modelling can allow children insights into the way an experienced reader thinks as s/he reads.

In the time when children work independently they can be helped to *investigate* how texts work using DARTS (Directed Activities Related to Texts). Here cloze activities, highlighting, reordering and representing text in another form are all ways in which readers can gain more familiarity and confidence with text.

As well as the whole class time at the start of the lesson, a plenary gives the opportunity for *evaluation* of texts and the chance for children to *discuss* their ideas and opinions.

Reading to learn

The clear-cut separation of the literacy lesson from the rest of the curriculum can be looked on as a positive feature of language across the curriculum. It releases teachers from the dilemma which used to face them when, for example, using information books in other subjects. What was the purpose of the lesson? Were children learning about a subject or were they learning how to locate information in reference books? So often what happened was that the children's experience did not quite achieve either objective. Although the extra time afforded to core subjects has reduced the amount of time available to other subjects, this time is now able to be dedicated to the subject. Literacy is one of many tools that can be used to learn more about the topic or subject to be studied. In addition, this provides a useful demonstration of the uses of different texts in the context for which they were written.

Using literacy to explore and find out about things is an important skill both for later schoolwork and for life at home. Using an encyclopaedia is not just a source of information for schoolwork but alphabetically arranged information is in constant use in our daily lives, e.g. the telephone directory. We live in an information rich society: reading and using information is part of our everyday lives.

Critical reading

It is fascinating how critical children are of others' opinions when it relates to their favourite football team or TV show but how accepting they can be of opinions found in books relating to work in school. When using texts to locate information for use at home or school, the reader needs to be able to evaluate how accurate that information might be and judge any bias in the presentation and in their own interpretation of it. Take, for example, this extract on farming taken from a child's information book. The choice of content and use of vocabulary indicate the stance of the writer.

> The chickens peck quietly in the farmyard under the watchful eye of the cock, perched proudly on the dung heap. Occasionally, as he has done since dawn, he throws back his head and crows: 'Cock-a-doodle-do!'
>
> (Halley, 1996)

Morgan (1997) identifies four principal ideas to underpin critical reading:

1 Any text is made in a particular society at a particular time. This influences the form it takes and the ideas it represents.
2 Any text gives you a particular version (or part of) a story: it emphasises certain things; and has its gaps and is silent about certain things.
3 Texts don't contain one fixed, definite meaning put there by the author. Different kinds of readers in different societies and times can produce different meanings for the same text because of what they bring to it.
4 Any text offers you a way of seeing and valuing things and invites you to accept its version as the truth, the way things are meant to be.
  (pp39–42)

Even beginning readers can evaluate the effectiveness of the medium and the perspective of the message presented in the texts they encounter. Many books provide illustrations to assist the beginning reader in his or her search for information. In the extracts below the author has made a choice about what information is given and how it is portrayed. Children could be asked to make similar maps or factsheets of their own areas then compare and discuss each other's choice of content. They could look at different sources of information on the Caribbean and create their own maps or factsheets, again comparing and discussing their choices. See Figures 4.3 and 4.4

Interrelatedness

I see there being a useful symbiotic relationship between literacy as it is *taught* inside the literacy lesson and literacy as it is *used* outside this time

Jamaica

Jamaica is an island in the Caribbean Sea, south of Cuba.

Key facts

Size: 10,991 sq km
Population: Over 2 million
Currency: Jamaican dollar
Main language: English

Capital city: Kingston. Built by a deep, sheltered harbour, this city was once ruled by a pirate, Captain Morgan, and his Buccaneers.

Landscape: Jamaica is a tropical island with lush rainforests, pretty waterfalls and dazzling white beaches. It is actually the tip of an undersea mountain range. Blue Mountain Peak (2256 m) is the highest mountain on the island.

Captain Morgan

Places to visit: As well as beaches, there are wildlife parks and bird sanctuaries where some of the world's most exotic birds can be seen. There are working sugar and banana plantations.

Industries

Tourism
Minerals
Farming

A Jamaican beach

Figure 4.3 Pirate picture and text (Butterfield, 1992)

Figure 4.4 Map from *My Big Book of the World* (Royston and Hawsley, 1995).

(although, of course, children are still learning about literacy while using texts). The interrelatedness of literacy inside the literacy lesson and beyond should be drawn upon where possible. There is a great deal of scope in planning work in other subjects backed by the study of supporting text types in the literacy lesson. Topics based in other curriculum areas could be scheduled to coincide with coverage of the appropriate text type in the National Literacy Framework. All the experiences children have with texts will work together to create the picture they develop of texts and reading: whether they are studying a text inside the literacy lesson; whether using the text elsewhere in the school day or at home; whether enjoying a text for the pleasure it brings. How much more complete will be their understanding of the joys and usefulness of reading if these experiences overlap and inform each other.

Use of narrative

Compare the following two extracts of text which tell about hurricanes in the Caribbean:

> In 1988 a hurricane called Hurricane Gilbert hit Jamaica. It did a lot of damage. Most of the banana plants and many coffee bushes were destroyed.
>
> (Barraclough, 1995)

This can be brought to life by the use of narrative as is illustrated in this extract from an autobiographical story:

> The winds howled round our door and shook the house. The rain beat down on the tin roof and sounded like a hundred steel drums. Grandma took Em and me by the hand and led us out into the wild night. As we struggled down the lane, the wind tugged at our clothes and tried to drive us back and knock us down. On and on we pushed. There were people all around us, all running for the strong shelter that was our school.
>
> (Linden, 1994)

In Figure 4.5 you can see from extracts from texts about the Caribbean how different types of text written for different purposes can be used to increase children's understanding of what they are learning. The figure shows how features of particular text types are useful and how they may complement each other.

Information Text	Narrative (Linden 1994)
Where is it?	
In the Caribbean sea, south of Cuba (Butterfield, 1993 p15)	Long ago and far away
What is it?	
a tropical island with lush rainforests, pretty waterfalls and dazzling white beaches (Butterfield, 1993 p15)	A coral island
What is it like?	
Most people are farmers. They grow coffee, sugar and fruit. Tropical fruits, sugar and spices also grow well …. (Royston and Hawsley 1995)	We ate good food on the island, food that you've possibly never seen in your whole life …. Boy! everything on that island tasted sweet.
Textual features	
Technical vocabulary Impersonal Precision	Text helps comprehension Personal commentary Atmosphere

Figure 4.5 Information about a Caribbean island

Learning about texts and using texts

As well as capitalising on the ways in which narrative and information text can work together to enrich children's understanding, we can also look at the aspects of texts that can be taught inside the literacy lesson and how this knowledge can then be used in other subjects. Figure 4.6 summarises this relationship. I have worded the title of the figure deliberately. Instead of writing 'using information books' I have used the word 'texts' to include the use of fiction and/or narrative. We have all gained some of our knowledge of the world from the novels we read. This source of vicarious experience should not be ignored – though it must, of course, be evaluated like any other information source.

Conclusion

Reading is an enjoyable and useful activity. As teachers, we need to enable children to read for a wide range of purposes: including for pleasure and to find information. We need to help them to see that reading is something

Inside	Outside
• Reading symbols on maps and charts	• Looking at a map of the Caribbean to locate …
• Looking at charts and discussing how they present information	• Looking at charts to find out …
• Looking for bias in texts and talking about how it is recognised	• Evaluating related texts and matching own knowledge against that found in text.
• Looking at structure and language features of texts	• Finding and using most appropriate sources of information
• Looking at headings, captions and other signposts in text which facilitate the reader	• As above
• Studying narrative text or poetry; considering fact and fiction, characterisation, setting and so on	• Considering information gained from reading narrative and poetry and evaluating it against other sources of information

Figure 4.6 Using texts to find information inside and outside the literacy lesson

that happens everyday in their lives outside school and that it is something that is useful in school and in the world of work. We need to help them gain the experience of a wide range of text types and help them to become familiar with the language and structure of the different texts they will meet. They need to understand how this language and structure is related to the purpose the author had when he or she was writing, who he or she was writing for and what the author's own view is of the topic. Children need also to know that they do not have to be dictated to by the author's purposes but can read a range of texts for their own purposes and can bring their own interpretations to that reading.

Teachers can help children to gain this experience both inside the literacy lesson and outside. All the experience children have of reading and writing both in school and outside will contribute to the knowledge they accumulate and, ultimately to the skill with which they read and the pleasure and use that it affords them.

Questions for personal reflection or group discussion

1 Look at the texts available for children to read in your classroom. What picture of reading will children draw from your collection.
2 Think of all the reading you do as part of your daily life: is this range reflected in school?
3 Does your class have the chance to read information books for pleasure and draw on their reading of fiction as a source of information?
4 Does your planning for literacy link with other curriculum areas and vice versa?
5 Are there still sufficient opportunities for children to read (or have read to them) full length novels for pleasure?
6 What opportunities do you use to think aloud (metacognitive modelling) as a reader to show children how readers think as they read?
7 How can children gain experience of questioning texts as to the author's beliefs, purposes and credentials?

Recommended readings

Christie, F. and Misson, R. (Eds) (1998) *Literacy and Schooling* London: Routledge.
Derewianka, B. (1996) *Exploring the Writing of Genres* Royston, Hertfordshire: UKRA.
Hall, C. and Coles, M. (1999) *Children's Reading Choices* London: Routledge.
Littlefair, A.B. (1992) *Genres in the Classroom* Royston, Hertfordshire: UKRA.
Marsh J. and Hallet, E. (Eds) (1999) *Desirable Literacies. Approaches to Language and Literacy in the Early Years* London: Chapman.
Meek, M. (1996) *Information and Book Learning* Stroud: Thimble Press.
S.C.A.A. (1995) *One Week in March: a survey of the literature pupils read* Discussion Paper 4.
Wray, D. and Lewis, M. (1997) *Exending Literacy: Children Reading and Writing Non-fiction* London: Routledge.
www.qca.org.uk for where National Literacy Strategy non-fiction objectives are mapped on to QCA schemes of work in other curriculum areas.

Bibliography

A Love Supreme (1998) *The Independent Sunderland Supporters' Magazine* Issue no. 75.
Barraclough, J. (1995) *Jamaica* Worldfocus Series Oxford: Heinemann.
Butterfield, M. (1993) *Countries* Factfinders Series London: Watts Books.
D.E.S. (1975) *A Language for Life* (The Bullock Report) London: HMSO.
DfEE (1998) *The National Literacy Strategy: Framework for Teaching.* London: DfEE.
Derewianka, B. (1996) *Exploring the Writing of Genres* Royston, Hertfordshire: UKRA.

Fisher, R. (1997) 'Children's Understanding of Narrative and Information Genres on Starting School' *Early Years* Vol. 18, No. 1 pp15–19.

Fisher, R. (1999) 'Children's Developing Understanding of Narrative and Information Genres in their First Year of School' *Education* Vol 16, No. 1 pp3–13.

Halley, N. (1996) *Farm* Eyewitness Guides London: Dorling Kindersley.

Jongsma, K. (1991) 'Critical Literacy: Questions and Answers' *The Reading Teacher* Vol. 44, pp518–19.

Linden. A.M. (1994) *Emerald Blue* London: Egmont Children's Books.

Littlefair, A.B. (1992) *Genres in the Classroom* Royston, Hertfordshire: UKRA.

Magorian, M. (1981) *Goodnight Mr Tom* London: Kestrel Books.

Mallett, M. (1991) *Making Facts Matter* London: Paul Chapman.

Morgan, W. (1997) *Critical Literacy in the Classroom: the art of the possible* London: Routledge.

Neate, B. (1992). *Finding Out about Finding Out* Sevenoaks: Hodder and Stoughton.

Oxford Children's Encyclopaedia (1994) Oxford: Oxford University Press.

Pappas, C.C. (1991) 'Fostering Full Access to Literacy by Including Information Books' *Language Arts* Vol. 68, October 1991 pp449–62.

Rawston, A. and Hawsley, G. (1995) *My Big Book of the World* London: Ultimate Editions.

Rosenblatt, L.M. (1991) 'Literature S.O.S.!' in *Language Arts* Vol. 68, October 1991.

Theodorou, R. and Telford, C. (1996) *Polar Bear and Grizzly Bear* Oxford: Heinemann.

Wray, D. and Lewis, M. (1997) *Extending Literacy: Children Reading and Writing Non-fiction* London: Routledge.

Part III

How should we encourage children to be readers?

5 Reading for real in the classroom

Observation, coaching and practice

Martin Coles

I intend in this chapter to consider just one aspect of the review a school might undertake of the methods it uses for developing children's reading – the organisation and practice of reading in the classroom. Of course, that aspect of teaching reading has been dramatically altered by the National Literacy Strategy (NLS) in England and its teaching framework that insists on a daily literacy hour.

One of the recurring themes of this book is to do with an understanding that those schools which decide to think seriously about their teaching of reading (perhaps as a result of the National Literacy Strategy) must do much more than simply think about the texts they offer children – scheme books or real books? A curriculum review of literacy practice in a school should mean that the school review the approach they take to the whole of the reading curriculum, not just the texts used but also the reading instruction offered by the teacher, classroom organisation of reading, assessment and record-keeping, and the involvement of parents. Such a review is a necessary part of any move towards a 'reading for real' approach, and the National Literacy Strategy despite the concentration on the importance of one hour of literacy teaching each day confirms the needs to pay attention to all these aspects of the reading curriculum.

I want first to look at an idea that not so long ago held sway in many primary classrooms, that is the notion of the beginning reader as an apprentice, sharing reading in the classroom with the teacher. Do recent changes in the practice of teaching reading in primary schools, which have resulted in England at least from government initiatives, mean that the concept of apprenticeship is now redundant or anachronistic?

Liz Waterland whose short book *Read With Me* (1985)is often credited as the key text in the real books movement explains her understanding of the concept of apprenticeship as it relates to beginning readers thus:

> I came to adopt instead, a view of the learner not as passive and dependant like a cuckoo chick but rather as an active and already partly

competent sharer in the task of learning to read. Here the model is apprenticeship to a craftsman. Consider the way apprenticeship works; the learner first undertakes the simplest parts of the job, then gradually the more complex ones, increasing the share he can cope with and all the time working alongside, under the control of, and with the help of, the craftsman. The apprentice does not sit passively with his mouth open; he works actively with the tools of trade in his hand.

On the face of it this last sentence indicates a serious weakness in the analogy. Traditional apprenticeship occurs in the field of manual tasks. Reading on the other hand is a mainly cognitive activity. Even recognising the place of cognitive plans in motor skills and the necessity for a certain level of hand–eye co-ordination in reading, drawing parallels between tasks which are different in so many respects might well lead to inappropriate descriptions of beginning reading. There are other problems too with Waterland's brief analysis. She asks us to consider the way apprenticeship works: 'the learner first undertakes the simplest parts of the job then gradually the more complex ones'. Now this is certainly how some classrooms work. Tasks and problems can be chosen to suit the stage of learning that the child is at. Teachers can, for instance, slowly increase the complexity of reading tasks and materials provided for children. But traditional apprenticeship is set in the workplace and the problems and tasks that are given to learners arise from the demands of the workplace. Tasks are therefore clearly and obviously purposeful. Letting the job demands select the tasks for students to practise is still one of the great inefficiencies of traditional apprenticeship.

So in traditional apprenticeship the tasks are selected either by job demands, or by the 'master', who takes the job demands into account. Yet many advocates of 'real reading' suggest allowing the child, not the teachers, to specify the task in reading apprenticeship. Children choose their own books. In this way at least, the child is in charge and controls the actions of the adult, a reversal of the traditional master–apprentice relationship.

Furthermore, apprenticeship often works on the basis of building subskills to the point where they can be integrated in the efficient performance of the target task. But, as Colin Harrison's chapter explains, reading is not a series of small skills fluently used; it is not a simple process where an individual takes a situation detail by detail and meticulously builds up a whole. For instance, in order to fulfil the basic goal of creating the meaning of a text, interpretations must be made that go well beyond the text itself, however simple the text. But the ability to do this cannot be separated from the ability to recognise the individual words within the text.

Criticisms of this kind imply that the notion of apprenticeship used as an exact model for teaching and learning reading is flawed. But if we look at apprenticeship as suggestive of what might be good classroom practice, rather than as an exact analogy, there are lessons to be learned that have a strong theoretical base and match current official orthodoxy. What then are the structural features of traditional apprenticeship and what lessons might it have for teaching and learning reading in the classroom? How does the model match with the official *approved images* of teaching reading that are coming to teachers in the form of Framework for Teaching offered by the National Literacy Strategy? There are I think some essential features of traditional apprenticeship which can be usefully applied to learning to read and which carry implications for classroom practice and which are very much in tune with these *approved images*. Those features are to do first with observation, coaching and practice, and second with social context. These features point up ways of sharing reading in the classroom. They are both ways of seeing teaching and learning reading in the classroom as assisted performance.

Apprenticeship highlights methods for carrying out a task. Apprentices learn their methods through observation, coaching and practice. The apprentice repeatedly observes the master carrying out a task, modelling the process. An apprentice then attempts to execute the same process with help and guidance from the master, i.e. coaching. A key aspect of this coaching is aid in the form of reminders and other help that the apprentice needs to complete the task. Once the apprentice has a grasp of the skill, the master reduces participation, providing only limited hints and feedback to the learner who continues to practice until the skill approximates to that of the master. It might be argued that the National Literacy Strategy's Framework for Teaching follows this model in miniature in its literacy hour recommendations by explicitly recommending teacher demonstration and modelling, scaffolding via shared reading activities, and independent work by pupils.

If we consider this model as apprenticeship, it becomes obvious that an apprenticeship approach is not a matter of *laissez-faire*. An apprenticeship approach following this paradigm does not mean just providing children with good books and assuming that it is enough simply to apprentice children to the authors and illustrators, important as good books are. Rather it is a case of being apprenticed to a teacher, of sharing reading. The pattern is one where, broadly, the child moves from listening to the adult read (observation), through reading with the adult (coaching), to reading independently (practice).

This is the path through what Vygotsky called the zone of proximal development which is the distance between the actual developmental level as determined by individual problem solving and the level of potential development as determined through problem solving under adult guidance or in collaboration with more capable peers (Vygotsky 1978 p.86) i.e. it is the gap between a child's ability working on their own and that ability working with assistance.

In the zone of proximal development assistance is provided by the teacher, the adult, the expert, the more capable peer whatever the activity and through this assistance learning awakens a variety of internal developmental processes that are able to operate only when the child is interacting with people in his environment and in Cupertino with his peers. Once these processes are internalised, they become part of the child's independent developmental achievement. (Vygotsky 1978 p.90).

Observation

Good reading teaching must be to do with assisting performance along a pathway through the zone of proximal development. The pathway starts at the point of observation where the child has a very limited understanding of the concept of reading, the reading task, or the goal to be achieved; at this level the teacher offers a model and the child's response is acquiescent observation. Only gradually does a child come to an understanding of what it might mean to read. The child gains some conception of the overall performance through listening, through conversation about a book, through questions and feedback. In this way the teacher is providing what the psychologists would call cognitive structuring in order to encourage the learner's belief that they can turn print into sense. So the child's notion of what it is to read, and what it is to be a reader, are both in the zone of proximal development. Knowing what reading is all about is the most crucial first lesson of all.

Several points are worth emphasising here. Traditional apprenticeship works in domains where the skills are usually external and readily available in both learner and teacher for observation. Applying apprenticeship methods to largely cognitive skills requires an externalisation of processes, which are usually carried out internally, in order that the learner can observe the expert strategies that the teacher is using. Of course, at the stage of observation, this means reading aloud, but also implies incidental conversation about the text and a commentary on the reading aloud in any one-to-one situation. So, for instance, the teacher might mention their change of voice as the speech marks provide a signal; they might at a certain point ask for a summary of the passage since summarising forms the basis for comprehension monitoring; they might ask questions of the text which require the reader to predict in order to encourage an overall reading strategy of hypothesis formulation and testing. The teacher might sometimes model these activities for the learner by summarising herself or, in a conversational way, making a prediction about the way the story is going in an attempt to reflect the fact that skilled reading involves developing expectations and evaluating them as evidence accumulates from the text. She might too offer some interpretative comments on the text as a demonstration that meaning is not somehow all in the text, to be extracted entirely through decoding, but relies to some extent on the reader's response. The literacy hour instructions, taking as they do the perspective of the teacher rather than the pupil, call all this *demonstration* and offer as an example teaching pupils how to read punctuation.

Of course all this has to be done with some sensitivity remembering that the eventual goal is for the teacher to fade from the scene, though when and whether this happens will depend entirely on the text and context. The zone is always with us! There is an important sense in which even undergraduates studying English are being taught, or are learning to read. The teacher becomes less obtrusive but certainly has not disappeared which is why the National Literacy Strategy format for primary school remains the same through to the end of key stage 2. Nevertheless the learner must be helped to move from observation, through coaching to practice, and overwhelming interruption from the text itself is unlikely to help motivate a reader or allow pleasure to be gained from the book. Judging the what, when, and how of intervention, and matching this to the learner's experience calls for sensitive, informed judgement. In practice a sensible compromise has to be reached between the need for commentary on the reading process and the need to provide a pleasurable and coherent reading experience. Still it is the case that there is a need to sensitise learners to the details of expert performance, which can be done by highlighting with skilful verbal description.

What else might be said about the observation stage? Well most obvious is the need for interesting materials that make sense to the learner. This point has been discussed at some length in the chapters by Jack Ousbey and Gervase Phinn. It is sufficient here to remind ourselves that if the texts used are interesting and meaningful to the child then they will not only offer motivation but also teach about 'the nature and variety of written discourse' (Meek 1982). Bamberger (1976) talks about the chief task of the teacher being to 'lure' children into reading. Teachers of the youngest children begin this luring process by storytelling and reading aloud so that children *know* the delights to be obtained from books.

Reading to children should not be confined to fiction of course. Interesting material is available in a variety of forms. The National Literacy Strategy is very clear that pupils ought to be introduced to a range of fiction, poetry and non-fiction. To become attuned to this variety of genre children must have early experience of texts other than simple narrative. Even young children might listen to newspaper accounts of current events. Comics, with their direct relationship of story to visual display through captions, stimulate a lively interest in most children. Children's own interests and hobbies might be a starting point for gathering other material.

Above all though children benefit from hearing the shape and form of written language which good stories, read well, offer. Reading aloud is a skill, which all teachers ought to continuously develop. There may well be a place for story reading that is carried out by a classroom assistant or other adult in the school, but story reading is a skilled job which ought not to be delegated lightly. Good reading will supply intonation and emphases that offer a message of meaningful reading. It is also important that children observe in the teacher an adequate image of a literate adult. Children who observe their teacher genuinely enjoying the stories she is reading will begin to see reading as something personal, not something which is carried out simply for the sake of instruction. It is important that young children do not see reading as a performance simply for the teacher's sake, irrelevant and purposeless outside the classroom. In this respect the teacher's role and attitude is crucial. Skilled readers show apprentices what it is like to be a reader, show them what kinds of choices are made about reading, and demonstrate the whole task complete.

Sometimes this reading aloud might be from an enlarged text, preferably in book form, from what the National Literacy Strategy calls *Big Books*, though sometimes perhaps enlarged by using overhead projector transparencies of books children can read for themselves, or even hurriedly produced text on large sheets or flipcharts with felt-tips. Making large text this way does have the benefit of allowing the teacher to tailor the text to the particular needs of the group, perhaps underlining certain phrases, or highlighting particular words or letters in different colours. In this way the book becomes an enjoyable shared experience which easily allows discussion about the way language is written down, about the elements of language which children recognise or about what is happening in the information text or story that is being read. Holdaway (1979) noticing the difficulty of matching the ideal of individualised teaching with the reality of large class sizes points out that corporate learning (for instance in initiation ceremonies, playground games and church services) has always been a powerful mode. The examples he offers have in common a lack of competitiveness, rather '… they are entered into to be *like* other people … if we can achieve this corporate spirit, there is no reason why a large class cannot learn together'. The group reading experience so strongly emphasised in the National Literacy Strategy, is not only for instructional purposes; it has the advantages of a co-operative social occasion in which participants share mutual enjoyment of the reading. This practice is an obvious way to connect story-time, the teacher reading, the enjoyment of narrative, the excitement of shared experience, with the child's 'learning to read' process. It should avoid the misunderstanding evident in this story told by Helen Arnold:

A child who was able to read, with natural intonation, at a normal rate, many books at home, took a copy of the reading scheme home to his mother and chanted it out word by word to her. When asked why he was reading it out in such a 'funny' way, he replied that this was how you were supposed to read your book at school. 'Everybody does it like that'.

(Arnold, 1982)

It is worth saying again that this kind of reading does not have to be confined to fiction. The sharing of songs and rhymes ought to be a fundamental part of any early reading curriculum. The benefits of early familiarity with rhyme have been dramatically demonstrated by the work of Bryant and Bradley (1985). Familiar stories and rhymes from the whole range of cultures represented in the classroom can be shared orally and then in written form, perhaps as large 'home-made' books.

- Sometimes the teacher will select books to share, which have no words, so that children will 'read' the story through the illustrations.
- Sometimes she will share the children's own writing in books, which have been placed in the book corner collection of books.
- Sometimes the teacher will read from the collection of books that children are able to read independently. Doing this will familiarise children with the form and language of the story and make independent reading easier.

It is important here to point out that the sequence of observation, coaching and practice is descriptive of a sequence of learning phases, but these phases are not simply linear in terms of time and it should not be assumed therefore that they offer a simple guide to a sequence of teaching activities. So for instance, reading aloud to a class should not be confined to young children and certainly should not stop when children can read independently. In any apprenticeship learning there is always movement back and forth between the stages of observation, coaching and performance. Perhaps Bruner's (1966) notion of the spiral curriculum, in which children continually return to the same piece of learning but at a more sophisticated level, is a useful one to keep in mind here.

Coaching

We have so far considered the stage of observation, but of course listening and watching are not enough to turn an apprentice into a skilled craftsman. It is crucial that running alongside classroom practices which offer opportunities for observation are chances to practice with coaching. This is the element of the reading curriculum which, many critics complain, has been missing in recent years, and which the National Literacy Strategy is designed to improve. Learners must try out the skilled activity for themselves but need help to do this. So what defines the stage of coaching?

Here we need to return to the Vygotskyian theory of teaching as assisted performance and remind ourselves of the main tenets of the theory. Assisted performance defines what a child can do with help, with the support of the learning environment, with others and of the self. The contrast between assisted performance and unassisted performance identifies the most important space between development and learning, which is the zone of proximal development. For Vygotsky, assistance should be offered in those interactional contexts that are most likely to generate joint performance. During the earliest periods in the zone of proximal development the child may have only a limited understanding of the task or goal to be achieved. The teacher offers a model and the child responds by observing and imitating. Gradually the child comes to understand the point and purpose of the activity and the way different parts of the activity relate to one another.

In terms of reading this happens through all those activities outlined above. Then when some conception of the overall performance has been acquired the child can be assisted by other means, by joint performance, feedback, questions and further cognitive structuring. For instance, even before interacting with a child a teacher assists by age-grading of materials. The selection of appropriate texts for an apprentice reader is one of the most important features of assisting performance.

During the coaching stage there should be a steady decrease in the teacher's responsibility for the task performance and a steady increase in the learner's proportion of responsibility. This is Bruner's 'handover principle' – the child who was once an observer, now becomes participant (Bruner 1983). Children gradually take over the structuring of the task themselves, for instance by asking questions of the adult – 'what does that say' – rather than only responding to adult questions, or by making choices about their own reading materials. The adult's task is to accurately tailor assistance to the child by being responsive to their current effort and understanding. The child's questions – what does this mean? – assist the adult to assist.

Attempts by skilled assisting adults to assess a child's readiness for greater responsibility are most often subtle rather than explicit, more usefully embedded in the ongoing interaction than separated out as assessment activities. Careful reflective listening and attention will allow appropriate coaching 'input'. This is the most essential skill in being a good teacher of reading.

In a good master–apprentice relationship the teacher graduates the coaching in response to the child's performance: the more the apprentice can do, the less the master does so that the coaching task is accomplished when responsibility for tailoring assistance and performing the task itself has been effectively handed over to the learner.

All this is theory. What does it mean for classroom practice? Essentially it means that at the stage of coaching the teacher will read *with* the child, or children, sharing and helping and enjoying the book.

> The adult's job is to read with him what both can enjoy, to let him see how the story goes, to help him observe what there is to be read and to tell him what he needs to know when he finds it difficult.
>
> (Meek 1982)

Reading with a child then is not at all the same as 'hearing a child read'. It is not just a regular check on quantity read, nor just a way of making individual contact with a child. It is not an activity in which a teacher listens to a child perform, but rather a joint performance, a collaborative activity. Seen thus, it is an activity that might be carried out with the class as a whole during what the National Literacy Strategy calls *shared reading* periods. But it might also occur with small groups or individuals during that part of the literacy hour that is dedicated to individual work.

It might also occur outside the literacy hour as part of the longer, but not frequent, pupil-teacher conference advocated by the Schools Council Report (Southgate *et al.* 1981) published some years ago but still containing much good sense. Helen Arnold (1982) describes this activity, in what she calls a 'shared reading interview', as 'a relaxed and enthusiastic dialogue between teacher and pupil'. She offers a particular recipe for the activity, made up of the following ingredients:

- Teacher reads some of the text.
- Child reads some of the text.
- Teacher sets a purpose at beginning of interview to encourage skimming and scanning to find certain elements in text.
- Teacher asks child to read a paragraph silently first and then to read it aloud.
- Teacher asks child to read a paragraph silently and then questions s/he on it.
- Teacher encourages a child to ask questions about a text that has just been read.
- Teacher discusses decoding problems with child.
- Teacher and child discuss contents of text in terms of appreciative/emotional response.
- Teacher discusses child's difficulties in reading in general, attitudes, likes, dislikes, and so on.

Arnold does point out that these ingredients would vary from reading to reading, and would very much depend on the text that had been chosen.

A particular element which Arnold omits from her recipe is that in which the child and teacher read together quite literally. The child reading with the teacher gradually gains confidence and begins to take over more of the reading. The child's contribution is supported by teacher guidance of the sort contained in the list above so that the child becomes more autonomous. In this way children achieve an understanding of the interaction of print and text, start to build a sight vocabulary, and learn to make informed guesses based on semantic, syntactic, grapho-phonemic, and bibliographic information, bringing to the activity all they know and can do in order to make the text meaningful.

It is this kind of interaction which occurs in the best parent/child story-reading times. Minns demonstrates that in the best domestic situations the parent approaches the activity:

> With warmth, confidence and intelligence. Most notably perhaps they make no outward distinction between reading and learning to read, and thus put no pressure on the child to become word-perfect ... Their aim, whether stated explicitly or not, is to involve the child as much as possible in understanding the author's words. They recognise that the child needs to talk about the story and give them time to do this. So the words of the story become intertwined with conversational talk; there are regular pauses to laugh at the funny bits, to enjoy repetitions aloud and to talk about things the story reminds them of ...
>
> (Minns 1990)

There are of course difficulties with shared reading of this kind. It would be foolish to pretend that the sustained one-to-one contact of shared reading is easy to achieve in the classroom, which is one reason why perhaps the National Literacy Strategy takes the pragmatic view that most reading teaching ought to be carried out with the whole class and groups. However, many teachers do organise their classrooms for such interactions to occur, mainly by creating a classroom ethos of self-reliance, so reducing the constant call on the teacher's attention. It is perhaps a question of priorities in terms of classroom organisation.

In shared reading the essential role of the teacher is to be an opportunist, a guide rather than an instructor, just as the master craftsman is a guide who provides feedback to the apprentice who is practising. Southgate, more than thirty years ago, was aware of how this relationship between the master reader and the reading apprentice should best work:

Teachers need to acquire an extensive knowledge of what requires to be learned if the skills of literacy are to be effectively mastered. Their expertise could be considered as a store of background knowledge from which they could draw at appropriate moments, rather than as an elaborately detailed curriculum of which every item has to be earnestly taught. The teacher would thus be in a strong position when the moment for a small amount of direct teaching arises to help the child to take the next minute step forward and so channel learning towards the ultimate goal of efficient reading.

(Southgate 1972)

What specific advice might be offered in regard to this kind of coaching and guidance? Well, the National Literacy Strategy Framework for Teaching contains a term by term list of those items which it considers ought to be drip fed into pupils during coaching and guidance, but the important point made by Southgate, i.e. any list must be part of a store of background knowledge to be drawn upon at appropriate moments, should not to be forgotten. It must be remembered too that the major objective in any reading session is to retain interest in and enjoyment of the text and so teaching must be sensitive to the danger of destroying the essential element of attending to and appreciating the reading experience. This does not have to be an alternative to an emphasis on cognitive learning. Showing children what the reading process is, and how to use the cueing systems available to them, does not destroy reading enjoyment. Indeed it should positively influence motivation towards the task as the apprentice readers observe their own improvement and increasing success. So what follows are five pieces of practical advice about shared reading coaching:

1 In any master–apprentice relationship the master's job is eventually to make himself redundant as a teacher. Likewise, in reading coaching the eventual goal should be nil intervention (although it is worth repeating what was said before that when this might happen will depend very much on text and context). Do not always interrupt the reader to correct errors. To do this is to risk offering the child a message that reading is to do with pronouncing rather than comprehending. Rather, take note that some 'errors' or 'miscues' are productive of comprehension while others are a hindrance. Some miscues, as for instance in 'the child went back to his home' for 'the child went back to his house', provide evidence that the child is on the right track in the search for meaning.

2 Offer children a range of strategies, what the National Reading Strategy

call *searchlghts* which they might use to work out the meaning of unknown words. Sometimes this might be by 'cloze' technique, encouraging children to make intelligent guesses from the rest of the sentence using both syntactic and semantic clues. Sometimes it might be by pointing out the initial sound of the unknown word, or some other letter/sound association. Sometimes it might be by demonstrating how long words can be broken into constituent syllables, as in cat-a-ma-ran. Sometimes a scrutiny of an illustration may provide a clue. Sometimes comparison with a more familiar word may present a clue, for example 'starts like', 'ends like' or just 'like'. Very often it will be appropriate simply to offer the word to the child in order to maintain fluency and motivation. Reliance by the teacher on a single strategy will encourage a similar narrow attack on the part of the child. In particular the earlier a word appears in the sentence, or the greater its isolation from a familiar grammatical context, the more necessary will be alternative cues.

3 Stop occasionally in the reading and ask questions about the text as part of the reading conversation, in order to cause the reader to interact with key ideas and information. An example question might be 'What do you think will happen next?' Sometimes it is a good idea to offer questions prior to the reading in order to direct attention to the text rather than asking the reader to use memory after the reading has finished. So, for instance, 'As we read together I want you to listen very hard for the parts of the story that tells us ...' Sometimes it might be appropriate to follow simple cohesive chains to trace the events of a story, perhaps playing 'detective', following clues to answer questions such as 'How do we know that the author means this or that person?'

4 Reading support with new texts is offered if some preparation takes place before the reading begins. A context for the story, or information passage can be provided by talking about the setting and characters in the story, or discussing the background to some new information, building up the general meaning of the text. Sometimes at the end of the session the child might be asked to investigate specific problems to do with the text as part of private reading; perhaps to answer questions which would encourage scanning rather than word-by-word reading; perhaps to answer questions which would allow a start to be made in appreciating the different levels of interpretation which can operate in fully understanding a text.

5 The way a learner approaches a task is crucially important. In reading, the way the text is approached will influence an understanding of what is read. In forming their strategies for reading children may have ideas about what they should do, but actually do something completely different. So in any shared reading act the teacher ought to take note

of the child's overall attitudes and styles of learning in order to tailor the coaching more appropriately to individual needs. For instance, a child who initially lacks confidence in word-attack skills should not find the teacher prompting too quickly on each hesitation.

Practice

We need once again now to return to our apprenticeship model of observation, coaching, practice. The move from coaching to practice comes once the task has been internalised, when assistance from adults or more capable peers is no longer needed. Indeed 'assistance' now might be disruptive since once this stage is reached instructions can be irritating and counterproductive. At this point self-consciousness, attempting an awareness of strategies being used is detrimental to the smooth integration of all elements of the task. Of course, dependant on the context and material, a child may be at more than one stage at a time as I have pointed out earlier. The child who can read certain stories independently, might still be in the zone of proximal development when it comes to understanding exactly how to extract information from a non-fiction text. Reading is a highly complex skill. It must be regarded as a continuously developing skill and thus the apprenticeship is a long one that continues through all levels of schooling and often beyond.

Thus once a child has mastered particular reading skills they should not have to rely solely on 'internal mediation'. They should be encouraged to ask for help when stuck. Any good reading classroom must allow for situations where, when a child is having difficulty, they may seek out more competent others.

So, the more competent a child becomes, the closer they move to the stage of independent practice, the more the coaching must become responsive, contingent and patient; the more the child can do, the less the adult should do. *Assistance* offered at too high a level is not effective teaching. Constant and careful assessment of where the child is in reading ability relative to the zone of proximal development is required. But at the 'internalised' stage practice should be the chief ingredient. The paradox that many teachers intuitively understand, is that many children do not read books because they cannot read well enough. They cannot read well enough because they do not read books. There needs to be a balance among the three elements of apprenticeship. Concentration on coaching is important, but equally, if not more important, is to develop children's reading through the development of a reading habit where pupils read regularly their own stories and favourite books. There certainly needs to be an understanding in the class that silent, individual or small group reading activities are central to the learning to read process not merely supplementary to the reading for instruction that occurs in the literacy hour. Whether a child is a habitual reader will depend to a great extent on how much satisfaction and enjoyment they come to expect from books.

There are several things a teacher needs to do to promote and encourage private reading. First, reading aloud to children is, as the earlier part of this chapter explained, one way in which children can be 'lured' into reading by themselves. It is important that reading to the whole class doesn't always become the starting point for some word or sentence level work – as might happen in the literacy hour. Second, though it should hardly need saying, it is essential to have a wide range of books freely available in the classroom attractively displayed. This collection needs to contain both fiction and non-fiction, both prose and verse, and books at varying levels of reading difficulty, both to meet demand and to create it. Third, it is important to give children time for sustained independent reading, not just to fill in when other work is finished or when the teacher is marking the register or collecting dinner money. Classroom organisation must allow space both in terms of time and location for a child to sit quietly and read when they wish and are ready to concentrate on reading.

There is though a tendency for reading to be restricted to short bursts. One way to overcome this tendency is to attempt to give children a period of uninterrupted, sustained, silent reading (USSR), otherwise known as ERIC (Everyone Reading in Class), or SQUIRT (Sustained, Quiet, Uninterrupted, Independent Reading Time). The National Literacy Strategy literacy hour arrangements do not make this time, which operates very successfully in many schools, redundant. Remembering what was said earlier about the role of the teacher as a literacy model, during this time teachers should be reading silently their own choice of book. The Schools Council Project (Southgate *et al.* 1981) offered a model of how this practice might take place:

1 Set aside a particular period every day for personal reading – perhaps the end of the morning or afternoon.
2 See that every child has a personally selected book at a level which he is likely to be able to understand, and, if he has nearly completed reading it, a second one to hand.
3 Tell the children that they will be allowed, say, ten minutes to enjoy their chosen books without anyone interrupting them.
4 The teacher should sit … preferably also quietly reading and trying to avoid speaking, for example by merely catching the eye of any child who is not reading and perhaps raising an eyebrow.
5 Every effort should be made to establish that pattern that children neither talk nor leave their seats during this period.
6 A notice on the door might read: 'Class reading – please do not disturb'.

7 As children become accustomed to this procedure, gradually increase
   the period devoted to this personal, uninterrupted reading.

A word about silent reading may be appropriate here. Many children do
not become capable of inaudible reading for some years. It is preferable
during USSR sessions that children read as quietly as possible if they are
not capable of completely silent reading, but this should not become a major
concern. It is now understood that even the most able adult readers sub-
vocalise. The crucial distinction is not between oral and silent reading, but
between reading for personal understanding and satisfaction on the one
hand, and reading for the understanding and satisfaction of an audience on
the other. It is not important for children actually to suppress audible
vocalisation in the early years of reading. The important thing is that they
should *read to themselves*.

Social context

We need, finally, to look at one other key feature of traditional
apprenticeship. It concerns the embedding social context in which learning
takes place. Apprenticeship derives many of its characteristics from its
embedding in a subculture in which most members are visible participants
in the target skills. Apprentices have continual access to models of expertise-
in-use. It is not uncommon for apprentices to have access to several masters
and thus to a variety of models of expertise. Moreover apprentices have the
opportunity to observe other learners who have varying degrees of skill.
Among other things this encourages them to view learning as an incremental
staged process while providing them with benchmarks against which they
can measure their own progress.

Margaret Donaldson's book *Children's Minds* (1978) is one of the best
known of many inquiries which are helping us to understand the importance
of the social context in all learning. Donaldson explains how thought and
language depend upon the interpersonal contexts within which they
develop. The apprenticeship approach to teaching reading recognises the
significance of this aspect of learning by carrying with it a package of practical
measures that help to create the embedding social context of apprenticeship
in general. Some of these measures, such as USSR where readers are made
very obviously aware that they are part of a community of readers, have
been described earlier in this chapter. The importance of the shared
experience of the teacher reading to the class, perhaps with copies available
to the children to allow the children to follow, has also been mentioned.
The common sense of enjoyment and the resulting sense of being part of a
reading community is a deeply educative process. There are other ways of
ensuring that, within the school at least; children begin to feel part of the

'literacy club'. For instance, many schools are adopting an approach which ensures that the child has access to more than one reading teacher by ensuring that parents play a crucial role in the reading 'life' of the child; some schools make arrangements for members of the local community to come regularly and share books with children; some schools adopt peer tutoring and paired-reading practices where older children within the school partner younger children, reading and talking about books together; or where friends within the classroom get together and share a book with the more competent reader taking the lead. In these ways children can play the role of both teacher and learner and thus begin to understand the nature of progress in reading by meeting and reading with other learners of varying degrees of skill.

There are still other practices that can be promoted to create an appropriate social context:

- On occasions children might be asked to bring their favourite books from home. These are then spread around the room in a way that allows the class to browse before each child chooses one or two to take back to their desk to read for a set period.
- Children might be asked simply to 'share' books they have enjoyed by telling the class about them.
- The teacher might read to the class part of something she has enjoyed reading – a letter, an extract from a book, a newspaper or magazine article.
- There might be a corner set up permanently in the classroom where children can go to listen on headphones to taped stories.
- Older children might write brief book reports, perhaps on a pro forma which is kept in a specified folder or file for other children to consult when they want to obtain recommendations from their peers about which books to read.

The practice of buying multiple copies for group reading, where five or six children read the same book, offers many learning opportunities. The National Literacy Strategy calls this *Guided Reading* and emphasises once again the teacher's role:

> The teacher should introduce the text to the group, to familiarise them with the overall context of the story and point out any key words they need to know. Pupils then read it independently, while the teacher assesses and supports each pupil in the group.

But there will also be occasions when pupils can support each other's reading, offer each other information about the text, discussing the characters and plot, sharing jokes or elements which are significant to them, and possible interpretations etc.

These are simply a few suggestions. Experienced teachers will have many more ideas for corporate activities. For instance some teachers start each morning with a collecting-together of reading experiences from the previous day, when small excerpts are read out by the teacher and children, and when what is read is briefly discussed. Reading plans for the day are then proposed. So children will be reading out snippets that they have already prepared to an audience who are used to listening to each other and there is also the implication that reading may be brought from home for sharing.

The crucial element in all these practical measures is the intention to create a classroom subculture of shared reading experience which contains all the benefits of co-operative and social activities, one in which participants read together and together enjoy the reading experience.

But there is a further relevant aspect of the social context in which traditional apprenticeship takes place. It has to do with the economic bias in traditional apprenticeship. Apprentices are encouraged at an early stage to learn that their skills are useful and therefore meaningful within the social context of the workplace. Apprentices have the opportunity to realise the value, in concrete economic terms, of these skills: well-executed skills result in saleable products. Apprenticeship reading, as well as finding a way to create in the school a culture of expert practice for children to participate in and aspire to, must devise incentives for progress parallel to the economic incentives of traditional apprenticeship if it is to follow that model.

So how can apprentice readers realise the value of their developing skills? Well, primarily perhaps through the pleasure principle. The joy of reading good books can itself be the reward for increasing independence in reading. Moreover reading fiction can, even for very young children be an experience which as many have noted, helps extend an understanding of life and what it means to be human, and offers rewards in those terms. But it is also the case that reading is linked to work and instrumental effort. If this is to be recognised, the classroom must provide a literacy environment and genuine literacy activities where children can 'cash in' the skills and begin to see the purpose of acquiring them for instrumental reasons too. Ros Fisher's Chapter 4 in this book, dealing as it does with the reading of non-fiction texts, explains one crucial way in which this can be done.

Summary

If, when considering reading, we treat apprenticeship as a suggestive, rather than an exact analogy, there are useful insights to be drawn from traditional apprenticeship with regard to the business of teaching reading in the classroom. Two features particularly hold messages for how we help children learn to read.

First, the movement in traditional apprenticeship from observation, through coaching, to practice can act as a model for reading 'instruction'. It highlights, for instance, that no approach to reading teaching can be *laissez-faire*, that coaching is required, but that coaching will be most effective if it is seen as a way of assisting performance, and as a way of making explicit to the learner processes which are usually internalised in skilled performance. The implications for teachers are radical. A number of traditional practices, such as hearing children read as a kind of ritual, almost a magical laying on of hands requires major revision. This is not a new point. It is continually being made by various commentators on the teaching of reading. And the Framework for Teaching and literacy hour recommendations contained in the National Literacy Strategy clearly imply that this poor practice should end and be superseded by more direct instruction. This instruction however need not be confined to the National Literacy Strategy points for action. This chapter has attempted to explain that many other subtle skills and understandings are required than those described by the National Literacy Strategy *Framework for Teaching*.

Second, a close look a traditional apprenticeship provides evidence for the importance of the social context in which learning takes place. Again, reading teachers can use the apprenticeship model to reflect on their own school/classroom practices to see whether they help create a culture of expert practice for instance, whether there is a genuine feeling of sharing reading, whether they offer the opportunity for learners to realise the value of their increasing skills.

I hope the theme of this chapter is clear. Good reading teaching is about assisting performance along a pathway through the zone of proximal development, to go together with children where at present they cannot go alone. There is a Chinese saying which is: 'the best sort of leader is hardly noticed by people; the next best is honoured and praised; the next best is feared, and the next best is hated. But when the best sort of leader has finished, people say, "We did it ourselves"'. Surely that's true of reading teachers too?

Questions for self-reflection and staff discussion

1 Do children in your class ever see you reading for enjoyment?
2 How much opportunity do you have to read aloud to children – as a group or on a one-to-one basis – purely for enjoyment rather than for direct instructional purposes?

3 Is your reading aloud to children confined to fiction or do children in your class get a chance to listen to an adult reading other types of material, perhaps outside a literacy hour?

4 Do you ever offer children the opportunity to group read a range of texts outside the literacy hour? How might this be beneficial?

5 What do you see as the prime purpose of a child reading to you? Are there other important purposes that you don't normally take into consideration? How can you organise the class to allow you uninterrupted time with individual children during reading conferences?

6 Consider your coaching strategies when holding reading conferences with individual children. Compare your strategies with the list in this chapter. What do you do which is not suggested here? Could you improve your practice by incorporating any of the suggestions into your normal practice?

7 How much time do children in your class get for sustained *independent* reading? Is this enough? If not would it be feasible to organise your classroom in such a way as to allow space both in terms of time and location for a child to sit quietly and read?

8 What opportunities does a child have in your classroom to share a book with a more competent reader other than the teacher? Would it be useful and possible to increase these opportunities?

9 Consider the list of suggestions for creating a reading community in this chapter. Would it be worthwhile trying to adopt any in your classroom?

Recommended readings

Cambell, Robin (1990), *Reading Together*, Open University Press. This short book deals with story reading, shared reading, hearing children read and sustained silent reading. Throughout the book, the role of the teacher as a systematic, responsive adult who offers good models to learners is stressed. It is full of ideas to enliven and instruct on INSET days.

The Teacher Training Agency (1999), *Effective Teachers of Literacy*. This is not a book, but a report of research at the University of Exeter, commissioned by The Teacher Training Agency, into the characteristics of teachers who can be shown to be effective in teaching literacy. It is short, very readable and contains important messages for all teachers, identifying key factors in the sample of teachers whose pupils make effective learning gains in literacy.

Graves, D. (1991), *Build a Literate Classroom*, Heinemann. Graves book, rich with specific approaches and suggestions, is a book for teachers about making reading/ writing decisions in the classroom. Like *Literacy in Action* it has an interactive style which is intended to encourage readers to rethink their classroom practice and in particular to change their use of time in order to set children on the road to becoming lifelong readers and writers.

McClelland, N. (ed) (1997), *Building A Literate Nation*, Trentham Books. This book, written under the auspices of The National Literacy Trust, is a platform for many of the United Kingdom's leading academics and major literacy organisations to offer perspectives and advice on the strategic grounds for literacy. The thirty-six chapters are all short, the topics covered are very wide-ranging, and there is much food for thought for any reader – student, teacher or academic.

Wood, D. (1988), *How Children Think and Learn*, Basil Blackwell. This book explores critically conflicting views about how children think and learn. In particular it compares Piaget's approach with those offered by Bruner and Vygotsky, establishing areas of common ground. It then considers what contribution these researchers can make to current debates in education asking, among other questions, what is the value of literacy and why do some children have such problems in reading and writing?

Wray, D., Bloom W., Hall N., (1989), *Literacy in Action*, Falmer Press. *Literacy in Action* takes a contemporary view of the way children learn to be literate and suggests ways in which teachers can facilitate this learning. It is primarily a *teaching* book, in interactive format, which encourages observation in classrooms and reflection on these observations in the light of theory.

Bibliography

Arnold, H. (1982) *Listening to Children Reading*, London: Hodder & Stoughton.

Bamberger, R. (1976) 'Literature and Development' in Merritt, J.E.(Ed) *New Horizons in Reading*, International Reading Association.

Bruner, J.S. (1966) *Toward a Theory of Instruction*, Cambridge Massachusetts: Harvard University Press.

Bruner, J.S. (1983) *Child's Talk: Learning to Use Language*, Oxford: Oxford University Press.

Bryant, P and Bradley, L (1985) *Children's Reading Problems*, Oxford: Blackwell.

DfEE, (1998) *The National Literacy Strategy Framework for Teaching*, HMSO.

Donaldson, M. (1978) *Children's Minds*, London: Fontana.

Holdaway, D.(1979) *Foundations of Literacy*, Sydney: Ashton Scholastic.

Holdaway, D. (1980) *Independence in Reading*, Sydney: Ashton Scholastic.

Meek, M. (1982) *Learning to Read*, London: The Bodley Head.

Meek, M. (1988) *How Texts Teach What Readers Learn*, Stroud, Glos: Thimble Press.

Minns, H. (1990) *Read It To Me Now*, London: Virago Press.

Southgate, V. (1972) *Beginning Reading*, London: University of London Press.

Southgate, V. *et al.* (1981) *Extending Beginning Reading*, London: Heinemann Educational Books.

Southgate, V. (1984) *Reading: Teaching for Learning*, London: Macmillan.

Vygotsky, L.S. (1978) *Mind In Society. The Development of Higher Psychological Processes*, Harvard: Harvard University Press.

Waterland, E. (1985) *Read With Me: An Apprenticeship Approach to Reading*, Stroud, Glos: Thimble Press.

6 The literacy environment of the classroom

Carol Fox

When I wrote my contribution to the original *Reading For Real Handbook* I drew upon my own extensive research on the oral storytelling of five pre-school children who had had a very extensive exposure to books and stories read aloud to them at home. That study began in 1981 and now is nearly 20 years old. In my article I tried to show how the literacy environment of the classroom in some ways needs to reflect and to produce some of the effects of pre-school literacy practices typical of homes where reading is highly valued and has high priority. In 1993 I published a book which contains most of the implications of my findings, so in the present up-dating of my piece I do not wish to replicate what I have said very fully elsewhere (Fox 1993). However, what I found in my research remains relevant; my five young children's oral invented stories revealed the extensive linguistic and cognitive development that is associated with hearing powerful stories read aloud in the early years. I asserted then, and still believe, that the emotional force of their favourite stories for my young children was fundamental to the stories they were able to tell themselves and to all the related thought and language that emerged from my analyses.

There have been some big changes in the educational climate in recent years, affecting the ways in which reading is construed and taught very dramatically – not only have there been two revisions of the National Curriculum, but there is the National Literacy Strategy and the Literacy Hour, which include, among other things, the 'new Grammar' teaching, phonics, and the three 'levels' of reading texts – word, sentence and whole text. There are other current concerns around reading too, notably the issue of whether the reading interests of boys are being adequately served in the curriculum (OFSTED 1993, QCA 1998) and, after the Stephen Lawrence inquiry, whether enough is being done in schools to counter racism and develop multi-cultural approaches; essentially these both arise from a concern with equal educational opportunities. In this revised article I shall argue that literacy practices which are strongly associated with play, powerful affects, and pleasure in books and stories, ought to be able to survive recent developments.

The new literacy curricula have certainly brought about changes in the literacy environment of the classroom. Big books (which have been around in Primary schools for a very long time but which are now more varied and prevalent), overhead transparencies, and flip charts are frequently employed for the whole-class presentation of reading material. Reading together as a class has become a formalised and regular daily activity occupying the first segment of the Literacy Hour, to some extent replacing the individual reading aloud to the teacher that used to go on. However, there is nothing really new about this. Indeed it can be seen as a more regular and formal application of the kind of shared reading described by Pidgeon, Lathey and Alam in the CLPE booklet *Shared Reading, Shared Writing* (CLPE 1991) which sometimes takes place around the book corner, but in many classrooms happens at the front of the room. The fact that the NLS now asks teachers to include word and sentence level activities in the Literacy Hour should not imply any dilution of the power of the really good stories and poems that teachers have always known work best in involving children in literacy learning.

Certainly my five children's oral stories sometimes showed that they were aware explicitly and implicitly of several aspects of words and sentences. For example, five-year old Sundari's stories included Edward Lear type nonsense stories where she showed that she knew very well how to segment phonemes and syllables in words. The occasional rhymes and poems the children experimented with revealed that their early literacy experiences had given them the phonological and metalinguistic awareness that current research demonstrates is a good predictor of reading success (Goswami and Bryant 1990; Goswami 1999). A reading environment which does not capitalise on children's natural propensity to make story metaphors for the fundamental aspects of their own living will surely be inadequate to persuade children that it is worth making the effort to understand (i.e. read) what the words on the page say. Making words 'say' in reading probably has more in common with joining in with the words, sounds, and rhythms of familiar catchy tunes than with plucking sounds off the page, letter by letter, word by word. The latter may be a logical process but it is incredibly tedious, because it takes so long and so much concentration to synthesise the sounds that all sense is lost. Children soon become bored and think that reading must be very difficult. Texts to support beginning readers, especially those chosen by the teacher to share with everybody, need not be constructed at the expense of the gripping stories children carry in their heads and tell themselves all the time; young readers should turn the page not to learn the 'new' word in the scheme but to find out what happens next. We may not be able to supply hundreds of books in our classrooms but, especially if resources are limited, the ones we choose should be powerful – powerful enough to offer strong competition to TV soaps, the daily news, videos and computer games. We do need a wide variety of books, as the National Curriculum urges, but we cannot afford to lose sight of the motivating force of really powerful stories. If texts are going to be focused upon in the concentrated way that the NLS suggests, with activities at the word and sentence levels as well as the whole text level, then they need more than ever to be worth young children's efforts.

All the five children in my study also showed awareness that words have definitions that are capable of explanation. They knew too about the way the word order of ordinary speech gets changed in sentences in writing and they knew about sentence rhythms and structures, though at such a young age they had no grammatical terminology to describe them. Their story dialogues showed that they had learned that the representation of speech in stories has its own forms that are not the same as real speech in life. What I am saying here is that the Literacy Hour need not threaten what children can learn from reading good stories if only we remember that choice of story or poem is crucial; children's pleasure and satisfaction in reading material must have priority, and we must resist any temptation to choose reading material primarily on the basis that it will readily produce word and sentence level exercises. For word and sentence level work to become interesting and inspiring to children the activities we offer them at these levels need to be rich, taking them further *into* the texts they read, not regarding the texts as props for the mundane and repetitive.

I found that in their storytelling my five children were highly creative and extremely competent at every level of linguistic analysis – the sound, or phoneme, the word, the phrase, the sentence, and the narrative discourse itself. They showed competencies that are surprisingly advanced – I say 'surprisingly' because I think we still know very little about language development after the early stages of acquisition. The vocabularies of the five children are very striking not only for obviously 'literary' words ('perished', 'astonished', 'scolded', 'dismay', 'realised', 'evil' etc.), but also for the creative ways in which the children invent the language they need at any given time. There is for instance the verb 'weared' from the adjective 'weary' from Sundari, and the noun phrase '*icicled snowball* person' from four-year old Jimmy. In one of five-year old Josh's stories Robin Hood goes 'through the town snatching foolish money for poor people', and, in another tall tale, Sundari's narrator announces a 'nearly crying story, nearly, nearly, nearly'. One of three-year old Robert's 'baddie' characters 'wasted things', Sundari's witch 'collects' a 7-year old to put in her stew', and Josh's super heroes are out of action because 'Robin's got chest-ache and Batman's got flu'. Names are invented with amusing originality – Cletcher (a boy), a Choryda (a monster), Truggle and Mubble (witch's daughters). In unconventional but highly colourful usages like these the children show themselves ready to take risks with words, to use them when they think they *may* be appropriate, to use what makes the discourse sound like real stories sound, to use grammatical knowledge to coin new words out of old ones, and to get them occasionally wrong – 'It was humble in the sea' (Sundari); 'He looked through his kaleidoscope and what did he see? The English riding out to sea' (Josh).

There is no doubt that books have been part of what has created these children's interest in and enjoyment of strange, unusual, colourful, and sonorous terms. Indeed some words are very unlikely indeed to have occurred anywhere but in a story from a book – 'As morning approached the little dewer man spread his dewdrops to meet the day' (Josh). This sort of thing is not parrot memorisation; Josh has not quoted verbatim from the original text but made several changes. Their frequent encounters with book language that is strange or unusual have given these children an experimental and creative focus on words, and that focus is intimately bound up with the power of the stories the words tell. Word level work in the Literacy Hour needs to be exciting and creative as well as analytic. The data in my story study imply that children are very capable of analysing and segmenting words, but they do it in powerful and meaningful contexts. I suspect that we learn new words when we need them to make new meanings *and* when we have the opportunity to use them, to try them out for the appropriate fit. Communication with others, including the physically absent authors of children's books, soon teaches us whether we are putting words in the right places or not. Yet learning language is a matter not only of learning the conventions, but also of learning to play with them, to change them, to recreate them or to make new ones, and writers and poets are particularly good teachers of invented, created languages. It seems obvious that if children frequently meet unconventional and original uses of language they will learn as a matter of course that that is the way language works, these are the things you can make it do. We have known for some time now that children do not learn language by copying adults or by adding on new words until they arrive at longer and longer sentences. They learn it by discovering underlying regularities in contexts that are highly meaningful and in situations where there is maximum feedback, and then they use those regularities to recreate words, phrases, and sentences for themselves. Literacy makes an enormous contribution to this process, for when they go to school children are still learning language in the ways they have learned it from the start.

The book corner, which was a kind of cosy and inviting class library, may now be being seen in some schools as a background or supplementary resource rather than the central focus of reading activity. Indeed reading now may wear two aspects – a 'work' face when it is done in the literacy hour and a more playful and relaxed face when children listen to the teacher reading stories in the book corner. If I may refer again to my story study, the children involved, who were very young, all invented the stories they told, and heard the stories that were read aloud to them, as part of voluntary play at home, where many other kinds of enjoyable activity were available and on offer. This is not to say that their play was not serious. It involved formidable concentration on the part of the young storytellers and an extraordinary degree of self-discipline and effort together with a great deal of emotional energy and drive (Fox 1998). Schools and teachers of course cannot afford to wait for older children, who have begun their education, to 'volunteer' to achieve literacy in this way. What they might do, though, especially when considering children who do not come to school with rich literacy experiences, is consider what cannot be sacrificed to the new structures but needs to be bound tightly into them. It is in the book corner that children are able to express choices and preferences and to explore a whole range of reading matter. If the National Literacy Strategy means that daily shared reading is chosen and structured by the teacher, then children's more personal experiences of reading become more, not less, important. The new literacy practices ought to strengthen and increase the resources for reading available to children all day long, especially if we are to avoid any fragmentation of reading that might result in creating a highly structured hour devoted to it. One of the best accounts of the resources for reading that ought to be available in Primary classrooms is given by Graham and Kelly (1988).

There are many positive ways of looking at the literacy hour. In some classrooms children could be experiencing a broader range of texts and genres than they were formerly. 'Coverage' of non-fiction, poetry, drama, multi-cultural literature as well as a wide range of classic and popular literature is built into the format of the literacy hour, though they were all already included in the national curriculum for English. This ought to mean that a wider range of reading tastes are guaranteed a place in children's reading experiences. The danger of course is that these might be regarded as 'covered' by the literacy hour rather than developed, fostered and extended. Given that the literacy and numeracy hours now consume nearly all of a morning's work in most primary schools, and that teachers must fit the rest of the curriculum into the remaining parts of the school day, what can teachers do to add both width and depth to children's reading? The strategies that they were using before must surely become much more important now, among them the involvement of parents and helpers in the classroom (Wragg, 1998), after-school book clubs, school book-shops, reading weeks, whole-school or class silent reading, and home-school partnerships in reading. All of these tactics pre-date the National Literacy Strategy in a large number of schools and need to be maintained if reading is not to become something that happens in twenty minute slots and is then 'done'.

The success of the National Literacy Strategy should not judged by SAT scores alone. A more rigorous evaluation of its success would involve finding out how many more children are reading extensively in their leisure time because they want to – how many children are becoming habitual and committed readers. Teachers may well feel at the moment that they do not have the space in their working lives to monitor these aspects of their pupils' reading but they can do a lot to the environment of the classroom to ensure that the pleasures of reading for oneself have not been replaced by some of the more workmanlike materials that are now making an appearance in many schools. Phonics charts may have their uses, particularly for teachers, but they must not *replace* the poems, verses, rhymes, jingles and word games that develop phonological awareness – indeed if the principle of the fun and enjoyment of word play and poetry is maintained there may ultimately be less need for materials that are detached from meaningful language contexts. In other words the new phonics ought to mean that the books of poetry and verse in classrooms increase in number and range. Children's literature can teach many interesting and fascinating aspects of language study (including grammar) in a way that does not intrude on children's pleasure in books (Taylor 1994). The present 'official' requirement that children learn phonics and the basics of grammatical structure can mean enrichment if it is interpreted imaginatively as well as rigorously. The issue here is really about *abstraction*. It can be easy, if somewhat mindless, for children to hunt for nouns, spelling patterns or phonic blends if these are abstracted into routine tasks that do not relate to ongoing literacy activity. Children often find that they are highly successful at repetitive exercises – a kind of busy-work that can be got right and thereby bring some satisfaction, especially to those who struggle to read. But they will develop their competencies in these areas more securely if they have some curiosity and interest, even fascination, with what they are about, and these are more likely to develop if learning about the technicalities of writing and literacy follow children's own ideas and theories. For example, it is quite possible for children to develop an interest in punctuation as an aspect of making meaning clearer rather than to regard punctuation as something that gets added to texts or becomes a form of correction (Hall and Robinson, 1996). Learning about adjectives and adverbs can be part of interesting experiments with children's own written texts. It would be an enormous waste if the superb work and ideas that formed the Language in the National Curriculum (LINC) project (Carter, 1990) were to be rejected in favour of more limited and less imaginative approaches to learning about language. So the fact that literacy education has become centralised and uniform should not mean that the pleasures of reading now have a lower profile. All the attractive and gripping books, comfortable reading areas, poetry posters and displays that motivate and inspire children to read should not now be marginalised or regarded as being of supplementary or secondary importance. On the contrary they are vital to supply the context within which the short sharp bursts of activity that characterise the Literacy Hour become meaningful.

The National Literacy Strategy takes a multi-genre approach to reading and gives attention to non-fiction genres in English in ways that might well be new to many teachers. The literacy environment of the classroom in the past always included information texts, often focused around a project or topic that was a cross-disciplinary enterprise. The collection of topic books around a theme often meant that books were selected because they fitted the theme rather than for their intrinsic quality, with the result that there were, and are, many poor quality books around. Colourful and expensive information books have proliferated in recent years and it has been suggested by Meek (1996) that teachers need to appraise them more critically before committing scarce funds to them. This is actually quite difficult for teachers to do, because sometimes they lack the specialist subject expertise necessary to bring a critical focus to such books. Perhaps recent developments in the way that lessons are planned and structured, with an emphasis on specific learning outcomes, could be helpful here. Looking at information and non-fiction texts in terms of *how they invite the reader to read them* could then be checked against what it is that we want children to use a particular literary genre for and what we want them to learn through and about that genre. In other words we need to check non-fiction and information texts against our learning outcomes, as I think we have always done with fiction and poetry. If some boys prefer non-fiction or 'factual' written genres (Millard, 1997), then we need to be guiding them towards really high-quality texts in those genres, texts that will extend and develop them as readers, *texts*, to use Meek's words, *that teach*. There is also evidence from a range of practitioners that quality of English teaching may be a very important factor in involving boys in reading (Barrs and Pidgeon, 1993). It would certainly be counter-productive to expect boys not to enjoy powerful stories and poems – imagine the outcry if girls were not expected to enjoy scientific or mathematical texts. Classrooms have always had plenty of non-fiction texts in them, and school libraries have sometimes even been allowed to become swamped with information books. Perhaps what is new and encouraging about the current multi-genre approaches to reading are that they demand a greater critical awareness from us all about just what it is that information texts are offering children as reading experiences. If the Literacy Hour now takes the time formerly allocated in schools to *English* we need to think carefully about two implications – what is there that belongs to what we think of as English that might become restricted by the daily literacy hour framework? What experiences of non-fiction genres belong to other subject genres? Literacy learning has always been part of the whole curriculum (see Wood *et al.* in Bearne, Ed, 1998, for accounts of the language needs of mathematics, science and music). We certainly need to maintain and develop that perspective or we risk losing the special contribution that English has to make to literacy development.

So far I have tried to suggest that current official othodoxies need not threaten the literacy practices that engage children's interest and turn them into readers and writers. This is an optimistic stance. I do though see some dangers in current approaches. Perhaps the development that I find most worrying is the possible threat to learning through play that lurks behind new curricula for the very youngest children. The more that nursery age children's learning becomes formally prescribed, the less opportunity there will be for the kind of spontaneous verbal play which the five children in my story study enjoyed to emerge. Though the children's stories grew out of their rich early literacy experiences the storytelling itself, that is the subjects of the tales, the genres, the words, the plots, the characters and all the extraordinary linguistic and cognitive operations that came in the wake of these, were solely in the children's own control because the stories were told as part of playful, voluntary and spontaneous activity. If such activity becomes marginalised in early curricula then we will become cut off from the knowledge we need of what children can do actively by themselves. I remain convinced, as I was ten years ago, that a literacy environment that does not communicate the fun, playfulness and pleasure of becoming literate is an impoverished one.

Questions for personal reflection or group discussion

1 Is there a school policy for communicating the importance of storytelling and story reading at home and at school to parents?
2 Are there enough emotionally powerful stories in the book collection for each class? If you use a reading scheme are the stories in the scheme books sufficiently srong to be as satisfying to young readers as some of the books mentioned in this chapter?
3 Do you have ways of observing and recording which stories are most meaningful to individual children? Have you thought about getting parents to help with this?
4 Are the children in your class getting enough repititions of the stories they like most? Have you considered the introduction of extra readers into the classroom to read to children on a one-to-one basis or in small

groups (e.g. parents and other relatives, older pupils from secondary schools, friends of the school and so on)?

5 Are your pupils hearing enough book language which is rich, colourful or unusual? Or do you worry that strange words will be outside the children's comprehension? What strategies can be used to introduce new words to children without destroying their pleasure in stories?

6 Do you have a small stock of special, more grown-up books, especially information or reference books, for the children to browse through? Can you think of any which would appeal to the children in your class?

7 Are poems, rhymes, jingles, verbal jokes and games an everyday part of oral activity in the class? Can you compile a list of books which could be a central resource for you and your pupils (e.g. Allan Ahlberg's *Old Joke Book* or, for teachers, the Opies' *Lore and Language of School Children*)?

8 Do you regularly invite groups of children to change or expand on stories you have read to them? Can you think of any stories or picture books which particularly lend themselves to this kind of imaginative exploration?

9 Have you thought of making a collection of story tapes for children to listen to as they read the books themselves? Is it possible for a group of staff to make some tapes together, thereby getting a variety of voices and accents on the tapes?

10 Have you though of inviting parents and grandparents to record autobiographical stories for your children to listen to?

Recommended readings

Applebee, A. (1978) *The Child's Concept of Story*. Chicago: University of Chicage Press. This book explains children's understanding of story structure using a model adapted from Vygotsky's developmental model of concepts.

Fox, C. (1989) 'Children thinking through story'. *English in Education*, **23**, (2). An article which relates the language of children's invented fantasies to the different discourses of school subjects. Shows how 'narrative must do for all' in the early years.

Meek, M. (1988) *On Being Literate*. London: Bodley Head. In her latest book Margaret Meek relates literacy to culture. This is the best available account of what membership of the literacy club actually looks like.

Meek, M. (1989) *How Texts Teach What Readers Learn*. Stroud: Thimble Press. A short but very dense booklet showing how the authors of really good children's books give readers lessons in reading. It takes the view that reading is much more than lifting words off the page and links literacy to literature. A reader who unpicked the references in the text would arrive at a very full understanding of Meek's arguments.

Sutton-Smith. (1981) *The Folk Stories of Children*. Philadelphia, PA: University of Pennsylvania Press. The introduction gives an account of the nature of this very large collection of children's oral stories. The bulk of the book gives us the stories themselves, at every age and stage.

Vgotsky, L. (1978) *Mind in Society*. Cambridge, MA: Harvard University Press. Essential for 'The role of play in mental development' in which Vygotsky claims that play lays the foundations of future abstract mental operations.

Bibliography

Barrs, M. and Pidgeon, S. (Eds) (1993) *Reading the Difference* London: CLPE.

Bearne, E. (Ed) (1998) *Use of language Across the Primary Curriculum*, London: Routledge.

Carter, R. (Ed) (1990) *Knowledge about Language and the Curriculum*, London: Hodder & Stoughton.

Centre for Language in Primary Education (1991) *Shared Reading/Shared Writing*, London: CLPE.

Cox, B. (Ed) (1998) *Literacy is not Enough* Manchester: Manchester Univ Press.

Fox, C. (1993) *At the Very Edge of the Forest*, London: Cassell.

Fox, C. (1998) 'Serious play: the relationship between young children's oral invented stories and their learning', *Current Psychology of Cognition*, Vol.17 No. 2.

Goswami, U. (1999) 'Phonological Development and Reading by Analogy: Epilinguistic and Metalinguistic issues' in: Oakhill, J. and Beard, R. (Eds) *Reading Development and the Teaching of Reading: a psychological perspective* Oxford: Blackwell.

Goswami, U. and Bryant, P. (1990) *Phonological Skills and Learning to Read*, Hove: Lawrence Erlbaum.

Graham, J. and Kelly, A. (Eds) (1988) *Reading under Control*, London: David Fulton.

Hall, N. and Robinson, A. (Eds) (1996) *Learning About Punctuation*, Clevedon: Multilingual Matters Ltd.

Meek, M. (1996) *Information and Book Learning*, Stroud: Thimble Press.

Millard, E. (1997) *Differently Literate*, London: The Falmer Press.

OFSTED (1993) *Boys and Reading*, Ref 2/93/NS: DfEE.

QCA (1998) *Can do Better: Raising Boys' Achievement in English*, London: Qualifications and Curriculum Authority.

Taylor, M. (1994) 'What Children's Books tell us about Teaching Language' in Styles, M. *et al.* (Eds) *The Prose and the Passion*, London: Cassell.

Wragg, E. C. *et al.* (1998) *Improving Literacy in the Primary school*, London: Routledge.

7 Forward to fundamentals – the foundations of literacy

The need for a comprehensive approach to language and literacy

Eric Ashworth

Perhaps the biggest formal change in the schools' fostering of literacy since the advent in 1988 of the National Curriculum and its attendant requirements such as SATs is the introduction of the Literacy Hour into English primary schools.

This has been greeted with mixed feelings. Some thought that it was a further unjustifiable encroachment on the responsibility of schools to devise their own curricula, approaches and ways of teaching. Others felt that it would lend a high degree of certainty to what schools were required to do. And whilst some were glad that the Literacy Hour would serve to focus literacy teaching, others feared that it might ruin a more pervasive view of literacy which saw it as running through the whole curriculum and that it might in the long run bring standards of attainment down rather than put them up. On such matters we must remain uncommitted and await evidence.

However, It is important to recognise that crucial matters concerned with literacy cannot be neatly confined within time-tabled periods or taught in any narrowly didactic way and that these are not trivial matters but are the bases of future success.

Irrespective of the merits or shortcomings of the Literacy Hour, this chapter suggests siz general propositions which seem to be necessary if literacy is to improve. They are:

1 that language and literacy events are basic in children's learning;
2 that we should consider literacy as a whole – not just reading but writing too;
3 that literacy should be treated as part of a wider language programme;
4 that we should move towards wider and deeper models of reading;
5 that the case for 'good' books is founded in relation to language development as a whole;
6 that 'positive affect' is both an excellent way to judge past attainment and is the condition for further successful learning.

Proposition 1. That language and literacy events are basic in children's learning

Language events

Quite simply, language events are occasions when an individual comes into contact with a person or persons speaking and listening. The individual may be either a participant or an observer. Such events occur throughout the lifetimes of all normal individuals. Indeed, they precede independent life, for it is certain that in a rudimentary but possibly significant way they begin before birth.

It is generally accepted that the power to speak and to understand speech grows in an interpersonal context. This context exists well before the child can speak. There is strong evidence that the child's pre-language vocalisings are influenced, certainly as far as quantity is concerned, by what we might call the linguistically-relevant attention paid to the child. It begins with eye-gaze and with talk to the child. The child reacts physiologically and by vocalising. Thus children learn the form of the conversation (A-B-A-B and so on where A and B are the participants) before they themselves can utter language and they exploit this form by responding vocally to other people's language. In these matters the mother or other major carer plays a vital role. Accompanying these transactions are dominant emotions, occasionally of rage but very often of pleasure, linked to feelings of dependence and physical comfort.

Soon children begin to babble, exercising their vocal mechanisms and usually, according to the amount of speech directed to them, that babble begins to approximate to, or incorporate, the sounds of the language around them. It is not only the smaller sounds that the child learns. From very early he listens to, responds to and himself begins to make the 'tunes' which are themselves meaningful and which envelope utterances. So at this stage children are learning the constituent sounds as well as the conversational structure of utterance and response.

This early learning goes much further. Children begin to associate the language that they hear with references and meanings. In such ways, even before they can speak, children learn what will be indispensable to them later. When the process is satisfactory the amount that they learn is massive.

Literacy events

In many ways literacy events are similar to language events and indeed may overlap with them. They are encounters in which a person comes across printed or written language, or sees people reading or writing, or tries to read or write him or herself, or plays at reading or writing. In children's early years they provide opportunities to learn a great deal that lies deep at the heart of the writing system and thus ultimately of reading and writing. They can learn how print is arranged and how it takes a typical order inside books, how the horizontal and directional principles work, what a word is and how it is made up of letters, what the alphabet is, what writing is used for, and so on. These are all matters of intellectual endeavour and generally it takes years before the successive understandings that children form come into line with adult conventions. When children are read to as part of these events, they learn also about how language can be ordered into texts and how information can be structured to give shape to a text. They take in literary forms in grammar, literary uses of vocabulary, and literary style, much of it well before they themselves can read in the conventional sense of that term.

Further, literacy events exemplify the ways in which literacy is woven into the fabric of the lives around a child. Writing and reading begin to be seen as valued activities. Literacy events provide examples and, most importantly, stimulate motivation for future endeavour.

Within the spectrum of literacy events much has been made of the importance of environmental print – the print on packets, labels, hoardings, television and so on. It is a very important element (Goodman and Altwerger, 1981), but it is not everything. There is a great distance between appreciating the significance of such print and the rather odd claim that, because of it, reading is 'natural', for there are other factors that should not be overlooked. For example, when we examine successful readers and look particularly at early readers (Clark, 1976; Durkin, 1966; Van Lierop, 1985; Sutton, 1985) we usually find, even among claims that they are self-taught, that close at hand has been an interested supportive adult or sibling, ready and willing to help and to answer questions. Even independent children need support, information, models, and feedback, and these come from interactions with others within literacy events. What has frequently been noted among early successful readers, whether they are 'self-taught' or not, is the initiatives they show. They are often found to take the lead, but even this may depend on adults and others who support and validate, sometimes by little more than being an approving presence, sometimes by more active participation, the children's literacy activities and the initiatives they feel they can take. Independent initiative, in other words, may itself often be derived from other people's support.

On the way to literacy children will, hopefully, come across hundreds of examples which are instances of what we can call 'modelling', and as they get closer to a text so they will become more aware of what adults and other practitioners actually do when they read and write. Thus, literacy events not only shape attitudes and interests, they give children chances to learn about some of the techniques that are being employed.[1]

The formative potency of literacy events and of what takes place within them is illustrated by cultural differences. There is plenty of documentation that shows not only their powerfulness but that they differ with different cultures. For example, Ron Scollon (Scollon and Scollon, 1981) has shown how his daughter was 'orientated' towards literacy by the time she was two and how she differed from the Athabaskan children in Fort Chipewyan who had a radically different regard for books and reading. Similarly, Brice Heath in an exhaustive study of language events and literacy events among three communities in the Carolinas – black industrial, white industrial and white 'mainstream' – has shown substantive differences in the kinds and totals of literacy-relevant learning that occur in the pre-school years (Brice Heath, 1983).

Let us look at one estimate of the possible scale of literacy events. Teale (1986) studied a group of low-income children aged between 2.8 and 3.8 years in San Diego, California. His data give an impressive picture of the incidence of such events over a period of a year. He looked at both the frequency and the duration of literacy events and found that the frequency ranged from 0.34 to 4.06 per hour and that the minutes spent in each encounter ranged from 3.09 to 34.72 per hour. Teale estimated that, as children were awake about 13 hours per day, they experienced reading and writing from approximately 5 to 53 times a day and spent on average between 40 minutes and 7.5 hours per day on such activities. Even a child who experienced literacy somewhat less frequently than others might encounter reading or writing over 2,000 times and for almost 500 hours in the course of a year. Encouragingly, every child in the sample 'was somehow involved with reading and writing during the course of everyday home experiences', but among them were considerable differences.

The scale and frequency of such encounters provoke several thoughts. The first is that if any child were to miss them completely his preparation for literacy would be very severely impaired – perhaps even to the extent of keeping him non-literate. The second is that even among the vast majority who do experience literacy events there are wide differences. As a result, whilst some children are richly provided for, others are *relatively* deprived. The third is that the scale of such events throws the literacy hour now embraced and required by the Department for Education and Employment into perspective. An hour each day, if that were all, compares only with the time spent by those towards the least-advantaged of Teale's groups. The comparison is still illuminating, even when we recognise in fairness that nobody advocates that literacy learning should be confined to that hour alone for, hopefully, language and literacy will extend over the curriculum and over living itself.

Teale had little to say about the *quality* of literacy events. We can guess that there are considerable differences so that some children are more fortunate than others. Low quality coupled with low frequency spells out warnings about whether the very foundations for future literacy are being soundly laid or not. Children who may have missed out will go into more formal work in literacy without secure foundations and, probably, without the accompanying feelings of pleasure, interest and competence that are engendered in more fortunate children. Life and school may well become uphill struggles for them.

Children's early writing

Vygotsky (1878) saw writing as developing from gesture. To him scribble was gesture on the page and that was the earliest 'writing'. (In this respect we can note in passing, and encourage parents to agree, that a child needs to enjoy a long career as a scribbler and maker of marks – preferably with different sorts of instruments on different sorts of surfaces – as a preparation for handwriting.)

Writing had, according to Vygotsky, another root. This was in pretend-play.[2] Such play, when something 'stood for' something else was a notable instance of symbolic activity and as time went on a developing idea of the symbol had somehow to be married to the gesture and its descendants in order to make writing which had an abstract quality – that is, which represented something, namely speech (and, presumably, whatever lay beyond speech).

So we have a wide range of outcomes in children's early writing. There is writing that is more or less spontaneous, writing that is a broad emulation of what the child sees around him or her, writing that takes on symbolic or representative character, writing that more closely resembles that of adult convention in being truly alphabetic, and so on. As with the rest of writing, including spelling and even handwriting, all this early learning has a strong conceptual basis. Learning to write, whatever else it is, is basically a cognitive exercise. It is founded on various understandings, which may change gradually or untidily over a period of time. It is some of these that I want to discuss next.

As I do, I must mention two adjacent ideas put forward by Vernon (1967) and by Downing (1973) about reading, not writing, but highly relevant to our concerns. Vernon believed that one of the causes that disabled children from reading was that they suffered from 'cognitive confusion'. They had no clear idea of what they should do when they read and so they could not do it. Downing took a similar tack and called for 'cognitive clarity'. Both may have misunderstood somewhat the true nature of children's early efforts to read for some, at least, of the 'confusion' that they detected may have been highly principled. However, they were right in that clarity is vital.

We can mention some of the many concepts that children may entertain as they move towards an 'adult' or conventional understanding of the nature of writing. It is wrong to call these misconceptions. Although they are indeed not conventionally 'correct', they are for the most parts triumphs of reasoning and sheer good sense, evidence of cognitive activity, persistent, and dynamic in that they typically reshape understandings under the pressure of changing evidence.

Investigations by Clay, by Ferreiro, and by Gundlach and colleagues, among others, have shown that children read and write (according to the model or set of understandings that they possess at that particular moment) in ways that are interesting but which may not immediately result in 'real' reading and writing.

The early history of literacy in the individual is therefore of encounters with prints and books, of seemingly endogenous (but probably ultimately triggered by social contexts) attempts to read and write which apparently owe much to inner momentum and are part of early semiotic development, and of the activation of succeeding schemata which operate to control literacy behaviour and which gradually come to terms with the essentials of conventional or 'real' reading and writing of English.

The concept of 'word', to which we have already referred, provides us with one instance. It would be a mistake to suppose, simply because young children use words in speaking, or because they understand words addressed to them, that they understand what a word is or that they grasp that speech can in principle be segmented down into words. Still less may they understand that all words in a message may be written down, or that the length of a word is in general (with the exception of many plurals) unrelated to the quantity, size, or any other quality of what it refers to, but that a general but not quite exclusive principle prevails that the word when written is linked alphabetically to the sound of that word when spoken.

The following instances are no more than a peep into the conceptual learning that is necessary before the children come to this sort of sophisticated understanding.

The 'undifferentiated signs and squiggles' noted by Vygotsky frequently begin to take on certain characteristics. They may proceed roughly from left to right. They may incorporate odd letters and letter-like forms. Clay (1975) noted a 'sign' concept which she saw as reaching out to mature writing, and also a 'message' concept when the child understands that messages can be written down but when there is still no real correspondence between the message and what is written. Another important understanding is what Clay calls the 'recurring' principle when the child incorporates the same elements again and again in his or her writing. As yet the child is far from fully understanding the alphabetic principle but the alphabet is the real key to the recurring that the child is now aware of. Also, the child becomes aware of a contrary or supplementary principle – the 'flexibility' principle which allows variation in what is put down. Clay, in fact, was among the first to systematise these early understandings.

Ferreiro (Ferreiro, 1985; Ferreiro and Teberosky, 1982) has also shed much light on early literacy. She has tracked children's understandings from their beginnings through the 'syllabic hypothesis', when signs are believed to stand for whole syllables, to the acceptance and utilisation of the alphabetic principle. She has investigated the ability of children to recognise (not yet read) print and to discriminate it from other markings including random marks, pictures, numerals and punctuation marks. She has done fascinating work within a Piagetian framework on children's notions of the necessary length of words. She has demonstrated that some children at various points in their early development will use the same number of letters as there are members of the group that is being written about. Thus 'four stars' would have 'stars' or whatever stood for stars at this time, written with only four 'letters' and 'three bears' would have 'bears' with only three. Sometimes the 'letters' are written large for big objects and small for little objects. Important objects and people may be given more letters. 'Daddy' is written bigger or longer than 'Mummy'. Ferreiro also investigated what her children understood as constituting a word. She found that many children believed that what was written could not be a word unless it contained a minimum number of letters, three being the critical number.

The development of writing is not just a simple matter of executive ability. Underlying it are greater understandings at a conceptual level. This conceptual basis is part of the deep foundation of literacy and not just of reading or writing singly, for the deepening of understanding revealed in writing also shows itself in reading. In particular, we can note such gradual understandings as that of the equivalence of the spoken and written word in that the same word may be spoken or written and of the use of the alphabet. and, pedagogically, the practical partnership between the parent (or teacher) and child which encourages and shapes the child's spontaneous efforts. We should also note the practical partnership between the parent (or teacher) and child which encourages and shapes the child's spontaneous efforts.

In writing, time and again we find the same story as we found in reading. Children who develop well before school and who are thus best prepared for schools as they exist usually come from a background in which literacy is valued and where encouragement and approval – direct through personal interactions and indirect through the provision of materials and opportunities – are common. Books, environmental print and supportive adults and siblings all have a role to play. It is important that, in addition to learning the basic concepts which allow entry into the world of literacy, children should emerge with a strong sense of interest, believing that written matter is fascinating, able to write, knowing what they are doing and with an appetite for more learning. If this is to be so they must not only learn these foundational concepts, they must feel happy and at ease when they employ them.

Children's early reading

When we turn back to reading we must stress two matters. The first is that good books are the only ones worth using (for it is too risky to chance using books that are dross), but they are not homogeneous. Picture books with little or no text can be very important. Through them the young child will be helped to grasp the vital distinction between picture and text. On the other hand a central criterion of the text of a good book is its employment of linguistic resources – grammar, vocabulary, style, structure and its use of metaphor and other tropes. Different sorts of good books offer different sorts of opportunities and the same book may offer new opportunities when it is revisited. Put differently, good books are important at each successive stage and with each succeeding model of the reading process that the child adopts.

The second is that there is a strong and continuing place for a range of supportive activities from the adult or others. It supplies the flywheel of gentle discipline, as well as the scaffolding for tackling texts.

Now we come to the central matter. Even a non-literate child is used to processing language for meaning. Spoken language is, or rather seems to be, natural in a culture, and so when children speak they are hardly conscious of what they are doing. But with print it is different. Embedded sentences, hierarchical processing (when one has to return to part of a text *after* one has gone further on), the possible abundance of non-literal language – which seems to mean something different from what it seems to say – the relevance of the text as a whole to meaning are heightened in much print as compared to speech[3] and are difficult matters which may call for conscious treatment. The point for us is that texts must be rich enough to present such features, for they represent not just difficulties but opportunities to learn. Hence the importance of support. Hence, too, the importance of gaining that massive background knowledge from books, from being read to,[4] and from elsewhere, that we have characterised as crucial.

Again, we come back to the notion of being read to from *quality* books. We need also to consider the further notion that being read to while one follows the print is one very good road into reading. This is discussed by Pugh (1978) and elsewhere by the present author (Ashworth, 1988, Ch 4). And whenever a story is revisited this offers a chance to do what the Language Experience Approach and Breakthrough to Literacy both allow – the opportunity to fit the meaning (which one already knows) to the text.[5] It seems to go without saying that if there is to be such re-acquaintance, there ought to be real quality in the book.

Proposition 2. That we should consider literacy as a whole – not just reading but writing too

There are two *modes* of English – the spoken and the written. Reading and writing are skills exercised upon the written mode and have a common conceptual basis. The two modes have different uses and use different resources: each employs grammar that is far from identical with that of the other. The learner of the written mode has to cope with the alphabetic nature of English, with the whole of the writing system – which includes numerals, short forms, punctuation as well as with spacing and lay-out requirements. He has to learn to leave to one side the systems of pauses, variable pitch, volume and speed in which he has enveloped his spoken English and which themselves constitute meaning-carrying elements of speech. These meaningful elements are still there to be used as an aid to reading. But, in their own time, children must gradually leave them behind as they metamorphose into silent readers, reading for meaning.

There is much common ground between reading and writing, as we have pointed out. However there are also profound differences. Margaret Peters once said that spelling is not the flip side of reading. Both children and adults can frequently read what they cannot write and a little more surprisingly can sometimes write what they cannot read (Bryant and Bradley, 1980; Frith, 1980). The language policy of each school, particularly those dealing with young children, needs to be conscious of these matters and to take steps to help the child's understandings.

Proposition 3. That literacy should be treated as part of a wider language programme

Somewhat different considerations make it doubly necessary to take a language-wide view of spelling development. It seems to be a matter of good sense that to be a good speller cannot be equated simply with being a correct speller. A correct speller who can spell only a few words is by no means a good speller (except of course in the case of absolute beginners). Extensions of vocabulary, through listening and reading are therefore potentially highly relevant to spelling ability, even though they may seem to 'belong' to other parts of a language programme.

Looking at reading and writing as a whole, one could say that there are two grand routes into literacy. The first is from within the child, a creative rather than a copying venture, when the child may invent or reconstruct literacy, or a version of it, for him- or herself. The second, which concerns us now, is the move from speaking and listening into more conventional reading and writing.

Even old-fashioned class reading books (particularly the early books among such sets) worked on the assumption that the words in them were already well-known to the reader. Somewhat newer approaches, also assuming previous knowledge, are based on what we might call idiolect: that is, they are based on the language – not just the vocabulary – that the child already possesses. The Language Experience Approach (Goddard 1974) is an instance of this. It has the merit of extending, or at least identifying, experiences – for example, a shopping expedition – and then of using them to make up a text. Children would talk about the experience and then with the teacher's help refine the language which they would then write down. This text would be used as a basis for reading. As with the second example, the approach has the inestimable advantage for early readers that they would know what a text 'meant' before they actually read it. The second example is Breakthrough to Literacy (Mackay *et al.* 1978). Here the child who cannot necessarily handwrite (i.e. in the conventional way) is helped by materials and the teacher to find a written version of what has been said and to acquire gradually increasing independence of the teacher as this takes place. This written version becomes the text for the child's early reading. Both the language experience approach and Breakthrough – and they are not exclusive alternatives – have much to commend them. Both are literacy approaches not just reading methods and both are rooted in the experiences and in the spoken language of children.

When we return again to the question: where does a child's familiarity with written language come from? I would suggest three sources. First, there is the child's previous knowledge of spoken language together with all the referencing, meaning, ordering, shaping for purpose and dips into vocabulary, sound patterns and grammar that this entails. Some of this will be simply transmuted into written form; some will be used to process print for meaning.

Then there is the direct knowledge of written language which comes from being read to and later from the child's own reading. Reading aloud to a listener always involves the reader in utilising the devices of pitch, pauses and stress and of chunking information to help the listener and so make texts accessible that otherwise would not be.[6] It allows the listener to gain an expanding knowledge of written language, the styles it takes and the genres into which it falls. It also provides an opportunity for adults to discuss the text and the act of reading with children, thus helping with their development of models.

The third source is really a subset of this. It is language gained in revisiting the same book. Worthwhile books in which a child is interested are worth visiting time and again. Sometimes children themselves demand such repetition. These encounters are valuable quite apart from their usefulness in preparing the child for reading. A revisit is almost never identical to an earlier encounter. Different matters come up. The rhythm is different. Meaning and the process of achieving meaning can be tackled in greater depth. Discussion tends to focus on different places or on different matters. Probes for meaning tend to go deeper. Less familiar words become more familiar.

In all of this book quality is a major factor. Quality is what makes the book worth revisiting. It may be the pictures, the language, or the movement into metaphor and away from the literal. It may be its efficacy in prompting talk, its ability to interest, engage, or enthral, or to create feelings of suspense, excitement and curiosity. Whatever the particular nature, it is quality that makes the activity worthwhile, though we should note that it may also require a willing and compliant adult to help matters along.

Speaking and listening, including being read to and talking about books, are not just important in their own right, they are important elements of work towards literacy.

Proposition 4. That we should move towards wider and deeper models of reading

It is an error to regard reading as being *mainly* the recognition of words (through 'look and say' or whole-word techniques) or their identification through sounding out (or phonics).

What we actually read is *language* which is made up of more than words and is organised into texts which may be of any length. 'Look and say', whole-word recognition and phonics are all word-bound. Neither alone nor together can they serve as a complete model of reading behaviour, first because they ignore so much of language and second because they do not deal with the achievement of meaning and response and tend to take them for granted.

What word-bound approaches mainly ignore is grammar and yet grammar is essential to all the uses to which language is put. It is a major part of language's potential for meaning, and is itself an indispensable, integral and absolutely vital part of all language.

From the teacher's point of view grammar is a major resource, possession of which allows children to make many different kinds of meanings, to exemplify relationships both human and material, and to generate language which can be used for many different purposes. Briefly, this resource is massive and consists of systems and structures. The *structures* comprise words, parts of words (morphemes), phrases, clauses, sentences and structures that are above the level of a sentence, including what is really the rhetorical device of story structure or 'story grammar'. These structures package the language and incidentally allow the experienced reader to make certain kinds of predictions because such a reader will have a good idea of how the structure will turn out. From one point of view all texts are made up of such structures.

Grammatical *systems* are even more various. They include ways of indicating whether nouns, pronouns and verbs are singular or plural, ways of making relative time references through the use of tenses and aspect, ways of asking questions, of making statements and commands. They include systems with such markers as 'may', which puts us into the hypothetical world of possibilities, and 'if', which moves us into the world of hypothetical conditions. The importance of many of these systems is that they get us well beyond the bald labelling statements of name or 'fact' and allow us to make more complex meanings. What I should claim here is that we are dealing, in a very important and fundamental way with nothing less than the growth of intellect – the stocking and orientation of the mind itself.

One other system, which is so pervasive that it often seems to be unnoticed, is the set of rules which is used to put words in the order in which they must be spoken or written. Much, probably most, of all this grammar is learned at an implicit rather than an explicit level. The knowledge remains tacit but its effects are powerful.

So much for the extension of the concern with words into a concern with language. However, a viable model of reading needs to spread wider and deeper still. If we take it as obvious that the goal is the construction, or reconstruction, or creation of meaning (and let us beg a question here by referring only to the 'achieving of meaning') and with it the engendering of response, it is clear that there is more involved in reading than just the language on the page. *There is also the reader's previous knowledge of language and his or her knowledge of the world. All readers always have to work with these. The sheer quantity of knowledge and information that the reader needs to bring to the successful interpretation of a text – any text, even a 'simple' one – is enormous.*

A comprehensive model of reading would try to show how readers would use the information that is picked up from the page, previous knowledge of language and how it works, and previous worldly knowledge and treat them all as being potentially available in the process of achieving meaning. These resources are sometimes alternatives, especially with more sophisticated readers; if one uses some, one does not need others, and therefore there is redundancy. This is just as true of stores of language as of worldly knowledge. Together they allow expectations to be built up about both local and global or overall meanings. They also permit inferences – which are always knowledge-based – to be made when appropriate.

Thus, reading, as it progresses towards meaning and response, is *always* a matter of language not just words and it is *always* a matter of more than language.

In the process of going from text to meaning, which is the essence of reading, various psychological mechanisms soon become involved. Three, at least, are very important. They are the building up of expectations and the drawing of inferences, to both of which we have already referred, and the development of the ability to monitor one's own behaviour and its outcomes as one reads.

All these are knowledge-based. Expectations arise partly through sensitivity to (i.e knowledge of) a particular situation, and with familiarity with the genre that is being explored, for we expect stories, for example, to proceed in a certain way.[7] Also, the language itself sometimes gives a strong clue – 'Once upon a time … ' sets up a mode of dealing with a text as well as exciting pleasurable anticipations. Familiarity with texts and the ways in which they bind together allows us to build firmer expectations. As far as the readers are concerned, when they are moved by such expectations, they are then searching for language and meaning that they expect to find. It makes the task much easier than it would otherwise be. The same thing happens with the grammatical structures and systems of language. For example knowing the word-order rules permits them to have a good idea of what sort of word may come next and it certainly allows them to rule out some possibilities altogether.

Inferences are also important. Also dependent on previous knowledge, they allow us to fill gaps in a text or to make more explicit what has only been hinted at. For example, if we read 'Without looking, the child ran across the road. There was a screech of brakes. The child lay lifeless by the side of the pavement.' we shall infer what has happened, even though the text does not tell us. This is only a dramatic instance of a process that goes on throughout texts. We, the readers, make them more complete, and inferring is a major way in which we do this.

A third process that goes on is that of self-monitoring. We become alert to the possibility that something that we are reading 'doesn't seem right'. And so we may read it again to see if we or perhaps the author or printer has made a mistake. If meaning does not tally with previous meaning we note the incongruity and, quite possibly re-read. This monitoring, of course, is only engendered when the meanings really are available to be achieved. Some texts are more meaningful than others and the meanings associated with some are more vivid than others. It is inescapable that children need good texts that are rich in meanings and rich also in the language that allows the reader to achieve more and more subtle and complex meanings.[8] Again, we should note that many of the judgements of self-monitoring are based on previously acquired knowledge. Often there is an implied comparison of the text with what the reader knows to be 'correct' or 'usual' or 'fitting' or 'likely'. A model of reading which does not incorporate these processes cannot be considered to be final because it is not yet complete.

There are, I suggest, four underlying criteria for models of reading beyond the obvious one that they should be useful for whatever purpose is in hand.

First, we should take into account development. This might mean that several models are needed successively and not just one, for the beginning reader does not read exactly like the expert reader but relies on different resources and uses different strategies.

Second, a reading model should be dynamic. That is to say that it should not deal with a static structure so much as with a process.

Third, it should be interactive – some of the dynamism is in moving between different strategies and sources of information, on the page and elsewhere, with each in principle liable to affect whether, or to what degree, use is made of the others. So the finished model will be complicated and it may be that only in exceptional cases will processing show a simple, straight, linear pattern.

Fourth, it should allow for variation and variety. One person's strategies may legitimately differ from another's even when both are reading the same text, and the same person may use different strategies as he or she encounters different sorts of texts or reads for different purposes. A viable model or set of models would allow the reader to go well beyond the information on the page – it would take account of the ability to hypothesise and to build expectations, to make inferences and to monitor and self-correct at different levels and to behave as much like a creative artist as a communicator (Smith 1985).

Learning *about* reading is among the most important learning to be done as these early foundations are laid. The 'cognitive confusion' to which Vernon and others have referred needs to be replaced by a positive picture within the child's mind. This is where what has been called 'feed-forward' is so important.

It is a commonplace of psychology that much conscious action among humans is in an important way pre-formed. One stands, walks, sits down, runs, articulates, speaks and so on, not completely afresh but because previous learning (and, maybe in a few instances, instinct) has laid down a pattern or schema that can be followed again. It is true that further and even continuous adaptation may take place whilst the activity is under way but the broad pattern remains even as it is being modified. With psychomotor activities the variations are often limited by comparison and may be taken without any apparent conscious effort. Thus we may divert our path when walking if we notice an obstacle in the way or, in a crowd, seem in danger of bumping into someone. Still, in a broad way our actions are mapped out for us by what we already have learned or acquired. The same is true of highly complex activities such as reading. The actions of readers are determined or highly influenced by what they think they must do as readers. (And the same is true of writers.) Some children believe that the object of reading is to say out loud words that are printed. Others will tell you, without further specifying, that the purpose of reading is to learn, which sounds more promising. One child's early model of reading might be such that it causes that child to look at the marks on the page and then make up a story. Another model might incorporate the linear nature of English writing and, a little more advanced, the way pagination works. Another part of a model might be the incorporation of phonemic clues – perhaps to assist with the initial sound of a word. Some would incorporate knowledge previously gained elsewhere. Others would envisage the build-up of expectations from the evidence of genre, grammar, and from the direction of story and events. A later model might involve a built-in tentativeness, necessary because with embedded clauses and with what is sometimes called the hierarchical principle, reading becomes less exclusively linear in the order in which it needs to be processed. This means that the reader must hold something from the text in reserve until the rest is coped with – an important principle in much reading.

Actually, we are dealing with two kinds of models. One kind is the child's which will change progressively. The other is the teacher's which sets the agenda for what the child has to accomplish if he is to be competent to work his own particular model and to develop it further. This accomplishment will be gradual, spread over several years. Without a consciously held model the teacher can hardly be fully effective. Tenable models for children and adults both 'feed-forward' and also help us to avoid that 'cognitive confusion' which Vernon and others have seen as a cause of failure.

Proposition 5. That the case for 'good' books is founded in relation to language development as a whole

We can now summarise the case for good books under several headings. Some of these pertain to reading others apply to other parts of the language spectrum. As I have tried to show, the language skills of reading, writing, speaking and listening are to an important extent mutually constitutive, though in different ways at different points in development, so that, for example, the use by adults of good books to bring on speaking and listening will have an indirect effect on literacy.

Speaking and listening

A book, whether it is a picture book or one with written text, provides a sort of changing focus for talk. Snow and Ferguson (1977) found that the mother's talk in encounters with picture books was richer than in free play with toys. There are different matters on the page, different parts of a picture, a range of characters and incidents, all of which are grist for possible discussion. Talk about books tends to be very rich. It changes, too, with successive revisits, provided that the book is of sufficient quality and interest, provided, that is to say, that it is a good book. One probable reason is that the book provides the topic and what remains is to elaborate this and to add comment.

Actually, using real books itself may include a wide range of activities: looking, pointing, reading, discussing content, linking content to experience, re-reading, using the text as a basis for further play, revisiting, answering questions, retelling the story, extending ranges of interest, collecting and storing books, learning a metalanguage, and so on. Many such activities insinuate themselves into the regular routines and rituals of family and later of school life. For example, Ninio and Brubner (1978) found that early speaking behaviour was routinised in the sense that encounters were typically made up of a series of small units each with only a few utterances. One partner would try to get the other to focus attention. Then one would try to get the other to label. If this were done, the first would provide the other with feedback. If not, the first participant would provide the label. We can note that it was usually the mother who provided the source of stability in these rich and productive sequences.

A further reason for reading aloud to children is that the children then practise sustained listening, processing the language for meaning. When the book is good and the language is rich the opportunities for such processing are amplified. Children are now doing what we shall want them to do more independently when they read for themselves. Reading good books to them means that they are being prepared to read good books for themselves later.

Writing

It seems clear that a critical phase in the child's development as a writer is the gradual building of an 'adult' (i.e. conventional) understanding of what a word is. The importance of constant presentations of print in the environment and in books is therefore quite obvious. Words cease to be 'transparent' and become opaque. The advantage of good books is that, being intrinsically resourceful, they are potentially interesting and so will allow, and even demand, this sort of commerce.

The grammar that children use as writers diverges from that of their speaking and especially from their conversation.[9] As writers, children need access to the grammar of writing. This they get through books – fictional and factual. Books provide the store on which children can draw and the better the book the better the store. From books children also begin to note the ways in which information can be structured, the sequencing or other organisation of events, the ways in which a writer deals with the presumptions that are made about what readers already know and what those readers need to be told.

Closely linked to this is what has been called story grammar – the ways in which stories typically begin with the introduction of the main characters and set the scene and period in the very first sentences, progressing through familiar kinds of complications to the final resolution. Story grammar does not perhaps have the exactness that is characteristic of other grammars, but it is very powerful all the same.[10]

Almost certainly the story grammar learned from good books is useful in three respects – in remembering and recalling, when it provides a structure, in reading, when it enables one to 'know' what is likely to come next and in writing, where it provides the writer with a plan of action that becomes so familiar that it seems to be part of the furniture of the mind.

Finally, we can turn briefly to spelling, which is an important part of writing. When real spelling emerges after various conceptual excursions, children look for ways to handle the correspondence between sounds and letters. Typically children try various ploys – one sound one letter, one syllable one letter, straight correspondences with articulatory units and so on. There are at least two indispensable needs for the child who is to be counted a competent speller at this stage. The first, we have stressed, is an acquaintance with a wide range of vocabulary. The second is the clear articulation of that vocabulary. Early in their careers, children tend to spell as they articulate[11] (Read 1975) but the articulation is influenced by what has been heard. Reading good books to a child helps to meet both needs.

Proposition 6. That 'positive affect' is both an excellent way to evaluate past attainment and is the condition for future success

Throughout what I have written there has been an emphasis on fundamental learning. Now we must turn to the emotional and allied conditions which learning engenders and which, in turn, engender further learning.

Encounters with books need to be as pleasant, as satisfying and as interesting as it is possible to make them. We have stressed the necessary role of the supportive adult (or sibling). A major part of that role is to ease the path of the learner, to make some activities game-like or playful, challenging at times, but with success usually guaranteed. Discussion, praise, encouragement are as much part of helping a child to learn to read as is supplying words or investigating phonemic relationships. Early reading, whatever else it is, is an interpersonal activity and in that way may be a source of pleasure to the child. Dependence, and inter-dependence, are the roads to independence.

A great deal of what we can call positive affect – pleasure, the motivation to succeed, the increase of appetite for reading and so on – comes from success and ease. Perhaps we can imagine what is unfortunately sometimes the case. Suppose we had a learner whose foundations were not very secure who was therefore uneasy about the tasks of reading. It is almost unbelievable what may be in store for him. 'Graded' reading schemes, often of low intrinsic merit, mean that each time he has struggled through a book he is given another one which is designed to be a little harder, thus trapping him in a miserable round which makes for lack of success and risks turning him against reading altogether.

Forward to fundamentals

In the past there have been calls to get 'Back to Basics'. They have not met with much success and the reason, I believe, is that they have not been properly identified. Too often 'basics' have been seen as phonic analysis or synthesis, or as a concentration upon what are word-based strategies such as 'whole word' techniques.

What I have tried to do in this chapter is to identify fundamentals, the foundations[12] upon which increasing competence in the literacy skills can be based. Even for beginners this is already a complex business and depends on the child having previously acquired all sorts of information, understandings, and skills (such as that of drawing inferences). The experience of many able teachers is that unless these are in place, other work may be fruitless or even counter-productive. I have drawn attention also to the need for models and for the children to be encouraged to become more and more sophisticated in what they incorporate into their models. I think it is fair to say that this is a relatively neglected part of work in literacy.

It is clear from the time-scale involved and from the wide-ranging activities that are needed, that what the school by itself can do is not enough. A concentration of work into a Literacy Hour may or may not turn out to be profitable. What is certain is that parents need to be actively involved.

What children need often cannot be neatly timetabled. Having recognised this, we need a truly viable definition of teaching, one that is not about going through the particular motions so loved by OFSTED inspectors but which sees teaching as 'facilitating learning' or 'causing to learn' whether directly or indirectly, one that gives teachers the chance to be fully professional.

The slogan we should adopt for the future should not be 'Back to Basics' but 'Forward to Fundamentals'. When we do, a much brighter future beckons to children, parents and teachers alike.

Notes

1 This early understanding needs to grow eventually into the development of personal models of reading. See below.

2 What Vygotsky had to say about 'pretend-play' was very important. However, I think that he may have underestimated the 'symbolic nature', as he might have put it, of speech. It might have been better if he had claimed that what happens with the onset of literacy is that this symbolising process intensifies and takes on another layer as written and printed signs come to 'stand for' spoken language.

3 Of course spoken language can also be complicated. Most of it is not. We are dealing with matters of degree.

4 A major feature of being read to, apart from the close interpersonal bond that is involved, concerns the nature of language and its understanding. What a reader actually reads to a child is *written* language. However, by reading aloud the competent reader chunks the information which helps to make it digestible and thus meaningful. He or she also uses the resources of *spoken* language which are themselves aids to meaning – tone of voice, speed of utterance, pause, emphasis and the significant use of pitch. These provide crutches which allow the listener to comprehend texts that otherwise he might not be able to understand. However, being read to ought not to be just for the very young. I have found it helpful also with older children, with sixth formers and with undergraduate and postgraduate students.

5 I claim no more than that *sometimes*, depending on the teacher's judgement, having meaning before scrutinising the text can be very helpful indeed.

6 Teachers who are stuck with a word-bound approach may not pay sufficient regard to this because it essentially involves longer stretches of language.

7 Knowledge of what is sometimes (misleadingly, I think) called 'story grammar' is really knowledge about how stories usually proceed. Early on they name the principal character, they locate that character in time and space, they begin a chronological account which is complicated by some event or by the actions of another person and they move towards a resolution. Of course not all stories proceed in exactly this way but most do and as exceptions are met so the range of expectations widens.

8 The strong implication is that some of the reading fodder that we put in front of pupils may have deleterious effects.

9 The conversational form is ABAB and so on. What both B and A actually say may pick up what has just been said and may take over, without repeating it, some of its grammar. Thus it is very different from writing.

10 My feeling is that it is misnamed: I think it belongs to rhetoric rather than to grammar. Its importance remains.

11   By 'articulation' I refer not just to the sound but to the functioning of the articulatory mechanisms – involving lungs, palate, nasal cavity, tongue, dental ridge, lips and so on.

12   In one sense these fundamentals are 'early' learning, but they may not ber chronologically early. They may need to be dealt with in secondary schools where well over 10 per cent of the pupils have 'Special Educational Needs' – many of them to do with language and literacy.

13   I have shown a model as a diagram in Many Birds; Few Stones which is Chapter 11 of (eds) Colin Harrison and Eric Ashworth, Celebrating Literacy: Defending Literacy, Blackwell Education, 1991.

Questions for personal reflection or group discussion

1   Do you consider that language and literacy events as described in the chapter are as important as is claimed?

2   Do you consider that every school has a responsibility to parents to educate and encourage them in ways of developing children's language and literacy?

3   If you do consider that schools should have this responsibility would it mean a fundamental change in their nature? Should they become more like Family Centres? What would be the implications for staffing, accommodation and resources?

4   How far do teachers work from a model of reading? Are they able to say what model, if any, a particular child seems to be employing? How would they get a child, when the time is right, to move on to a more advanced version?[13]

5   What do you think makes a 'good' or 'quality' book? Are any of the books for your children *not* 'good' books?

6   How far do you regard literacy as being dependent on (a) worldly knowledge and (b) linguistic knowledge? And are these deliberately fostered with a view to developing reading and writing?

7   Do you think that it is an attainable aim that each child should leave every session concerned with literacy with positive feelings, i.e. that he or she should feel interested, to be improving, to be well-motivated for the next encounter and generally at ease because of a sense of pleasure and increasing mastery and because of the encouragement that he or she has received?

Recommended readings

Among the books referred to, the following complement the present chapter by extending the argument and relating it to other examples of good practice.

Ashworth, E. (1988) *Language Policy in the Primary School: Content and Management*. London: Croom Helm.

Clay, M. M. (1972) *Reading: The Patterning of Complex Behaviour*. Auckland: Heinemann Educational.

Ferreiro, E. and Teberosky, A. (1982) *Literacy before Schooling*. London: Heinemann Educational.

Heath, S. B. (1983) *Ways with Words: Language, Life and Work in Communities and Classrooms*. Cambridge: Cambridge University Press.

Bibliography

Ashworth, E. (1988) *Language Policy in the Primary School: Content and Management*. London: Croom Helm.

Bryant, P. E. and Bradley, L. (1980) 'Why young children sometimes write words they do not read'. In U. Frith (ed.) *Cognitive Processes in Spelling*. London: Academic Press.

Clark, M. M. (1976) *Young Fluent Readers*. London: Heinemann Educational.

Clay, M. M. (1972) *Reading; The Patterning of Complex Behaviour*. Auckland: Heinemann Educational.

Clay, M. M. (1975) *What Did I Write?* Auckland: Heinemann Educational.

Downing, J. (1973) 'The cognitive clarity theory of learning to read'. *Reading*, **7**, 63–70.

Durkin, D. (1966) *Children who Read Early*. New York: Teachers College Press.

Ferreiro, E. (1985) 'Literacy development: a psychogenetic perspective'. In D. R. Olson, N. Torrance and A. Hildyard (eds) *Literacy, Language and Learning*. Cambridge: Cambridge University Press.

Ferreiro, E. and Teberosky, A. (1982) *Literacy before Schooling*. London: Heinemann Educational.

Frith, U. (1980) 'Unexpected spelling problems'. In U. Frith, (ed.) *Cognitive Processes in Spelling*. London: Academic Press.

Goddard, N. (1974) 'The language experience approach'. In N. Goddard (ed.) *Literacy: Language Experience Approaches*. London: Macmillan.

Goodman, Y. and Altwerger, B. (1981) 'Print awareness in preschool children'. *Program in Language and Literacy*. Arizona Center for Research and Development, College of Education, Tucson.

Gundlach, R., McLane, J. B., Stott, F. M. and McNamee, G. D. (1985) 'The social foundations of children's early writing development'. In M. Farr (ed.) *Children's Early Writing Development*. Norwood, NJ: Ablex Publishing Company.

Heath, S. B. (1983) *Ways with Words: Language, Life and Work in Communities and Classrooms*. Cambridge: Cambridge University Press.

Mackay, D., Thompson, B. and Schaub, P. (1978) *Breakthrough to Literacy Teacher's Manual* (2nd edn). London: Longman for Schools Council.

Ninio, A. and Bruner, J.S. (1978) 'The achievement and antecedents of labelling'. *Journal of Child Language*, **5**, 1–14.

Pugh, A. K. (1978) *Silent Reading: an Introduction to its Study and Teaching*. London: Heinemann Educational.

Read, C. (1975) *Children's Categorization of Speech Sounds in English*. Urbana, IL: NCTE.

Scollon, R. and Scollon, S. (1981) *Narrative, Literacy and Face in Social Contexts.* Norwood, NJ: Ablex Publishing Company.

Smith, F. (1985) 'A metaphor for literacy'. In D. Olson, N. Torrance and A. Hildyard (eds) *Literacy, Language and Learning.* Cambridge: Cambridge University Press.

Snow, C. E. and Ferguson, C. A. (eds) (1977) *Talking to Children: Language Input and Acquisition.* Cambridge: Cambridge University Press.

Sutton, W. (1985) 'Some factors in preschool children of relevance to learning to read'. In M. M. Clark (ed.) *New Directions in the Study of Reading.* London: Falmer Press.

Teale, W. H. (1986) 'Home background and children's literacy development'. In W. H. Teale and E. Sulzby (eds) *Emergent Literacy: Writing and Reading.* Norwood, NJ. Ablex Publishing Company.

Van Lierop, M. (1985) 'Predisposing factors in early literacy: a case study'. In M. M. Clark (ed.) *New Directions in the Study of Reading.* London: Falmer Press.

Vernon, M. D. (1967) *Backwardness in Reading.* Cambridge: Cambridge University Press.

Vygotsky, L. S. (1978) 'Mind in Society: The development of higher psychological processes'. Trans. M. Cole, V. John-Steiner, S. Scribner and E. Souberman. Cambridge, MA: Harvard University Press.

8 Paired Reading with peers and parents

Factors in effectiveness and new developments.

Keith J. Topping

Paired Reading is one of the best researched, most effective, and most cost-effective methods of raising children's attainments in reading. In a recent review of the effectiveness of twenty interventions in reading, Paired Reading ranked as one of the most effective, surpassed only by one or two methods which seemed to have produced spectacular results, but which had only been evaluated with very small numbers of children (Brooks, Flanagan, Henkhuzens and Hutchison, 1998).

Of course, just because a method is effective does not ensure it continues to be used, and some teachers have been heard to express declining interest in Paired Reading because it is not 'the latest thing'. Fortunately most teachers are too sensible and pragmatic to be so easily influenced by concern with novelty. Indeed, amidst much talk of higher standards and targets, governments around the world are showing greatly increased interest in evidence–based education and issues of school effectiveness (see, for example, Postlethwaite and Ross, 1992; Teddlie and Reynolds, 1999). And as this chapter later outlines, there are a number of new developments and applications in the world of Paired Reading.

Nomenclature has been another problem – the phrase 'Paired Reading' has such a warm, comfortable feel to it, some teachers have loosely applied it to almost anything that two people do together with a book. Of course, the effectiveness research only applies to 'proper' Paired Reading – the specific and structured technique described below (and in more detail in Topping, 1995, 2001). Some teachers have invented their own procedure, cheerfully (mis-)labelled it Paired Reading, then found it did not work, and looked around for somebody else to blame. This dilution through problems of loose nomenclature and poor implementation integrity can easily result in muddled attitudes to the technique. Indeed, in the USA, the need was felt to re-label 'proper' Paired Reading to try to avoid this kind of confusion – teachers there felt the new name 'Duolog Reading' was unusual enough to remain clearly identifiable in an educational market-place overwhelmed with a plethora of methods.

Since the first edition of the *Reading for Real Handbook*, teachers in England have coped with a great deal: the development of a National Curriculum, the accompanying burden of assessment, devolution of finance to schools, a substantial increase in administrative work, the introduction of the National Literacy Strategy, and so on – all creating innovation fatigue and sometimes reducing the time, energy and perhaps even motivation available to teach. Teachers in many other western countries will find this picture familiar.

In the 1980s, there was a great surge of interest and activity in the UK in parental involvement in reading. In the 1990s, although parental involvement figured strongly in governmental rhetoric, the real effect of other changes and stresses seemed to be a slowing down in work with parents – at best a plateau phenomenon. However, the pressure to 'do more with less' increased. In striving to raise attainments, some schools turned increasingly to various forms of peer tutoring in reading.

It would be most unfortunate if peer tutoring were seen as a substitute for parental involvement. It is certainly potentially powerful and effective, and has the attractions to teachers of requiring relatively little teacher energy to establish, and being very much under the direct control of the school. Parental involvement tends to require more energy to establish (especially in the early days, when there can be frustrations and disappointments), and seems inherently more risky (who knows what those parents are saying and doing?). However, the positive side effects of parental involvement can be enormously potent. Peer tutoring can improve ethos and relationships between children in school, but parental involvement can improve ethos and relationships between adults and children through the whole local community.

Parents or peers as tutors?

For decades many ordinary primary (elementary) schools claimed to have a policy of sending reading books home, so that children could be 'heard read' by their parents. In fact, surveys indicated that practices even within one school were often very various, according to which class teacher a child happened to have. Often, little guidance might be given to parents as to why the child was reading what they were reading, and what the parent was actually expected to do at home in interaction with the child and the book.

The Haringey research led to both quantitative and qualitative changes in practice. In 1980, Jenny Hewison and Jack Tizard reported research on a disadvantaged area of inner London which demonstrated clearly that one of the largest factors in children's reading attainment in school was whether they read with their parents at home, irrespective of whether the school operated a formal parental involvement scheme. This was followed up by a direct intervention, and in 1982 Jack Tizard, Bill Schofield and Jenny Hewison were able to report on a project in which teachers had encouraged parents to hear their children read at home, given a little additional guidance and the support of home visits. The attainment of the project children rose substantially, in comparison to a control group and children who had received extra small-group help from qualified teachers. It was subsequently reported that these differentials had been maintained at long-term follow-up (Hewison, 1988). Suddenly it had become clear that it was actually more cost-effective for a teacher to spend some time encouraging and organising the involvement of parents in their own children's reading development, rather than spend all their time on the direct classroom teaching of reading.

Peer tutoring is also a long standing method. The idea is a very old one, first noted hundreds of years ago. In Britain, Bell and Lancaster used peer tutoring on a large scale about 200 years ago. By 1816, 100,000 children were learning in this way. However, in recent years it has become much clearer how to organise peer tutoring more effectively. Peer tutoring involves children purposely helping other children to learn, in role as tutors and tutees. Sometimes older children help younger children, and sometimes more able children help less able children of the same age. When peer tutoring is properly organised, tutors gain as much, if not more, than the tutees. To tutor a subject, you have to really strive to understand and communicate it well – this intellectual engagement benefits the tutor.

Reviews of research on peer tutoring consistently find that structured methods of tutoring are associated with better measured outcomes for both tutors and tutees (e.g. Sharpley and Sharpley, 1981; Cohen, Kulik and Kulik, 1982). Many studies show that peer tutoring also improves how both tutor and tutee *feel* about the subject area – they grow to like it more. Also, in many cases the tutor and tutee grow to like each other more, and get on better. There are many reports of both tutor and tutee showing more confidence and better behaviour.

Some primary schools are now offering all their younger children the chance to be a tutee, and all their older children the chance to be a tutor. This helps to settle the young children into the school socially, and gives a boost to the older children, who feel very grown-up and responsible. Like class-wide tutoring, this is important because it gives all children an equal opportunity to participate. (In other schools there is still a tendency to select a few of the 'best' children as tutors. These are often those who are most like the teachers and might be very disparate in ability from their tutees, creating an ethos of Victorian philanthropism, raising anxieties about any possible gains for the tutors, and implying that peer tutoring is a form of inferior surrogate teaching.)

Parental involvement and peer tutoring are thus both powerful methods for interactive learning. They should not be construed as alternatives to each other, although at some ages one might seem more developmentally appropriate and acceptable than another. For instance, in high schools parents can lose touch with what their children are doing, but peer tutoring is often more and more popular with children as they move up through the school.

What is Paired Reading (PR)?

The elements in the structure of the method are described below in relation to peer tutoring – minor adaptations are made for parent tutors.

Selecting material

The tutee chooses high interest reading material, from school, the community library or home. Newspapers and magazines are fine. Because Paired Reading is a kind of supported or assisted reading, tutees are encouraged to choose material above their independent readability level. Of course, the material must not be above the independent readability level of the tutor!

Contact time

Pairs commit themselves to an initial trial period of at least fifteen minutes per day at least three times per week for about eight weeks. At least some of this should be in regular scheduled class time, with the possibility of doing more during recess if the pair wish. This frequency of usage enables the pair to become fluent in the method and is sufficient to begin to see some change in the tutee's reading.

Position and discussion

Finding a relatively quiet and comfortable place is desirable – not easy in a busy school with many other pairs at work around you. It is important that both members of the pair can see the book equally easily – tutors who get neck-ache get irritable! Pairs are encouraged to talk about the book, to develop shared enthusiasm and to ensure the tutee really understands the content. Of course, discussion makes noise.

Correction

A very simple and ubiquitously applicable correction procedure is prescribed. When the tutee says a word wrong, the tutor just tells the tutee the correct way to say the word, has the tutee repeat it correctly, and the pair carry on. Saying 'No!' and giving phonic or any other prompts is forbidden.

Pause

However, tutors do not jump in and put the word right straight away. The rule is that tutors pause and give the tutee four seconds to see if they will put it right by themselves. Tutees will not learn to self-correct if not allowed the opportunity to practise this. Holding off for four seconds is not easy. Tutors can be encouraged to count slowly to four in their heads before allowing themselves to interrupt. (The exception to this rule is with the rushed and impulsive reader. In this case earlier intervention and a finger point from the tutor to guide racing eyes back to the error word is necessary.)

Praise

Praise for good reading is essential. Tutors should *look* pleased as well as saying a variety of positive things. Praise is particularly required for good reading of hard words, getting all the words in a sentence right and putting wrong words right before the tutor does (self-correction). PR engineers out undesirable behaviours by engineering in incompatible positive behaviours.

Reading together

So how can the tutee manage this difficult book s/he has chosen? Tutors support tutees through difficult text by Reading Together – both members of the pair read all the words out loud together, with the tutor modulating their speed to match that of the tutee, while giving a good model of competent reading. The tutee must read every word and errors are corrected as above.

Signalling for reading alone

When an easier section of text is encountered, the tutee may wish to read a little without support. Tutor and tutee agree on a way for the tutee to signal for the tutor to stop Reading Together. This could be a knock, a sign or a squeeze. When the tutee signals, the tutor stops reading out loud right away, while praising the tutee for being so confident.

Return to reading together

Sooner or later while Reading Alone the tutee will make an error which they cannot self-correct within four seconds. Then the tutor applies the usual correction procedure and joins back in Reading Together.

The Paired Reading cycle

The pair go on like this, switching from Reading Together to Reading Alone, to give the tutee just as much help as is needed at any moment. Tutees should never 'grow out of' Reading Together; they should always be ready to use it as they move on to harder and harder books.

Figure 8.1 outlines the flow of the method in use. Completely error-free reading is indicated by the left hand channel of the chart, with the error correction feedback loops for Reading Together and Reading Alone indicated on the right hand side.

Of course there is relatively little new about Paired Reading – some aspects of long-standing practice have merely been put together in a particularly successful package. However, it is this precise combination which has been proven. Remember PR does not constitute the whole reading curriculum, but is designed to complement professional teaching without interfering with it. Full details of how to organise PR successfully are given in Topping (1995, 2001).

Evidence on effectiveness

The Paired Reading method has now been very widely disseminated all over the world, and has been the subject of a great deal of research. This has been the subject of reviews by Topping and Lindsay (1992) and Topping (1995). Much of the evaluation has been in terms of gains on norm-referenced tests of reading before and after the initial intensive period of involvement. The general picture in published studies is that Paired Readers progress at about 4.2 times 'normal' rates in reading accuracy on test during the initial period of commitment.

Nor are these results confined to isolated and possibly atypical research projects. In the Kirklees LEA in Yorkshire the technique has been used widely by a large number of schools, and in a sample of 2372 children in 155 projects run by many different schools, average test gains of 3.3 times normal rates in reading accuracy and 4.4 times normal rates in reading comprehension were found. This represents a very substantial effect size. These results were supported by baseline and control group data. At follow-up the gains of Paired Readers had not 'washed out' (Topping, 1995). More

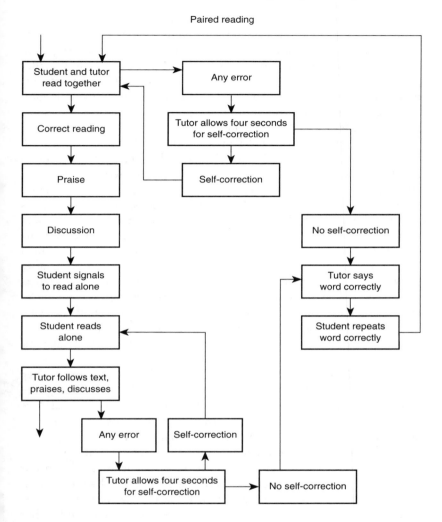

Figure 8.1 The Paired Reading Cycle

data were available for parent tutored than peer tutored projects, but no significant difference in outcomes between the two was found. The evidence suggested that tutors tended to gain more than tutees, although this difference did not reach statistical significance. There was less follow-up research on peer tutoring than parent tutoring.

Taking another approach to evaluation, the subjective views of tutors, tutees and teachers in the unselected projects were also gathered by structured questionnaire (Topping and Whiteley, 1990). In a sample of over

1000 tutors, after PR 70 per cent considered their tutee was now reading more accurately, more fluently and with better comprehension. Greater confidence in reading was noted by 78 per cent of tutors. Teachers reported generalised reading improvement in the classroom in a slightly smaller proportion of cases. Of a sample of 964 tutees, 95 per cent felt that after PR they were better at reading and 92 per cent liked reading more. Eighty-seven per cent found it easy to learn to do, 83 per cent liked doing it and 70 per cent said they would go on doing it.

In the PR phase of the pilot Paired Reading and Thinking project in Scotland during the National Year of Reading (Topping, 2001), 13 schools and 34 classes were involved (in 4 classes not all children were involved, often because they were mixed-age classes, so the equivalent of 32 full classes participated). For tutees in 16 full classes, 9 classes showed average gains well above normal which reached statistical significance, 6 classes showed gains above normal which did not reach statistical significance, and one class showed only normal gains. For tutors in 16 full classes, 7 classes showed gains well above normal which reached statistical significance, 8 classes showed gains above normal which did not reach statistical significance, and one class showed only normal gains. The aggregated gains for all tutors were highly statistically significant ($p<0.000$) (i.e. the probability of a gain of that size happening by chance was so small that when giving results only to three places of decimals it doesn't seem to exist at all). The same was true for the tutees.

An analysis was conducted of the relationship between pre-test reading ability and amount of reading test gain. Overall, the *least able tutees gained most, and the least able tutors gained most*. Low ability tutors produced tutee gains at least equivalent to those produced by high ability tutors, and low ability tutors themselves gained more than high ability tutors.

The relationship between reading gains and gender was also analysed. Overall, female tutees did better than male tutees, but male tutors did better than female tutors in terms of their own test gains. So perhaps boys learn better by being tutors than by being tutored. Teachers had been encouraged to match children by ability differential, disregarding gender, but nevertheless cross-gender matching proved to be less usual. However, cross-gender matching actually yielded better tutee gains than same-gender matching, and was good for tutors as well. Male-Male pairs appeared very good for the tutor, but not for the tutee (contrary to previous findings of high gains for both partners in this constellation, see Topping and Whiteley, 1993). Female-Female pairs did least well on aggregate.

Social gains were also widely reported. Each participating teacher was asked to record their summary observations of child behaviour. They were asked to comment only on children in their class whose reading they knew before Paired Reading started, and only indicate change if they had observed it, it was significant, and it had definitely occurred since PR started. The response rate was 33 out of 34 possible (97 per cent – one teacher had left the school). The summary results are displayed in Figure 8.2 for behaviour in the classroom during Paired Reading, and in Figure 8.3 for behaviour in other activities in the classroom and outside the classroom within school.

It is clear that for behaviour in the classroom during Paired Reading, very few teachers had *not* observed a positive shift in the majority of their children. Regarding generalisation of positive effects to other subject areas and outside the classroom, the effects were not as strong (as would be expected), but were still very positive. The improvement in motivation during the PR sessions was particularly striking. Especially worthy of note was the improvement in ability to relate to each other – and that the children's social competence improved both during PR and beyond it.

Factors in effectiveness: PR process studies

So it works. But *how* does it work? Relatively few of the very many studies of Paired Reading have reported detailed information on the behaviour of participants after training and during involvement in projects. It cannot be assumed that participants' behaviour was standard throughout, i.e. that training was actually effective, especially in the longer term.

Topping (1995, 1997a) reviewed process studies of PR, and readers should consult these sources for more detail – only the conclusions will be given here. In both the parent-tutored and peer-tutored process data, many contradictory findings were evident. Participants were more likely to show the required process behaviour in studies of smaller numbers of participants, especially when the training had been more detailed. In larger studies of parent-tutored Paired Reading, conformity to good technique has been found in from 75 to 43 per cent of participants, the higher figure being associated with home visits. Amount of time spent engaged with PR correlated relatively weakly with test outcomes, so other effects in addition to a practice effect appear to be operating. Degree of compliance with the procedure was related to test outcomes in only a minority of studies. Of course, there are issues about the sensitivity, reliability and validity of the reading tests which were the outcome measure. Thus, the relation between process and outcome remains more or less obscure, and the vast majority of studies have evaluated on a crude input–output model. Output variables may reflect the structure and quality of service delivery (training and follow-up) as much as the impact of a particular technique that is assumed to have been applied. Perhaps past process studies have not been addressing a sufficiently wide range of questions.

Indeed, the conception of PR as a unitary intervention might be over-simplistic. As with other methods for reading instruction and improvement,

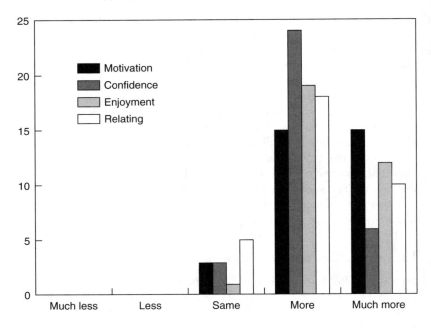

Figure 8.2: Teacher observations: during the PR sessions

what is taught and what is learned might not be identical. The PR experience might offer participants multiple pathways to improvements in multiple aspects of the reading process. Thus different components of the technique might be most potent for different subjects, these multiple aptitude × treatment interactions reducing the probability of finding one or a few process factors which are omnipotent for all.

Studies of the impact of PR on the reading style of participants might illuminate the processes and mechanism involved. Topping (1995) also reviewed this literature – again only the conclusions are given here. Considering parent, peer and teacher-tutored studies together, in eight of these studies error rates had been found to reduce in Paired Readers and in no cases had error rates increased (remember that Paired Readers choose harder books as they progress, so the error rate might have stayed the same or even worsened). In seven studies, Paired Readers showed decreases in refusal rates and in two cases an increase. In seven studies, use of context showed an increase, in one case no difference was found, and in no case was there a decrease. In four studies the rate or speed of reading showed an increase and in no case was there a decrease. In four studies, self-correction rate showed an increase and in no case a decrease. In three studies the use of phonics showed an increase and in no case was there a decrease.

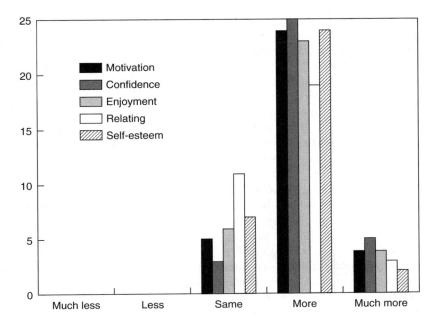

Figure 8.3 Teacher observations: outside the PR sessions

Although many of the differences cited did not reach statistical significance and only a few studies used either control or comparison groups who were non-participant or used another technique, strong consistent trends emerge from all these studies considered together. The general pattern is of Paired Reading resulting in fewer refusals (greater confidence), greater fluency, greater use of the context and a greater likelihood of self-correction, as well as fewer errors (greater accuracy) and better phonic skills. However, it is difficult to establish whether these are causal factors or themselves effects.

The empirical process and reading style studies thus leave us with a patchy and incoherent picture of how PR has its effects. Of course, PR might work through different pathways for different children, which could be why group studies seeking to find one mechanism which operates for all the children have shown such various results. Theoretical models of the processes involved, while often difficult to test directly, might elucidate some of the different mechanisms which might operate for different children.

Factors in effectiveness: process models

What can parents or peers offer that teachers cannot? The first of these factors is extra practice – children who read at home or with peers regularly simply get more practice at reading than those who do not. It is well established that practice consolidates a skill, promotes fluency and minimises forgetting. The amount of reading practice engaged in by children has recently again been emphasised as a critical variable (Snow, Burns and Griffin, 1998; Guthrie, Wigfield, Metsala and Cox, 1999; Topping and Paul, 1999).

In recognition of this, many primary school teachers have over the years allocated class time to independent silent reading of books chosen individually by the children themselves. However, simply increasing time allocated to silent reading practice might not be effective in raising achievement. Indeed, a review of the practice of allocating Sustained Silent Reading (SSR) time in schools noted mixed results, six studies finding a positive effect on reading scores, five no such effect (Manning-Dowd, 1985). 'Reading practice' is not a homogeneous, unitary activity, and the *quality* and *effectiveness* of reading practice also requires consideration.

It is important that the practice is positive – i.e. is practice at reading successfully. Teachers traditionally tried to keep error rates during reading in check by using carefully structured and graded reading schemes. But with close support from more able readers, it becomes possible for error rates to be kept low by the deployment of much more supportive tutoring techniques, coupled with carefully articulated correction procedures.

In a busy classroom, children receive relevant feedback from the teacher (about the correctness of their attempts to decode a particular word or deduce the semantic implications of a section of text) rather late and often in a less than clear manner. In the luxury of a one-to-one situation, feedback can be immediate, preventing the compounding of error upon error. Of course, immediate feedback will only be advantageous if it is supportive and positive in nature. Certainly, detailed guidance about the nature of feedback, particularly at the point of an error, is essential to incorporate in all parental or peer reading projects.

Weak readers by definition experience little success – they generate few opportunities for the teacher to meaningfully offer them praise. Teachers do not praise children as often as they would like to think they do, and the evidence suggests that natural rates of parental praise for children are a little lower than those of teachers, but not greatly so. In a parental involvement project, great attention is usually given to the development and application of parental praise. Parental praise has the big advantage of being offered by someone who is a very major and important figure in the child's life – certainly far more important than the teacher. A teacher figures in a child's life for less than a year, but parents are there more or less permanently, and have the advantage of association with tangible rewards! So the social reinforcement a parent dispenses for success in reading can be more powerful than the teacher's attempts in the same direction, and parents and peers can give praise more frequently and regularly (if required) than a teacher can manage.

The fourth crucial advantage that a parent has as a reading tutor at home is much greater scope for modelling or demonstration of the required behaviour. Many children want to 'be like' grown-ups, particularly the most significant grown-ups in their life, their parents. Thus where parents can demonstrate enthusiasm for books and appropriate and mature reading behaviour, the effect on the child is likely to be considerably more profound than that of innumerable verbal urgings in the classroom. Modelling is likely to be more powerful the more the child feels emotionally involved with, and wants to be like, the model. It follows that the father's role can be particularly crucial for boys. Peer tutoring (especially if cross-age) can also have a powerful modelling effect.

Thus, compared to teacher input, time actively engaged in reading is greater and practice is more regular, parental modelling is more powerful, parental feedback is more immediate, and parental reinforcement is more valuable.

Turning to specifically consider peer tutoring, the research literature concerning the theoretical underpinnings of Peer Assisted Learning (PAL) (discussed in chapter 1 of Topping and Ehly, 1998) may be summarized for the busy practitioner in a single chart (see Figure 8.4), highlighting mechanisms through which both tutor and tutee might gain.

This model assigns some of the main sub-processes into one of five categories. The first of these again includes organizational or structural features of the learning interaction, such as the need and press inherent in PAL toward increased time on task (t.o.t.) and time engaged with task (t.e.t.), the need for both helper and helped to elaborate goals and plans, the individualization of learning and immediacy of feedback possible within the one-on-one situation, and the sheer excitement and variety of a different kind of learning interaction.

Cognitively, PAL involves conflict and challenge (reflecting Piagetian schools of thought, and necessary to loosen blockages formed from old myths and false beliefs). It also involves support and scaffolding from a more competent other, within the Zone of Proximal Development of both parties (reflecting Vygotskian schools of thought, and necessary to balance any damaging excess of challenge). The cognitive demands upon the helper in terms of detecting, diagnosing, and correcting errors and misconceptions is substantial – and herein lies much of the cognitive exercise and benefit for the helper.

PAL also makes heavy demands upon the communication skills of both helper and helped, and in so doing develops those skills. For all participants, they might never have truly grasped a concept until they had to explain it to another, embodying and crystallizing thought into language – another

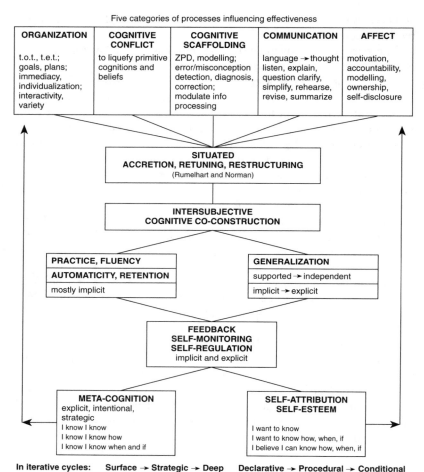

Five categories of processes influencing effectiveness

ORGANIZATION	COGNITIVE CONFLICT	COGNITIVE SCAFFOLDING	COMMUNICATION	AFFECT
t.o.t., t.e.t.; goals, plans; immediacy, individualization; interactivity, variety	to liquefy primitive cognitions and beliefs	ZPD, modelling; error/misconception detection, diagnosis, correction; modulate info processing	language → thought listen, explain, question clarify, simplify, rehearse, revise, summarize	motivation, accountability, modelling, ownership, self-disclosure

SITUATED
ACCRETION, RETUNING, RESTRUCTURING
(Rumelhart and Norman)

INTERSUBJECTIVE
COGNITIVE CO-CONSTRUCTION

PRACTICE, FLUENCY
AUTOMATICITY, RETENTION
mostly implicit

GENERALIZATION
supported → independent
implicit → explicit

FEEDBACK
SELF-MONITORING
SELF-REGULATION
implicit and explicit

META-COGNITION
explicit, intentional, strategic
I know I know
I know I know how
I know I know when and if

SELF-ATTRIBUTION
SELF-ESTEEM
I want to know
I want to know how, when, if
I believe I can know how, when, if

In iterative cycles: Surface → Strategic → Deep   Declarative → Procedural → Conditional

Figure 8.4 Theoretical model of peer-assisted learning

Vygotskian idea, of course. Listening, explaining, questioning and summarizing are all valuable transferable skills.

The affective component of PAL can also prove very powerful. A trusting relationship with a peer who holds no position of authority might facilitate self-disclosure of ignorance and misconception, enabling subsequent diagnosis and correction. Modeling of enthusiasm and competence and the simple possibility of success by the helper can influence the self-confidence of the helped, while a sense of loyalty and accountability to each other might help to keep the pair motivated and on-task.

These five categories of sub-process feed into a larger iterative process of extending each other's declarative knowledge, procedural skill and conditional and selective application of knowledge and skills by adding to and extending current capabilities (accretion), modifying current capabilities (re-tuning), and (in cases of gross misconception or error) rebuilding new understanding (restructuring). These labels for types of cognition are somewhat similar to Piagetian ideas of assimilation and accommodation. This leads to the joint construction of a shared understanding between helper and helped – which is adapted to the idiosyncrasies in their perceptions (i.e. is inter-subjective) and might not represent absolute truth (whatever that is), but certainly forms a foundation for further progress superior to whatever preceded it.

Subsequently, PAL enables further practice, leading to consolidation, fluency and automaticity of core skills. Much of this might occur implicitly, i.e. without the helper or helped being fully aware of what is happening with them. Simultaneously, PAL can lead to generalization from the specific example through which a concept is learned, to extending the ability to apply that concept to an ever widening range of alternative and varied contexts. As this occurs, as a result of the feedback they give to each other, both helper and helped should begin to become more consciously aware of what is happening to them in their learning interaction, and more able to monitor and regulate the effectiveness of their own learning strategies in different contexts.

This development into fully conscious explicit and strategic meta-cognition not only serves to promote more effective onward learning, it makes helper and helped more confident that they can achieve even more, and that their success is the result of their own efforts. These affective and cognitive outcomes feed back into the originating sub-processes – a virtuous circle.

New developments

The Paired Reading method was originally devised with a view to developing fluency and comprehension. The Reading Together and Reading Alone aspects proved to be relevant to readers of any level of ability, because everyone can be faced with a text which challenges their independent reading competence. Because PR supported the tutee and raised their confidence, it always tended to give them more time and spare processing capacity to think about what they were reading. However, the PR method has now been extended to enable a greater emphasis to be placed on higher-order reading skills and thinking about the reading.

'Paired Reading and Thinking' usually involves starting with regular PR, then in a second training session moving the participants on into 'reading and thinking', which involves training and prompting tutors and tutees to ask 'increasingly intelligent questions' of each other about what they have read together. Details will be found in Topping (2001) and the 'Resources' listing appended to this chapter. Paired Reading and Thinking is structured in four differentiated levels, so young and less able readers can participate, but the top level is certainly applicable to higher ability and age ranges. At all levels, the intellectual strain on the tutor is quite considerable (the tutors ruefully tell us), so the cognitively effortful nature of tutoring is transparent and unquestionable. Indeed, among both researchers and practitioners in general, more interest is now focusing on the impact of being a tutor than on the value of being a tutee.

Additionally, the PR type of method has been extended to spelling and to writing – so all aspects of literacy can be approached (see 'Resources').

New applications

Paired Reading started life as a method for weaker readers, then quickly became a method offered on an equal opportunity basis to readers of all abilities, including adults. Similarly, it started in the UK, but has spread to very many parts of the world, and is now widely used in developed countries (e.g. within the USA in volunteer tutoring schemes) and also in countries with great development needs (e.g. within family literacy programmes in the townships of South Africa and in provincial parts of Brazil).

In more advantaged countries, PR is connecting with the development of electronic literacy (Topping, 1997b). It can be used with material on the World Wide Web, or with a shared story loaded into an Ebook rather than on paper, for instance. Stemming from its reincarnation as Duolog Reading in the USA, PR is also linking to software for computerised self-assessment of reading comprehension of real books by children – an excellent additional form of motivation, monitoring and accountability for both members of a peer tutoring pair (e.g. Vollands, Topping and Evans, 1999).

As we have seen above, PR can be deployed to help address concerns about the under-achievement of boys in reading. It can be deployed to support the transition from primary school to high school both socially and academically, and has featured in many literacy summer schools. It can also be deployed to address issues of equal opportunities and social inclusion, and social competence and school ethos, especially in schools where different year groups, classes or other groups do not customarily relate well.

Over the years it has proved to be an extraordinarily flexible method. In the UK, it fits well into the current National Literacy Strategy. Indeed, it fits well into most strategies, and has proven to be philosophically and ethically acceptable by very diverse teachers who might not agree on anything else. There are undoubtedly many new applications still waiting to be found.

Paired Reading and 'real books'

Paired Reading encourages children to choose and read 'real books' – which are 'real' and highly motivating *to them* and relevant to *their* own interests and needs, life and culture. The purpose of education is to impart skills and motivation and belief in your ability to deploy those to achieve your *own* goals. Education is empowerment.

Whatever the ongoing debates, there is certainly little evidence that a 'real book' as distinct from a 'reading scheme' approach in school is of itself likely to result in any lowering of reading standards. Indeed, a review of 40 research studies by Tunnell and Jacobs (1989) reported the opposite – that in 24 studies the outcomes favoured the 'real books' approach, in only one study did the outcome favour the reading scheme, and in the remaining studies there was no significant difference.

But beware false dichotomies. Teaching mechanical reading skills to children is of limited use without also heightening their motivation to use those skills for their own purposes, and equally, flooding children with high quality 'real books' is pointless in the absence of a well-structured programme of skills tuition to enable them to access those books. Additionally, there is the constant danger that 'real books' is actually construed as a narrow collection of white middle class adult favourites – the concept of 'real books' can be culturally specific and imposed on children from above.

Of course, there is a great deal more to a 'real books' approach than merely the books involved, and arguably this approach puts greater demands on the organisational skill and awareness of the teacher than does proceeding through a pre-structured reading scheme. This may make a 'real books' approach less durable in the hands of inadequate, stressed or demoralised teachers than other approaches, and thus the published research findings may not truly reflect current day-to-day reality in schools.

Finally, then, remember that good organisation remains crucial as you begin to plan your PR initiative. Start small and do it well, rather than being over-ambitious. Even the most effective peer tutoring or parental involvement in reading technique will not survive a ramshackle attempt to deliver it.

Questions for personal reflection or group discussion

Parental tutoring

How much parental involvement in reading is there:

(a) in your class?
(b) in the school as a whole?
(c) what percentage of parents are involved?
(d) parents of what type of child?

Is your current practice on parental involvement:

(a) offering/ensuring equal opportunities?
(b) reducing or increasing relative disadvantage?

So what are you (and your colleagues) going to DO about it? Write down one small first step.

Peer tutoring

How much peer tutoring in reading is there:

(a) in your class?
(b) in the school as a whole?
(c) cross-age or same-age?
(d) class-wide or a select few children?
(e) are the selected few only 'goodies' and 'remedials'?
(f) are gains for tutors assured?

So what are you (and your colleagues) going to DO about it? Write down one small first step.

The PR process

(a) How well has your PR been organised in the past?
(b) How could the organisation be improved?
(c) What elements of the process do you think are most important for your children?
(d) Or are different elements important for different children?
(e) How can you test out the process model through action research in your class?
(f) How can you try out the new developments and applications?

Recommended readings

Paired reading

Morgan, R. (1986) *Helping children read: the Paired Reading handbook*. London: Methuen.

Topping, K. J. (1995) *Paired Reading, Spelling & Writing: the handbook for teachers and parents*. London & New York: Cassell (http://www.continuum-books.co.uk).

Topping, K. J. (2001) *Thinking Reading Writing: a practical guide in paired learning with peers, parents and volunteers*. New York & London: Continuum International. (http://www.continuum-books.co.uk).

Topping, K. J., *et al.* (1997) *Duolog Reading: video training pack*. Madison, WI: Institute for Academic Excellence (www.renlearn.com)

Topping, K. J. and Hogan, J. (1999) *Read On: Paired Reading and Thinking video resource pack*. London: BP Educational Services (nominal charge). Information and many resources can be freely downloaded from: http://www.dundee.ac.uk/psychology/ReadOn

A Teacher's Manual and NTSC training video titled '*Paired Reading: positive reading practice*' is available from the North Alberta Reading Specialists' Council, Box 9538, Edmonton, Alberta T6E 5X2, Canada, or from the International Reading Association, 800 Barksdale Road, P.O. Box 8139, Newark, Delaware 19714–8139, USA (http://www.reading.org).

Pause prompt praise

Merrett, F. (1994) *Improving Reading: a teacher's guide to peer-tutoring*. London: David Fulton (http://www.fultonbooks.co.uk).

'Listening' approaches

Branston, P. and Provis, M. (1999) *Children and Parents Enjoying Reading: parents and the literacy hour*. London: David Fulton (http://www.fultonbooks.co.uk).

General

Wolfendale, S. W. and Topping, K. J. (eds.) (1996) *Family Involvement in Literacy: effective partnerships in education*. London & New York: Cassell (http://www.continuum-books.co.uk).

Topping, K. J. and Ehly, S. (eds.) (1998) *Peer-Assisted Learning*. Mahwah, NJ & London, UK: Lawrence Erlbaum (http://www.erlbaum.com).

Topping, K. J. (2001) *Peer Assisted Learning: a practical guide for teachers*. Cambridge, MA: Brookline Books (http://brooklinebooks.com).

Other curricular areas

Topping (1995) covers writing and spelling as well as Paired Reading, and Topping (2001) extends this to thinking and higher-order comprehension skills. Also see:

Topping, K. J. and Bamford, J. (1998) *Parental Involvement and Peer Tutoring in Mathematics and Science: developing Paired Maths into Paired Science*. London: Fulton; Bristol, PA: Taylor & Francis (http://www.fultonbooks.co.uk).

Topping, K. J. and Bamford, J. (1998) *The Paired Maths Handbook: parental involvement and peer tutoring in mathematics*. London: Fulton; Bristol, PA: Taylor & Francis (http://www.fultonbooks.co.uk).

Topping, K. J. (1998) *The Paired Science Handbook: parental involvement and peer tutoring in science*. London: Fulton; Bristol, PA: Taylor & Francis (http:// www.fultonbooks.co.uk).

Bibliography

Brooks, G., Flanagan, N., Henkhuzens, Z. and Hutchison, D. (1998) *What Works for Slow Readers? The effectiveness of early intervention schemes*. Slough: National Foundation for Educational Research.

Cohen, P. A., Kulik, J. A. and Kulik, C-L. C. (1982). 'Educational outcomes of tutoring: a meta-analysis of findings'. *American Educational Research Journal*, **19**, (2), 237–48.

Guthrie, J. T., Wigfield, A., Metsala, J. L. and Cox, K. E. (1999) *Motivational and Cognitive Predictors of Text Comprehension and Reading Amount*. Scientific Studies of Reading, **3**, (3), 231–56.

Hewison, J. (1988) 'The long term effectiveness of parental involvement in reading: a follow-up to the Haringey Reading Project'. *British Journal of Educational Psychology* **58**, 184–90.

Hewison, J. and Tizard, J. (1980) 'Parental involvement and reading attainment'. *British Journal of Educational Psychology*, **50**, 209–15.

Manning-Dowd, A. (1985) *The effectiveness of SSR: a review of the research*. Educational Resources Information Centre Document Reproduction Service, No. ED 276 970.

Postlethwaite, T. N. and Ross, K. N. (1992) *Effective Schools in Reading: implications for educational planners*. The Hague: International Association for the Evaluation of Educational Achievement.

Sharpley, A. M. and Sharpley, C. F. (1981). 'Peer tutoring: a review of the literature'. *Collected Original Resources in Education*, **5**, (3), C–11.

Snow, C. E., Burns, M. S. and Griffin, P. (eds.) (1998) *Preventing Reading Difficulties in Young Children*. Report of the Committee on the Prevention of Reading Difficulties in Young Children. Washington, DC: National Research Council and National Academy of Sciences. (Educational Resources Information Centre Document Reproduction Service, No. ED 416 465).

Teddlie, C., and Reynolds, D. (eds.) (1999). *The International Handbook of School Effectiveness Research*. London & Philadelphia, PA: Taylor & Francis.

Tizard, J., Schofield, W. N. and Hewison, J. (1982) 'Collaboration between teachers and parents in assisting children's reading'. *British Journal of Educational Psychology*, **52**, 1–15.

Topping, K. J. (1995) *Paired Reading, Spelling & Writing: the handbook for teachers and parents*. London & New York: Cassell.

Topping, K. J. (1997a) 'Process and outcome in Paired Reading: a reply to Winter'. *Educational Psychology in Practice*, **13**, (2), 75–86.

Topping, K. J. (1997b) Electronic literacy in school and home: a look into the future. *Reading OnLine* (IRA) [Online], **1**, (1). Available:www.readingonline.org/international/future/index.html [June 1].

Topping, K. J. and Ehly, S. (eds.) (1998) *Peer-Assisted Learning*. Mahwah, NJ & London, UK: Lawrence Erlbaum.

Topping, K. J. and Lindsay, G. A. (1992) 'Paired Reading: a review of the literature'. *Research Papers in Education*, **7**, (3), 199–246.

Topping, K. J. and Paul, T. D. (1999) 'Computer-assisted assessment of practice at reading: a large scale survey'. *Reading and Writing Quarterly*, **15**, (3), 213–31. (themed issue on Electronic Literacy).

Topping, K. J. and Whiteley, M. (1990) 'Participant evaluation of parent-tutored and peer-tutored projects in reading'. *Educational Research*, **32**, (1), 14–32.

Topping, K. J. and Whiteley, M. (1993) 'Sex differences in the effectiveness of peer tutoring'. *School Psychology International*, **14**, (1), 57–67.

Tunnell, M. O. and Jacobs, J. S. (1989) 'Using "real" books: research findings on literature based instruction'. *The Reading Teacher*, **42**, (7), 470–7.

Vollands, S. R., Topping, K. J. and Evans, H. M. (1999) 'Computerized self-assessment of reading comprehension with the Accelerated Reader: action research'. *Reading & Writing Quarterly*, **15**, (3), 197–211 (themed issue on Electronic Literacy).

9 Real assessment for real readers

Margaret Cook

This chapter starts by attempting to describe what real reading and real assessment are, then looks at some aspects of their implementation in schools, including recording and reporting; and discusses aspects of real assessment; and lastly, reviews issues particularly relating to reading assessment, including whether real reading assessment is compatible with drives towards national norms and standards. Throughout, there is a firm assumption that although reading is the focus of the chapter, writing, speaking and listening and drama are essential to the successful learning and practice of reading and integral to its assessment, providing additional learning experiences, evidence of understanding and opportunities for response. Models of reading assessment which disregard this can give us interesting and valuable evidence about a reader's achievements but can never provide the whole picture of what a reader can do. The word 'reading' in this chapter is therefore always to be taken as including these other aspects of language.

Defining real reading

What makes a 'real' reader ?

The question 'what makes a "real" reader?' is a fundamental one in reading assessment, for children, parents, teachers, politicians, and statisticians concerned with national and international comparisons. Reading is a complex skill, which few of us fully acquire even in a lifetime. Much of what successful readers do is both hidden below the surface, and so dependent on a great variety of present and past experiences, that the very act of assessment may distort our picture of a rich and delicately constructed process. Assessment which is based on a single aspect of reading or which communicates a purely normative view of this process can never do justice to the totality of what is really happening. Standardised tests, for example, may be excellent in terms of validity and reliability, and useful in evaluating a single aspect of reading progress and establishing a (limited) standard of performance, but they can't tell us how someone is really progressing as an all-round reader. Only a good formative assessment procedure based on a wide-ranging knowledge of what readers do when they read can do this.

Several influential contemporary descriptions (for example, the Primary Language Record in England; the Western Australian First Steps material; the National Standards Project in the US; and the English National Curriculum and National Literacy Framework) provide definitions of reading which aim to be compatible with complex and real life descriptions of reading. They are underpinned by an understanding that reading is a quest for meaning, and in its pursuit, successful readers need many things: the knowledge and skills necessary to deal with the written code and how it is manipulated by writers; knowledge of how to read a for a variety of purposes and across a range of texts; understanding of what is read at a number of different levels; the ability to respond to texts appropriately, critically and pro-actively; and knowledge of the different forms of written language (see Figure 9.1). To follow up these national initiatives, please refer to Barrs (1998), Education Department of Western Australia (First Steps, 1997), Pearson (1998), the Revised National Curriculum for English (1995, 1999), and the English National Literacy Framework (DfEE, 1998).

But real readers are not just efficient and comprehending: they are also positive and enthusiastic about reading and its purposes, seeing it as a compelling and inescapable cradle-to-grave activity in which they respond to a wide range of authentic texts. These will include texts from a variety of media which real readers encounter in the course of ordinary life, and not just specially chosen ones. These additional qualities are not ones which it is easy to assess by traditional methods, yet they are what remain for most of those lifetime readers long after schooling is over, and good reading assessment recognises this in some way.

How can we structure what we know about readers?

In spite of the apparent hugeness of the task, it is, in fact perfectly possible to gather together and summarise all these characteristics of reading under three headings: *learners' responsiveness* to reading, including being enthusiastic and critical about what reading can do for them, and talking and writing about what they read; their *understanding* of what is read for the purposes of real activities and the application of this to real life situations; and their *capability* in using the written code in authentic, real life, texts, and being conscious of its forms. These organizing principles, or markers of progression, are what lend structure to reading assessment and enable us to

Enthusiasm for reading
Knowledge of the written code
Skill in using it
Ability to read different texts for many purposes
Critical perspective
Flexibility of approach
Appropriateness of response
Explicit knowledge of the forms of language
Lifelong practice

Figure 9.1 What makes a real reader

see a picture of the reader as a whole, albeit one which, like the portraits in Hogwarts, shift somewhat from time to time.

All these features of reading are essential to successful reading throughout life and for readers at every stage of development. They cannot be separated within the act of reading, its teaching and assessment, but the placing of responsiveness first suggests the importance of giving sufficient emphasis to how readers view and use reading throughout life. This is especially the case for more vulnerable learners, including some boys and second language learners, for whom reading experiences need to be consistently and coherently planned to reflect all aspects of the reading process (Martin 1990).

Markers of progression and stages of development

In order to meet this challenge of marking progression with economy and efficiency, the procedure needs to be structured in a way that acknowledges what remains the same about reading throughout readers' lives, the *markers of progression* mentioned earlier; and what differs according to their *stage of development*. Once reading achievements have been assessed against both these, appropriate learning experiences can be planned to support further progress. High quality assessment frameworks also describe these *learning opportunities*, sometimes adding teaching strategies, resources and contexts as well.

How can we tell if readers are making progress?

Progression through the structures, indicated in Figures 9.2 and 9.3, takes into account that children (and adults) move forward through stages of development which are characterised by particular skills and knowledge. These *critical features* are the indicators which provide the immediate means

---

2a Markers in some current frameworks

Primary Language record
- attitudes to reading
- strategies
- response

First steps
- making meaning using text
- making meaning using context
- making meaning at word level
- attitude

English National Curriculum 1999
- experience of textual range (fiction and non-fiction texts);
- skills leading to fluency, accuracy and understanding;
- understanding and appreciation of information, fiction and non-fiction texts;
- language study

English National Literacy Framework 1998
- Text level: reading comprehension (fiction and non-fiction); writing composition (fiction and non-fiction)
- Sentence level: grammatical awareness; sentence construction and punctuation;
- Word level: phonological awareness, phonics and spelling; word recognition; graphic knowledge and spelling; vocabulary extension; handwriting.

2b Markers common to several current frameworks

Responsiveness
Understanding
Capability

Figure 9.2 Organizing principles/markers of progression in real reading assessment

of collecting the *evidence of achievement* by which learners can be judged to be at a particular stage or level of development. An exact fit is not necessary or desirable. In this model, progression in learning is never even, although it is cyclical. All the skills and knowledge achieved contribute to the reader's development, but not all need to be equally developed all the time. This approach is therefore fundamentally different both from models which privilege one aspect of reading above others (for example, attitude and motivation, or phonic knowledge); and from those hierarchical ones where a reader's progress is judged against a narrow range of skills the whole of which must be acquired before moving on to a further stage.

Primary Language Record
- Stages of development with two five-step scales from beginner to exceptionally fluent and from inexperienced to exceptionally experienced.

First Steps
- Five (NLS version) or six (Australian version) phases of development from role play to conventional/advanced reading.

English National Curriculum 1999
- Key Stages, each with its own overall aims, and assigned assessment levels, for each of which there is a level description.

English National Literacy Framework
- No stages of development but staged teaching objectives indicate that achievement is progressive and cyclical.

Figure 9.3 Stages of development in some national and commercial frameworks

Four year old Nicola's reading with her teacher of a book of family photographs (see Figure 9.4a) demonstrates not only the practicality of this approach but the richness of the evidence of reading achievement it produces. Readers of this chapter might like to assess where she is in terms of her stage of development on the First Steps continuum (Australian version) and, more importantly, make a judgement about her overall progress as a reader in terms of her responsiveness, understanding, and capability in the use and knowledge of the language code.

Assessment frameworks such as these, helpful as they are, inevitably focus on reading/literacy achievement in educational settings, reinforcing the notion that reading as a legitimately assessable activity, happens mainly in school. To restrict reading assessment in this way to any set of skills, or to a single stage of development, however broadly conceived, is to deny what reading is really about. Like reading assessments based on a single aspect of reading, those which take place only in school cannot reflect what readers really do nor what teachers and others need to provide to help them on their way. They need to be complemented by observations of what readers commonly do in and out of school and college, by the involvement of parents, teachers and carers and, above all, by the development of readers' own habits of reflection and self evaluation, as in Figure 9.5, an extract from a child's reading record:.

If this broad, progressive and lifelong approach to reading is to underpin its assessment, everyone involved will need to share and understand the same perceptions of the reading process and develop the habit of talking about and recording significant aspects of its acquisition. This belief lies at

---

Nicola   [pointing to the caption and reading]; "A mucky puppy!" She added, "That's me being a mucky puppy."

Teacher: "I can see you're in your high-chair covered in food. You couldn't feed yourself then."

Nicola: "But I can now, I'm a big girl! I'm nearly five!"

Nicola   [turning the page and using her finger to point to each word in turn]: "I like dressing up, I'm a police lady in my brother's hat."

Teacher   [pointing to the next photograph]: "Is this where you love?"

Nicola: "That's my house and that's Daryl's and Sue's. That was when Daddy didn't go to work. It snowed and we made a snowman with a carrot for his nose."

Teacher: "What does this writing say?"

Nicola   [pointing along the line of writing]: "It says 'Nicola playing with her toys'."

Nicola read 'Nicola paying with her toys' independently. At this point she hesitated with her finger under the word 'at'. The teacher encourages her to sound the word out and then read 'Christmas time' with her.

Turning the page, Nicola pointed to the next caption and read 'This is my'. She stopped with her finger under the word 'friend'.

Teacher: "Do you know what that word begins with?"

Nicola: "E."

Teacher: "That's right, it says 'friend'."

Nicola pointed back to the beginning of the caption and read 'This is my friend Jessica'. Nicola was very proud of her new book, keeping it carefully in a plastic bag. She confidently approached the teacher to share the book with her, and enjoyed talking about herself and her family.

Figure 9.4a 'All About Nicola'

the heart of much teacher assessment, the portfolio movement and, out of school, those home school and family literacy programmes where parents and carers are encouraged to support their children's reading through observation and recording and where adults and children achieve through learning together. Real reading assessment will therefore always include some evidence from readers' home or community situation (see Figure 9.6).

Phase 1: Role Play Reading

Making Meaning at Text Level
- displays reading-like begaviour
  - holding the book the right way up
  - turning the pages appropriately
  - looking at words and pictures
  - using pictures to construct ideas
- realises that print carries a message but may read the writing differently each time, e.g. when 'reading scribble to parents
- focuses on the meaning of a television program, story, or other text viewed, listened to or 'read'. Responses reflect understanding.
- makes links to own experience when listening to or 'reading' books, e.g. points to illustration, saying 'My dog jumps up too.'
  - uses pictorial cues when sharing a book or 'reading', e.g. pointing to a picture in The Three Little Pigs, says 'The three little pigs left home.'
  - turns the pages of a book, telling the story from memory.
  - knows that writing and drawing are different, e.g. 'Mummy reads the black bits.'
  - selects favourite books from a range, e.g. chooses a book saying 'I want The Three Little Pigs.'
  - can talk about favourite stories and enjoys hearing them
  - is beginning to use some book language appropriately, e.g. 'Once upon a time ...' The child may use a 'reading' voice
  - responds to and uses simple terminology such as: book, right way up, front, back, upside down

Making Meaning Using Context
- uses pictorial and visual cues when watching television, listening to or 'reading' stories, i.e. talks about a television program, advertisement or picture in a magazine or book, relating it to own knowledge and experience
  - reacts to environmental print, e.g. noticing a fast food sign the child says, 'I want a hamburger.'

Making Meaning at Word Level
- recognises own name, or part of it, in print
  - is beginning to recognise some letters, e.g. Sam Says 'That's my name', pointing to 'Stop' sign

Attitude
- displays curiosity about print by experimenting with 'writing' and drawing and asking 'What does that say?'
- wants to look at books
- offers to 'read' writing and points to text while 'reading', indicating the beginning of having-a-go
- expresses enjoyment by joining in orally and responding emotively when listening to familiar stories
- eagerly anticipates book-reading events tat are part of daily routine

Figure 9.4b Phases

continued...

Phase 2: Experimental Reading

Making Meaning at Text Level
- realises that print contains a constant message, i.e. that the words of a written story remain the same, but the words of an oral story may change
- is focused on expressing the meaning of a story rather than on readingwords accurately
  - knows that print goes from left to right and from top to bottom of a page
  - responds to and uses terminology such as: letter, word, sentence, chapter
  - is beginning to demonstrate awareness of literary language, e.g. ' a long, long time ago …', 'by the fire sat a cat', 'No, no, no', said the …'
  - identifies the subject matter of a story through the use of titles and illustrations, e.g. 'I want this story about the big black cat'
  - shows an ability to connect ideas and events from stories heard or viewed by retelling events in sequence, using pictures, memory of the story and knowledge of story structure
  - expresses personal views about the actions of a character and speculates on own behaviour in a similar situation, e.g. 'If I had been … I would have …'
  - sub-vocalises or whispers when reading 'silently'

Making Meaning Using Context
- uses prior knowledge of context and personal experience to make meaning, e.g. uses memory of a text to match spoken with written words
  - demonstrates understanding of one-to-one correspondence between spoken and written words, for instance, the child slows down when dictating to an adult
  - asks for assistance with some words. May be aware that own reading is not accurate and may seek help, re-read or stop reading

Making Meaning at Word Level
- recognises some personally significant words in context, e.g. in job roster, weather chart or books
- matches some spoken words with written words when reading a book or environmental print
  - is developing the ability to separate a word from the object it represents. For instance, the child realises that 'Dad' is a little word, not that 'Dad' is a big word because Dad is bog
  - recognises some letters of the alphabet and is able to name them
  - demonstrates some knowledge of letter-sound relationships, for instance, the sound represented by the initial and most salient letters in words
  - points to specific known words as they are read
  - uses initial letter sounds to predict words in texts

Attitudes
  - is beginning to see self as a reader and talks about own reading
  - may ask for favourite stories to be read
  - joins in and acts out familiar stories if invited to do so
  - selects books to read for pleasure
  - self-selects texts on basis of interest or familiarity

Figure 9.4b Phases (continued)

Part C To be completed during the Summer Term*

C1 Comments on the record by child's parent(s)
Reading has improved a great deal. His biggest thrill is being able to read to his sister – she still has to tell him a couple of words now and again but he's delighted that he can read well enough for her to listen. His spelling is getting better and he's interested in it now.

C2 Record of language/literacy conference with child
'Sometimes I need help when I'm reading when I don't understand a word. I enjoy reading best when I'm in bed because you can concentrate and when I read stories to my sister. I like reading in school but only when it's quiet not when people come and annoy me. The bit of writing I like best is when I did it with S. – we had the same title, we decided it together then we went away, and wrote our own stories. When we read each others we both had Ghostbusters in it. Because S. writes fast, he finished before me but then he had to go through it and put in commas and full-stops, but I do it slowly and do them as I go along and it takes a long time.'

C3 Information for receiving teacher
This section is to ensure that information for the receiving teacher is as up to date as possible. Please comment on changes and development in any aspect of the child's language since Part B was completed.

D. has begun to view reading as a rewarding, satisfying thing 'to do' I think this has come from him being able to select his own reading material which he enjoys doing. In the last few weeks he has really come to grips with the fact that writing can be interesting and fun and has worked really well. He works very well in small groups. He has become a moderately fluent reader on reading Scale 2.

What experiences and teaching have helped/would help development? Record outcomes of any discussion with head teacher, other staff, or parent(s).

It could be helpful to him if he didn't *always* play safe in his choice of books so maybe encourage him to select a wide range of reading material. After talking to D's mother we both agreed that he would enjoy and benefit from writing his stories on the computer as it may make it easier to get his thoughts onto paper more quickly.

Signed: Parent(s) _____ Class Teacher _____

Date _____ Head Teacher _____

*To be completed by the Summer half-term for 4th year juniors

Figure 9.5 Example of Primary Language Record

Sefton FAST
Tel: 0151 933 6021

Child's Name: .... Week Beginning ....
Outreach Worker: ....

When you share books with your child – Remember:

Have a chat about the picture on the front. Read the title and author.
Did they notice anything new e.g. speech bubbles. How did they join in with the reading.

Remember children can read everything and everywhere. Were they aware of any print when you went out today - what did they notice?

We shared these books:

	Wed	Thurs	Friday	Sat	Sunday	Monday	Tuesday
Book opportunities	wakey wakey She laughed and enjoyed waking us up.	Bedtime She likes this book and enjoys baby going to bed.	Little bear at the beach we read this to show her what our holiday will be like.	wakey wakey She still enjoys waking us up when we pretend to be asleep.	Colours Her favourite colour seems to be yellow.	Playtime She enjoys seeing the children playing with the boys.	Little bear at school She enjoys the part where little bear makes cakes in his school.
Other reading opportunities	Courtney recognised McDonalds when we went to a friends party.	She pointed to tweenies book in Woolworth when we went shopping.	She noticed the lolly ices by looking at a poster.	She once again recognised McDonalds when we walked past, and asked for chip-chips.	She asked for choc when we passed the sweet shop.	She recognised the park by the sign on the gate.	She noticed the Doggy sign on the front of the play area which means no dogs.

Figure 9.6 Pre school and adult records from a family literacy programme

Defining real assessment

What makes assessment real?

As we have seen, real reading assessment must first be reflective of what reading really is, serve the purposes of individual readers and the reading community as a whole and be progressive. If reading assessment doesn't make us real readers, then it's really not worth doing. It must also be good assessment, encompassing the features shown in Figure 9.7: meaningful, economical and useful for a variety of purposes and audiences; valid and reliable (including the acknowledging and redressing of racial, cultural and gender bias); based on good evidence collected by different means from a wide range of authentic contexts in and out of school, including discussion with the learners; progressive; manageable; and reflective of the curriculum which has been taught and the manner of teaching it.

Real assessment must also be realistic, and must take account of the fact that, however comprehensive and elegant the design of its procedures, or interesting its findings, it is not an end in itself. Realism also demands the recognition and addressing of legitimate institutional and political purposes as part of the whole procedure, but never in such a way that these become the main aim and driving force. The major criterion for judging real assessment is that its primary purpose is for the benefit of the reader.

How do assessment and teaching relate to each other?

The primary use of assessment is to inform teaching. Nobody teaches in a vacuum. All teachers have theories about how and what to teach (especially, perhaps, those who say they haven't) and these theories are confirmed or confronted by the evidence of classroom and other learning produced by assessment. Getting assessment right is therefore an essential part of getting teaching right, of checking from an accurate description of the outcomes

---

Significance, economy and usefulness
Validity and reliability
Recognition of bias
Use of wide ranging evidence from school and home
Reader's involvement, including reflection
Progression
Manageability
Judgements made regularly
Curriculum fit
Shaped by learner's needs

Figure 9.7 What to look for in reading assessment

that your theory about what to do was valid in the first place. The role of assessment in this process is, as Fountas and Pinnell (1996) point out, as research, 'to collect data to inform teaching'. And the ways in which evidence is collected and organised – what is seen as essential and what peripheral (and what is absent) – will reveal what teachers consider to be important about what they teach and the principles which inform the curriculum and its realisation in practice.

Assessment in the school context

How do different purposes affect the forms of assessment?

How useful any assessment policy or procedure is will depend on its meaningfulness for the principal stakeholders' different purposes. Children, parents and class teachers will be mainly concerned with the progress of individual learners and whether they are fulfilling their potential. These purposes will be principally addressed by *formative assessment* largely based on the school's interpretation of what is required by their own and the national curriculum. Schools have these interests, too, but with greater publicity about assessment results, and in England at least, a very public system of inspection, they are also necessarily concerned about their image in their community, funding and staffing allocations, and even their very existence. Schools therefore are increasingly concerned with *summative assessment* which enables them to evaluate individual and school achievements in the context of similar individuals and schools elsewhere, and to see how they are achieving in relation to national, state and district expectations.

Learners, parents and teachers also have an interest in the results of summative assessment, since these enable teachers to assess progress over periods of time, to assess children's achievements in relation to similar children and to review and revise curriculum objectives and teaching methods and set realistic expectations. Those outside the school have an interest, too. Employers are anxious to know what assessment results tell them about an employee's suitability for the workplace. Governments, whether federal, national or state, are concerned with the feedback assessment will give them about the effects of public spending, the nation's position in world league tables, and their own political futures. See Figure 9.8 for the assessment guidelines as set out in the National Literacy Strategy.

What kind of evidence should we look for?

The role and form of evidence and its recording are clearly crucial in all this. A wide-ranging curriculum requires an equally wide range of evidence,

The purpose of assessments vary. They relate to the different uses made of the information by the teacher, the whole school community and at a national level.

The **class teacher** wants to know:
- has the class overall learned what I planned?
- are all the children making progress
- are they making sufficient progress against national expectations?
- which individuals need more help in which areas?
- which children need extension work?
- is my planning for activities, resources and staffing well targeted?
- how can I do it better next time?

The **headteacher** and **other teachers** want to know:
- are the children making progress?
- are there any major problems?
- how does their performance compare with those in parallel classes or in other years?
- is the children's in line with the school's targets?
- how is the school doing in comparison with other similar schools?
- what aspects of our curriculum and teaching need to be strengthened?

The **parents/carers** want to know:
- is my child making good progress?
- are there any major problems?
- how is my child doing compared with others of the same age?
- what can I do to help?

The **LEA and national government** want to know:
- how is the school and LEA progressing against their targets?
- are the school development plans working?
- what national curriculum levels are children achieving in teacher assessment and tests at ages seven and 11?
- how is the school doing in comparison with other similar schools?
- are the priorities of the LEA's Education Development Plan being met?

Figure 9.8 Target setting and assessment in the National Literacy Strategy

but this is useless if it is not also reliable and valid. Consistency is vital, in identifying what is to be assessed and the means of collecting evidence; in the curriculum provision and teaching methodology which produce classroom outcomes; in evaluating the texts and contexts for assessment; and in the use of the same recording frameworks and reporting contexts throughout the period of assessment (the whole of a child's school life, at least). In the end, only teachers and schools can ensure that everything

---

Teacher observation
Conferencing and interviews
Sharing texts
Written response
Discussion with peers and adults
Test results
Scrutiny of records

Figure 9.9 Sources of evidence for reading assessment

works together to inform teaching and support learners, and they are both helped and hindered in this by outside influences.

Also to be considered are the ease with which evidence can be used to form judgements which can usefully be communicated to others, and that other important reality, the fact that time, energy and opportunity are limited, and effectiveness must take into account manageability and economy. The methods used to collect evidence should be varied and should include, at the very least: observation; discussion with the learner in conferences and interviews; discussion with other adults and peers connected with the reader at home and at school; sharing texts (including electronic ones); written response; review of writing, dramatic representation and artefacts; tasks specifically directed to assessing the learner's ability to represent and evaluate, understand and decode what has been read; summative records such as the results of standardised , screening and diagnostic tests; and scrutiny of individual, class and school records. These methods are summarised in Figure 9.9, the Sources of Evidence for reading assessment.

How should judgements be made?

Teachers, as we've said earlier, make judgements all the time. Most of these are made in the course of teaching and it would be both impossible and wrong to suggest that written records should be consulted first, and for all decision making. Teachers have to depend for much of the time on an 'in the head' knowledge of children and the curriculum, which is why knowing what to expect of children and being familiar with the curriculum are so important to successful assessment. This makes it all the more important to ensure that time is set aside for the making of regular considered judgements on the basis of a range of evidence; for the drawing up of criteria for the collection and deployment of written evidence; and for discussion with all teachers about the timings for different kinds of judgements. A framework for making such judgments is presented in Figure 9.10.

Required judgements on the evidence of records should be determined by senior management together with times for review of evidence and completion of those records. Judgements need to be clearly articulated,

The table below outlines the key features of this systematic approach to assessment and record-keeping, which helps teachers see the connections between the different timeframes and judge the focus of work at any stage.

	daily/weekly	*termly*	*annually*
Who uses the ? assessments	teacher support staff	teacher children and parents/carers support staff	next teacher children and parents/carers whole school and beyond
Are the Assessments Recorded?	mainly no, yes for some aspects	some group and class records, individual pupil's targets, some individual notes/comments	yes, for each child
Should records be retained or discarded?	mainly discarded	keep only most recent work and targets	retained and passed on
How do the assessments relate to teaching and planning?	strong link to daily/ weekly planning	link to medium term (e.g.termly planning, target setting)	long term (balance overall, srength/ weakness)
What are the points of reference	National curriculum, National Literacy Strategy *Framework for teaching*	National curriculum, National Literacy Strategy *Framework for teaching*	predominantly national standards
Where will the information be used?	individual teacher	individual teacher, SENCO, school management	individual teacher school management LEA national agencies

Figure 9.10 Timescales for assessment

regularly reviewed and monitored, and communicated to those who need them, the most significant of these recipients being the learner. Records need, therefore, to be easily managed and to be in the same format throughout schooling.

What kind of assessment framework should we look for?

All the above will be made much easier, and consistency provided, if the school uses a common assessment framework, either a home grown one, or one based on published materials. The major features of an effective assessment framework are, as we have seen, that it is curriculum-based and compatible both with school beliefs about the teaching of reading and with any national or state requirements; that it uses assessment to inform teaching; that it acknowledges, values and plans for reading experiences in and out of school, throughout life and for those who progress in ways different from the expected; that it involves learners in their own assessment, uses a range of strategies and contexts to collect evidence and inform judgements, and responds efficiently and reliably to the needs of the major stakeholders, including those statutory bodies requiring summative assessments.

Assessment frameworks for reading such as those described earlier in this chapter are structured in this way, acknowledging that successful reading involves the exercise of the same processes and skills throughout a reader's life, although differently contextualised for different stages of the reader's development. The stages of development described provide sets of coherent expectations for reading behaviours at particular phases of a reader's progress and provide the basis for individual assessment. The markers for progression ensure a systematic framework for recording and reporting for the whole of a child's primary career so that teachers know in advance the categories of judgements they will need to make and the way in which the records they receive will be organised. Both consistency and development are supported and the frameworks support the formation of individual readers over periods of time. This is difficult if not impossible using frameworks which rely solely on either narrative descriptions or completion of checklists.

How can we address learners' different circumstances?

Effective assessment must also take into account the realities of schools' and learners' situations and should view these as strengths rather than weaknesses. Assessment evidence should include at least the learner's present and previous learning experience, schooling, age, gender, home language, cultural and family history and the school's social, cultural and economic

- conference record completed at least once a term (including a shared reading record)
- reading and writing log
- reading and writing journal
- record of genres read and written
- written response to literature and information texts
- notes of teachers' observations and discussions with the child and other adults
- any significant artefacts or photographs

Figure 9.11a Individual records

situation. This contextual evidence should not be viewed negatively, as an explanation for poor achievement, but rather as presenting positive opportunities for extending learning and providing assessment opportunities other than classroom ones. How learners actually read at home or in the community may be quite different from how they achieve in school (Brice Heath 1983) and may throw light particularly on the achievements of more and less able readers. Parents in particular should be made aware of the significance of these home experiences. Where parents are aware of the school's broad understanding of reading, the assessment evidence from these home experiences (and not just from books sent home by the school) should be valued and incorporated in their children's reading records.

Recording and reporting assessments

How should reading assessment evidence be recorded?

It is important to distinguish between the act of collecting evidence and that of making judgements on it. Collecting evidence is an ongoing process, which covers many diverse teaching and learning situations, and sometimes leads to perfectly valid, on the spot, teaching decisions. Evidence will, however, also include the results of one-off tests, assessments (such as those in the Reading Recovery programme) which are repeated, time specific tasks such as essays, assignments for course work, and pre-arranged contributions to portfolios. Some evidence will be purely oral and may be recorded only, if at all, in a teacher's observation notebook. Formal written records should cover major aspects of the reading curriculum as well as evidence from home, the results of summative assessments, and with older children, reading activities in the community. Figures 9.11 a, b, c and d give an indicative list, which includes both individual and class- or group-based records.

Keeping records which are relatively brief but consistent in range and format, and regularly scrutinized, will be much more helpful than keeping a large quantity of evidence which is narrow in its range or irregularly

- any required school, national or state objectives and curriculum targets
- learning experiences planned for the term
- range of genres covered
- titles of texts studied by the class as a whole
- termly summary of class achievements from the common assessment framework

Figure 9.11b Class records

matched to the school's criteria for reading. Individual portfolios can be helpful here, provided they are organised according to a clear set of requirements which hold good throughout the school. Children's reflections on the collected evidence of their achievement should be a regular part of the process, usually as part of the termly reading conference, and these reflections should then be entered in the record. Class, year or whole school portfolios can make a substantial contribution to consistency of teachers' judgements if they are carefully organized to show sample children's achievements, across the whole range of ability and in the same contexts throughout the year.

To whom should we report?

There is a growing recognition that the recording and reporting of assessment must be meaningful to education's most important stakeholders: to learners and their families as feedback and in providing a challenge and direction for further growth; to the teacher in planning the next step, setting objectives and identifying problems and concerns; to the school management in planning the whole curriculum, setting targets, assuring quality and allocating resources; to the community at large, including those in higher education and employers, in setting realistic expectations; to administrators and politicians in determining policy, and setting and evaluating national standards. Where there is an explicit national or federal programme to raise standards, it may be particularly important to recall this range of stakeholders and their purposes to avoid the assumption that the findings of assessment are only relevant to those with administrative, political or research interests.

Some issues in reading assessment

How can consistency be achieved?

Since 1980, the cause of consistent reading assessment has been furthered by two significant developments. Between the 1970s and 1990s there was,

Once a term

Individual Reading Record

Name: Year: Class/Teacher	Term I			Term II			Term III			AP	SA	Comment and Action
	Date:		AP	Date:		AP	Date:					
	✓✓	✓	?	✓✓	✓	?	✓✓	✓	?			
Capability												
• Competence in decoding complex and unfamiliar texts	✓✓	✓	?	✓✓	✓	?	✓✓	✓	?			
• Monitoring and adjusting reading style to meaning and purpose												
Understanding												
• Dealing with more challenging texts												
• Structuring meaning												
• Using reading for learning												
• Meanings beyond the literal												
Response												
• Enjoyment and enthusiasm												
• Experiencing a range												
• Reflection of language												
• Reflection on texts												
• Use of text knowledge in own talking and writing												

✓✓ Plenty of evidence   ✓ enough evidence   ? little or no evidence   AP assessment procedure

Figure 9.11c Specimen formats for individual and class records (unpublished inservice material)

Key Stage 2: Termly Record for Reading

Names	Response	Understanding	Capability	Experience of Range	Evaluation

Class   Code: ✓✓ = Plenty of evidence   Teacher:
        Date:
Year: ✓   = Enough evidence
                             ?   = Little or no evidence

Figure 9.11d   Specimen format for termly reading record

generally but perhaps especially in England, a 'paradigm shift' in assessment representing, a radical change in thinking about the purposes and processes of assessment (Coles and Jenkins 1998). This shift has moved us towards models and procedures in keeping with the features of 'real assessment' described earlier. These are (in intention at least) slanted towards positive achievement, relate to a broad curriculum held in common, and are aimed at assessing all children using tasks which reflect classroom activities (and, in the case of reading, require the use and construction of authentic texts).

A defining moment in England in this shift was the TGAT Report (1988) with its clear statement that the assessment process should be integral to the educational process and systematically incorporated into all teaching strategies and practices. Many teachers, particularly teachers of language and literacy, welcomed this model as one that fitted well with their own experience of teaching. (Much of the practical work on which this chapter is based, derives from various attempts to realise the TGAT model in practice.)

Recently, curriculum consistency in England has been further supported (some would say, hardened) by the introduction in 1997 of the (non-obligatory but almost universally implemented) National Literacy Framework, which assigns content derived from national curriculum programmes of study to specific year groups and terms. It also specifies a highly structured methodology (the Literacy Hour) to support its implementation. This move is intended to further support the establishment of national standards for English for seven, eleven and fourteen year olds and the assignment by central Government of numerical and curriculum targets linked to these, for those responsible for education at the local level, schools and, in the case of curriculum targets, year groups. Uniformity in progressing towards these norms in England is supported by guidance from the a central body (QCA – the Qualifications and Curriculum Authority) which outlines curriculum targets selected from the National Literacy Framework teaching objectives, together with exemplars of evidence from case studies (QCA 1999b).

There are current concerns in England that this highly structured approach to consistency in teaching and assessment may militate against the development of 'real readers' and in particular erode some aspects of provision for reading and writing. Some of these concerns are powerfully expressed in Eric Ashworth's chapter in this book. Teachers are especially concerned about a possible lack of provision for extended reading and writing. Specific time allocations for the development of speaking and listening may also be difficult to provide. If these concerns turn out to be justified, not only will curriculum opportunities be curtailed but it will be difficult to collect the full range of written and oral responses to reading which the model outlined above requires. The requirement for guided work in the literacy hour has also been seen by some English schools as necessitating the removal of time for individual reading and putting difficulties in the way of home school reading programmes. It is still too early to judge whether these are substantial problems but they underline the need for every innovation to be judged in the light of broad criteria for achievement and not just for short-term gains.

How far is reading assessment a high stakes activity?

What is clear in all this is that the time when classroom assessment could develop largely unaffected by the external world has passed. The drive in almost all English-speaking countries is now towards a system where any assessment procedures, internal or external, must now be capable of serving the needs of the individual, group, class and school, and be open to monitoring and evaluation by a number of agencies. Within this process, judgements on teachers' and school's effectiveness will inevitably include an evaluation on how far children are progressing in relation to norms. These days, the assessment of reading is very much a high stakes activity and it is thought by many outside education to be on the one hand, the bedrock of the system, and on the other, a simple process which is easily assessed. This makes it very vulnerable to political and cultural pressures and to the inevitable tensions between the different purposes of stakeholders, in particular between the needs of lifelong learners and those of policy makers.

Do national norms influence practice?

Alongside these moves towards a broad and evidence based approach to statutory assessment, the last ten years have, as we have seen, also edged a number of countries towards the establishment of national norms, some of which now form national standards. As Coles (Coles and Jenkins 1998) points out, norms are uneasy bedfellows with an evidence-based approach which, inevitably, is geared towards a positive view of individual achievements and progress, whatever they are. One result of all this is that we have the uncomfortable sight of test agencies struggling (in some cases at least) to provide assessment tasks which reflect a broad reading curriculum and use authentic texts but which also conform to constraints of time and format which will satisfy both politicians and the interested public. Another is that schools, required to deliver specified levels of performance at particular points in a child's school career, feel pressurised to restrict the language curriculum in order to do so. English schools have additional constraints in having to reconcile a number of different priorities, including those set by the external inspection system, national targets for the teaching of literacy and individual learning targets for identified vulnerable children.

Meanwhile, there is evidence that national reading standards in England as defined by other measures show a worryingly long tail of underachievement (Brooks *et al.* 1998) It remains to be seen whether the current English statutory initiatives reduce this tail and also support the development of a nation of readers as defined by a wide range of criteria.

Can national assessment tasks promote real reading?

Statutory assessment procedures in England have provided a common description of achievement against which to make assessments and record judgements, although the focus of formal assessment covers only a selection of the whole curriculum, a selection which, intentionally, changes from year to year to ensure coverage of the whole range of texts and skills covered by the National Curriculum in English. Close adherence to the intention as well as the requirements of the statutory documents has meant that, at least for children up to eleven, most tasks use authentic texts, and purposes often approximate to authentic ones and require understanding and use of a range of genres. For example, narrative is no longer privileged above other genres, the main 1999 texts for the national tests of reading at age eleven being a poem, a set of cartoons, and some diagrams. Information texts included graphics and the tests were illustrated in colour, using child-friendly formats and conventions.

Significantly, primary teachers have been involved in the composition of these tests and have also been given a role in making their own assessments in the three core subjects of English, mathematics and science. The results of these are published as part of the public record of their school's performance. This means that not only has teacher assessment in England at last been given a role in external assessment but, because any part of the curriculum can be externally assessed in any year, teachers cannot safely teach only part of the curriculum at any one time.

Other developments in the English assessment system have also impacted on the teaching of reading, in particular the introduction of running records and the inclusion of a test of reading aloud as part of the assessment of average and below-average seven year old readers. The first provided an incentive for teachers of young children to learn an assessment procedure which had been used for many years by teachers of broad based approaches to the teaching of reading, and, more recently, by the much praised Reading Recovery programme; the second provided for the first time, a required reading test common to all schools.

Is real reading compatible with the drive for national standards?

Governments in the contemporary 'developed' world seem sometimes to be obsessed by concern over standards of literacy and they take steps to assess these in different ways. (Governments in the 'developing world' are usually preoccupied with getting children into school, and the length of time they spend there is often used as the prime measure of that nation's literacy). It is a tribute to the influence of curriculum developers of the last thirty years, that both the scope and the methods of several new national assessment procedures attempt to meet the requirements of real reading outlined earlier. As we have seen, the US New Standards Project, for example, aims to encompass a wide definition of literacy, integrating reading and writing, requiring evidence from 'entire performance' and including portfolio assessment and level related descriptors of achievement. The descriptor for level four, for example, requires, among other things, that a complex response is shown , including understanding and interpretation of the text; and that the student can question and critically evaluate a text (Pearson *et al.* in Coles and Jenkins 1998).

What is worrying here, however, is that national standards such as these can be used without necessarily implementing the portfolio-based system for collecting evidence which the project design envisaged. Without the latter, it is difficult to see how a student's full range of reading achievements across these standards can be confidently established.

Conclusion

A consistent approach to the teaching and assessment of reading can help to ensure that both are informed by what really matters in reading as well as by clear thinking about how we collect evidence of real achievement, make useful and reliable judgements on it, communicate the results to those to whom it really matters and use it to inform how we view reading and its teaching in the future. Some healthy scepticism about innovations in curriculum and assessment is also in order, although it's also wise to recognise that no educational procedure is so perfect that it shouldn't occasionally be changed. Schools face a difficult challenge in managing all this, not least the importance of prioritising the needs, interest and enthusiasms of individual readers while still meeting statutory requirements and national targets. Determination is needed to take what is helpful from these without relinquishing the ideal that education for reading must always be more than satisfying national targets and standards. Finally, structures and systems don't of themselves make readers – that's done by readers themselves with the support of other readers, including parents, teachers, and schools.

Questions for personal reflection or group discussion

1   Does everyone in your institution (including parents) share the same view of what reading is?
2   Does everyone (as above) share the same view about what's important in assessment?
3   Does everyone look for evidence of readers' achievement everywhere and all the time?
4   Do you have a common way of recording reading achievements?
5   Are there set times by which these have to be completed?
6   Who checks that this has been done?
7   Who (other than the teacher) checks that learners are achieving as they ought?
8   What rewards does the institution have for 'real' readers?

Recommended readings

Barrs, M. *et al.* (1988) *The Primary Language Record: handbook for teachers*. London, ILEA/CLPE.

Coles, M., and Jenkins, R. (1998) *Assessing Reading 2: Changing Practice in Classrooms*. London, Routledge.

Education Department of Western Australia (1997) *First Steps: Reading Developmental Continuum*. Perth, Rigby Heinemann.

Meek, M. (1991) *On Learning to Read*. London, Bodley Head.

Bibliography

Arnold, H. L (1982) *Listening to Children Read*. London, Hodder & Stoughton.

Barrs, M. *et al.* (1988) *The Primary Language Record: handbook for teachers*. London, ILEA/CLPE.

Brooks, G., Flanagan, N., Henkhuzens, Z., and Hutchison, D. (1998) *What Works for Slow Readers? Effectiveness of Early Intervention Schemes*. Slough: NFER

Brice Heath (1983) *Ways with Words*. Cambridge. CUP.

Coles, M., and Jenkins, R. (1998) *Assessing Reading 2: Changing Practice in Classrooms*. London, Routledge.

Education Department of Western Australia(1997) *First Steps: Reading Resource Book*. Perth, Rigby Heinemann.

Education Department of Western Australia (1997) *First Steps: Reading Developmental Continuum*. Perth, Rigby Heinemann.

Education Department of Western Australia (1999) *Assessment, Teaching and Learning*. Oxford, GHPD.

Department for Education and Employment (1998) *The National Literacy Strategy: Framework for teaching*. London: DfEE.

DES(1988) *National Curriculum Report on Task Group on Assessment*. London, HMSO.

Fountas, L. and Pinnell, G. (1996) *Guided Reading: Good First Teaching for All Children*. London, Heinemann.

Harrison, C. and Coles, M. (eds) (1992) *The Reading for Real Handbook*. London, Routledge.

Martin, T. (1990) *The Strugglers*. London, Hodder and Stoughton.

Meek, M. (1991) *On Learning to Read*. London, Bodley Head.

Qualifications and Curriculum Authority (1999a) *Revised National Curriculum in English*. London, QCA.

Qualifications and Curriculum Authority(1999b) *Target Setting and Assessment in the National Literacy Strategy*. London, QCA.

Rowling, J. K.(1997) *Harry Potter and the Philosopher's Stone*. London, Bloomsbury.

SCAA (1996) *Standardised Literacy Tests in Primary Schools: their use and usefulness* London SCAA .

SCAA (1997a) *Looking at Children's Learning Desirable Outcomes for Children's Learning on Entering Compulsory Education* London SCAA.

SCAA(1997 b) *Teacher Assessment at Key Stage 2* London SCAA.

Sefton (undated) Unpublished Home–School Record. Sefton (Mersyside), Sefton Education Department.

10 Supporting readers with English as an additional language

Guy Merchant

> I started to learn English from the age of five. I am all right at speaking it alone in my mind. I hate reading it aloud. I started to speak Bengali from the age of two. I still have lessons at Palfrey School on Saturday and Sunday. I can read Arabic from the age of six. I started to take lessons off my mum. Now I can read Arabic well. I can understand Hindi – I picked it up from the films.
>
> (Azizul Islam)[1]

At the age of nine, Azizul was asked to write his own language profile. The picture that emerges is one of a child who is familiar with four quite distinct language systems. Azizul is literate in three of these languages. The extract from his profile is a powerful reminder of how the social and cultural worlds that children inhabit are reflected in their uses of language as well as in their knowledge about language. Azizul's feelings about the languages around him are also important. They help to shape his view of himself as a language user – take for instance his lack of confidence in reading aloud in English – and how this contrasts with his ability to read Arabic. Of course these attitudes are not fixed for ever. We would anticipate that Azizul's confidence in reading English will increase in the future: but not at the expense of those other languages in his repertoire.

Azizul's story is by no means unusual. Impressive though it is, his experience is similar to that of children in many parts of the country: speakers of a wide range of world languages. Nevertheless learning to read and write in more than one language is a significant achievement, representing a versatility to be celebrated. It enables the child to participate in a variety of social and cultural practices that are of central importance in a pluralist society.

Biliteracy[2] for Azizul means a great deal. Not only does it have immediate and tangible benefits as he interacts with his family and friends, it also links him with a wider community with its own distinct history and traditions. He is undoubtedly fortunate in possessing a rich and varied knowledge of language. But Azizul is fortunate in a more fundamental sense. He is part of a strong family that values and engages in a variety of literacy practices. Well before the start of compulsory schooling, Azizul was apprenticed to the 'literacy club' (Smith, 1988). He understood about the uses and functions of literacy and the different relationships between print and the spoken word in the languages around him. For Azizul and children like him from many different language backgrounds, maintaining a level of biliteracy and providing support for its development are important social and educational priorities.

Other bilingual children may not share Azizul's good fortune. Families may be isolated and community and social networks may be difficult to organise. Those opportunities for learning to read and write the home or community languages that have so clearly enriched Azizul's life may not be so readily available. As with monolingual children, it is difficult to make generalisations about the early literacy experiences of young bilinguals. Bilingual children in British schools will have varying levels of proficiency in their home, community or religious languages[3]. This variation is the result of a complex interplay of individual, family, social and community circumstances. So, we cannot always assume a level of literacy, instead we need to find out about the patterns of language and literacy in the communities that our school serves.

With something in the region of 200 distinct language groups in the school population, it is important that we acknowledge and learn about linguistic diversity. It has been argued that rapid changes in the linguistic profile of the school population suggest the need for a radical reappraisal of policy and practice in language education (Merchant, 1990; Gregory, 1996). Unfortunately, the 1988 Education Reform Act which transformed curriculum content, offered little in the way of encouragement or practical support for teachers working with bilingual pupils. So the resulting provision of a core curriculum paid lip service to cultural diversity whilst avoiding any serious consideration of the issues that it raises for language education (Savva, 1990). Since the introduction of the National Curriculum, professional development for teachers has tended to focus on implementation of the core and foundation subjects and debate over diversity has been marginalised. As Edwards observes 'Teachers were in effect given permission to sweep matters relating to the needs of bilingual pupils under the carpet'(Edwards, 1998).

This trend has continued with the development of the National Curriculum and the National Literacy Strategy. Recently concerns have been expressed over how well the Literacy Hour meets the needs of bilingual children. The DfEE have responded by producing additional guidance as part of an annex to the new literacy curriculum framework (DfEE, 1998,

Section 4). At this point, however, it is perhaps still worth reflecting on the sentiments expressed in the Cox Report:

> Work should start from the pupils' own linguistic competence. Many pupils are bilingual and sometimes biliterate, and quite often literally know more about language than their teachers, at least in some respects.
> (DES, 1988)

How can we build on this knowledge and experience of other languages? And how will it inform the teaching decisions which we take? Before exploring these questions it is worth looking at what is already known about biliteracy in the British context.

Biliteracy and British school children

The DES-funded Linguistic Minorities Project (LMP), set up in 1979, remains the single most reliable source of information on patterns of language use in multilingual Britain. In the survey sample the project team found that:

> Literacy in the minority language was never much less than 50 per cent ... literacy rates range from over 80 per cent of the Polish- and Ukranian-speaking respondents, through notably high proportions of the Gujerati, Turkish and Bengali speakers.
> (LMP, 1985)

These findings suggest that the majority of bilingual children in British classrooms are likely to experience either formal or informal instruction in the written form of a community language. Such instruction will in most cases take place in voluntary schools, at places of worship, or at home and not as part of compulsory schooling. This will certainly be the case for primary-age children in England, although it is worth noting that there have been some small scale successes in introducing minority community languages into the secondary school curriculum.

A significant part of the debate on 'mother-tongue teaching' in the early 1980s focused on the issue of maintaining and developing levels of literacy in minority community languages. Mahendra Verma, writing at the time, emphasised that 'a language is fostered, cultivated and preserved through reading and writing, not simply speaking ... Biliteracy is a prerequisite to sustained and stable bilingualism.' (Verma, 1981, p83)

Despite pressure from various quarters, the provision of community language teaching in primary schools has remained at the level of transitional bilingualism in which the spoken language of the home or minority community is used only until communicative English has been established. Other languages are used as a bridge to the language of instruction: classroom English. So, although teachers continue to work hard to value community languages in the primary classroom (Houlton, 1985; Edwards, 1998) it is likely that bilingual children's most influential experiences of another language will take place outside the school context.

A more comprehensive view of bilingual education – one that develops biliteracy – has not attracted a great deal of support, partly because of the prevailing ideology of a common curriculum in all schools and partly because of logistical difficulties. However, as Edwards observes:

> Bilingual education is, of course, a viable proposition only in situations where there are significant numbers of speakers of the same language and, very often, schools include small numbers of speakers of many different languages. It is important to remember, however, that the English-only classroom is not the sole viable alternative to bilingualism.
>
> (Edwards 1998)

Classrooms where the diversity of language and literacy is recognised, valued and used in the curriculum provide us with this sort of alternative. In other words, learning environments in which both children and teachers recognise the social and cultural importance of literacy in languages other than English as well as the cognitive benefits of bilingualism. One of the stronger features of the National Literacy Strategy's guidance on 'Children with English as an Additional Language' (DfEE 1998, Section 4) lies in the emphasis given to biliteracy. The document suggests that it is important for teachers to gather information on 'literacy skills in another language' (p 106), to talk about literacy in other languages (p 107), to use dual language texts (p 107) and to give opportunities for talking about text in other languages (p 110). Whilst the message is clearly about transitional bilingualism, the recognition of different (or 'other') language and literacy skills is welcome.

Finding out about children's use of language is clearly an important starting point. Language surveys draw our attention to some of the issues involved in looking at language repertoire and its social contexts. The orientation of community-organised provision for minority language teaching is one such issue. For example, many voluntary schools organised by minority groups closely associate literacy with religious instruction. Polish Saturday schools, Welsh language Sunday schools as well as classes held in mosques, temples and gurdwaras perform this function.

Children's accounts of learning to read two languages do not tend to dwell on these orientations. Instead they often refer to more fundamental characteristics of learning, such as the age at which they learnt to read, the environment in which they learnt and the approach of their teachers.

Inevitably they make comparison. Nine year-old Benares comments are interesting in this context:

> I went to Mosque from 7 years old. My dad took me and then I started learning it. I read English too. I'm learning to read good. You know at Mosque this big man he – this big man he give us Kaida [a primer]. You go and read to him and he tells you the word if you don't know. I learned English in the infants. Mrs Richardson said 'Read your reading book and then you can play in the Lego'.
>
> (Benares)[4]

Differences between the 'big man' who teaches reading by group recitation and Mrs Richardson who listens to individuals reading in turn may be understated in this account. In talking with young bilinguals we are often forced to recognise that teaching and learning styles may vary quite considerable within and between different cultural groups. These approaches may be quite different from those experienced in school. Another child's account suggests this difference in pedagogy:

> I go to reading at 5 o'clock: this lady teaches me. She writes them and I have to say them, it's hard because she writes them joined up. I want to be a teacher. The lady who teaches us shouts at us and we have to stand in the corner. We read her the book. If we don't know she tells us. Sometimes we go on to the next page.
>
> (Shaheen)[4]

In general such differences of approach are regarded by children as 'normal' and are not seen as a problem. As the fascinating case studies of Hilary Minns (1990) illustrate, literacy in a culturally diverse setting includes a wide variety of experiences. As a result we are led to consider new dimensions of literacy and what it means to be a reader in different cultural contexts.

Despite a growing awareness of minority languages we are still relatively ill informed about community literacy practices and tend to adopt a narrow view of literacy, defined in terms of an ability to read and write in English. This view has been re-enforced with the introduction of the literacy hour, although, as we have seen recent guidance takes a more enlightened view of the role of community language literacy.

Approaches to language teaching and learning to read English

So far I have suggested that an understanding of the development of literacy in bilingual children has to take into account their experiences of reading and writing in a variety of different contexts. Children's language repertoire may vary from emergent literacy in one language to fluency in two or more languages. Schools that recognise the importance of valuing and supporting community languages are clear that this is not done to the exclusion of English language teaching. In fact research and anecdotal evidence suggest that the use of the first language can be supportive in the development of the second. Clearly, English is not only essential for progression through the school curriculum, it is also vital for full participation in social and political processes. The importance of the majority language is clearly stated by Wallace, who observes that:

> While literacy in the mother tongue helps to ensure participation in the contexts of home and family, literacy in the standard language (English) is one necessary condition for access to the institutions of power in the wider society.
>
> (Wallace, 1988)

Although the domain of use of some community languages extends beyond the home and into the immediate community, Wallace is certainly right in emphasising the importance of literacy in English for bilingual pupils. Learning to read in English is essential in the multilingual classroom, just as it is in other contexts, but should there be any significant differences in teaching approaches?

We have already observed that knowledge about literacy may be quite varied in the multilingual classroom. Children's experiences outside the school setting may have provided them with different versions of what it means to be a reader and how to go about the task of learning to read. These experiences will be as diverse as the communities that the school serves and as a result it is very difficult to generalise. So, the best teaching will be based on an informed view of the child's experience of language and literacy. The sort of detailed profiling encouraged through the Primary Language Record (Barrs *et al.* 1988) and through school language surveys (Edwards, 1996) show how we can begin to gain more insight into the child as language learner.

Whilst effective teaching will be based on an understanding of what the learner brings to the task it will also be informed by the teacher's views about how language develops. This is particularly true when we consider bilingual learners. Successful teachers working with bilingual readers will build their practice on what they know about how pupils develop their use of spoken English.

Broadly speaking, English language teaching approaches are informed by two distinct strands of thinking (Levine, 1990). The first approach is the *structural-situationalist* pedagogy in which English language input and output are controlled by the teacher with an emphasis on achieving structural accuracy and grammatically complete utterances. The second is a *functional-communicative* approach, which encourages greater pupil interaction and stresses the communication of meaning over accuracy.

There are of course clear parallels between these two approaches and competing ideologies in the English curriculum and the teaching of reading. It is hardly surprising, then, that professional practice in the literacy development of bilingual pupils has raised some familiar issues. Advocates of the *structural-situationalist* approach have argued that texts with a carefully selected and familiar grammatical structure and a controlled vocabulary will be the most helpful for non-native speakers. The *structural-situationalists* tend to favour a graded language scheme with a controlled vocabulary as a means of teaching spoken English. It comes as no surprise then to find that the *structural-situationalists* usually advocate following a published reading scheme – or use teacher-made resources that mirror their approach to oral language teaching.

In contrast the *functional-communicative* approach finds itself more in sympathy with a pedagogy that emphasises reading for meaning and interest. Scheme materials tend to be used in a more flexible way and pupils will be encouraged to read a wide range of texts. Here reading is seen as enriching the language development of bilingual learners. (The Real Reading Project described in the following section shows this sort of approach in action.)

The National Literacy Strategy has yet to clarify its position on the learning processes of bilingual children. In fact, the wider area of oracy remains a cause for concern (Merchant and Marsh, 1998). The claim that the 'participative nature of whole class and group-work helps in teaching children who speak English as an additional language' (DfEE, 1998) is questionable. With forty minutes of the hour devoted to whole class work, even the most skilled teachers find it difficult to include all children in meaningful interaction, let alone to address the specific needs of bilinguals.

Working with bilingual learner readers

There has been relatively little research and development work on reading with bilingual children in the British context and opinion about approaches and materials is divided. For instance, some teachers believe that there is a need to establish a fairly high degree of oral fluency in English before beginning reading; others claim that the oral fluency of young children can be improved through early encounters with print. With little published guidance on such matters schools have tended to seek their own solutions, and have met with varying degrees of success.

The work of a group of teachers in Sheffield[4] shows how school-based development can begin to address the needs of bilingual readers. The teachers started with the observation that children showed little interest or enthusiasm for the reading material used in the school. Although basic decoding skills were efficiently taught and most children achieved a level of reading competence judged to be appropriate to their age, books were not generally regarded as a source of pleasure or enjoyment. This was seen primarily as a resource problem. A succession of budget cuts had meant that the school had been unable to update its stock of reading materials and had to rely on existing book stocks. The books, the majority of which came from reading schemes, were often uninspiring in content and unattractive in appearance.

The teachers drew up a list of reading activities and experiences that they wished to promote. These were turned into the set of principles listed below:

- Make reading easy and enjoyable
- Use interesting and appropriate materials (including good stories with a multicultural or anti-racist content)
- Encourage storytelling and reading from pictures and illustrations
- Set aside time and space for enjoying books
- Use high-quality dual language texts
- Make your own reading materials (eg; class books)
- Share an enthusiasm for different texts – talk about them!
- Read aloud regularly (remove the distinction between class stories and reading books)
- Hear children read a whole book or allow them to choose a stopping place
- Set up reading partnerships within the school
- Allow mistakes so long as they do not change the meaning of the text
- Teach word attack skills after initial confidence has been built up

Initially, books brought in by the teachers themselves were used to resource these new developments. This quite quickly had the effect of improving the quality of reading and influenced the children's enthusiasm. Bilingual children who had previously struggled to make sense of their reading were now able to enjoy such books as *Bringing the Rain to Kapiti Plain* (Aardeema) and *Cops and Robbers* (Ahlberg). Teachers began to feel that the rather stilted language of some of the reading scheme books, which often seemed confusing to those who spoke English as a first language, had actually caused further problems for bilingual learners. One teacher commented: 'It seems as if some of these reading books were written for no one in particular by no one in particular'. The newer texts, some in dual language editions, either provide support in their use of pattern and rhyme or were closer to the kind of everyday English that the children were used to hearing in their daily lives.

Teachers were beginning to use material that they were enthusiastic about; and this enthusiasm was contagious. Books bought by teachers, often at their own expense, were chosen for a reason – because they were 'good', 'interesting' and 'well-illustrated'. Discussions with bilingual children tended to focus on the reasons for choosing a particular book, its presentational features and favourite excerpts. Even with a relatively small collection of new and high quality materials children were keen to read and re-read. Homemade books were used to supplement this growing resource. A series of such books were produced, based on amusing incidents that had happened to members of staff in the school. These were illustrated with photographs, and captions were translated into various community languages. This material proved to be extremely popular with the children.

Emerging from the Sheffield work is the impression that building a stimulating reading environment in which good texts are created, appreciated and discussed is as important for bilingual learners as it is for their monolingual counterparts. The additional benefits of bringing an active multilingual element to this reading environment continue to inspire a growing number of both teachers and children.

The Linguistic Diversity Project (WMBEC, 1989; 1990) picked up on this theme of celebrating children's biliteracy. In one school[5] a class of Year 5 children were involved in producing a series of dual-language storybooks suitable for sharing with younger children in Nursery and key stage one classes. Stories were written in Punjabi and Gujerati, checked by parents and then read to younger children. This involved planning, drafting and re-drafting in two languages developing children's experience of the writing process and the skills of book production.

Most bilingual children learn to read English quickly and fluently in a supportive environment. Development work with bilingual children has emphasised the importance of:

- Recognising, valuing and using children's knowledge of other languages
- Providing an exciting and rich reading environment
- Emphasising reading for meaning and enjoyment
- Using and developing appropriate materials which provide positive images of children's language and culture

Bilingual children and English texts

In the previous section I suggested that good practice in the teaching of reading will have the same benefits for bilingual children as it does for their monolingual counterparts. I also drew attention to the variety of experiences of literacy in a multilingual setting and have attempted to outline how biliteracy can enrich schools and classrooms. Here, I categorise the skills that bilingual pupils draw on when working on English language texts.

So far I have argued that bilingual and monolingual children draw on the same skills and strategies in reading. For young bilinguals, their experience of another language system may influence the way they use these strategies. Goodman's work on cue systems (Goodman, 1964) recently adapted by the National Literacy Strategy (DfEE, 1998) as 'searchlights' provides a useful framework for looking at the ways in which bilingual readers approach English texts. Goodman describes reading cues drawn from the *semantic system*, the *syntactic structure* and the patterns of *grapho-phonemic representation* of the language. I will explore each of these in turn, but before doing so it is important to consider the *cultural context* of reading.

Cultural context

In an informative study, Halliday and Hasan have demonstrated how the understanding of texts is dependent upon a knowledge of the culture in which they are located (Halliday and Hasan, 1985). Our familiarity with the cultural context is often taken for granted in the process of reading. It is nevertheless true that a successful reader draws on cultural competence in order to construct meaning. As Wallace explains:

> Our cultural competence is a very complex package of beliefs, knowledge, feelings, attitudes and behaviours .... In terms of reading, the term might be used to refer to the ability to recognise, interpret and predict certain kinds of phenomena or behaviour described in texts.
>
> (Wallace, 1988)

Bilingual learners will have a repertoire of cultural competences and differing degrees of familiarity with aspects of mainstream culture. It is important to ensure that reading resources embody a similar variety of cultural perspectives. Materials written by bilingual writers set in a British context can be used to 'match' the experience of young bilinguals and to broaden the reading diet of monolingual children. Stories and other texts celebrating the heroines and heroes, the historical, scientific and cultural achievements of different communities are an important dimension to the range of texts used in the literacy hour and elsewhere in the school curriculum. Using the National Literacy Strategy as a starting point, we might begin by asking how different cultures, languages and scripts are represented in the texts we choose when looking for instance at traditional stories, instructions, or public information documents.

The semantic system

Successful reading involves making meaning by drawing on a prior knowledge of how texts 'work'. Our experience of story, information books and other written materials help us to recognise the significance of events, phrases and words that we read. This experience enables us to organise our reading comprehension, to understand a text's underlying structure and to make accurate predictions. Bilingual learners may not always be familiar with the structures and vocabulary that they encounter in reading. Reading with a limited vocabulary can mean that children are not aware of the semantic alternatives (such as collocations) that writers use. Rather than organising additional 'warm-up' sessions (DfEE, 1998) creative teachers have used more exciting and more meaningful ways of building understanding and vocabulary – as Dodwell describes:

> role-play areas can be turned into a setting based on a familiar book. *The Three Bears Cottage* is a favourite example, but equally powerful have been the cave featured in *Can't You Sleep, Little Bear?* and the train in *Oi! Get off our Train!* (complete with stuffed animals). Tables or trays can contain scenarios modelled on books, with appropriate props and small figures. These experiences enable children to retell stories, to practise chunks of language learned and to play with remembered words.
>
> (Dodwell, 1999)

Syntactic structure

Our knowledge about word order, the clause and sentence structure of written English help us to read in a way that makes grammatical sense. Children in the early stages of learning English will only have a limited understanding of the syntactic structure of the language. They will have varying degrees of proficiency in judging how grammatically 'complete' or 'correct' their reading is.

Although other languages use different syntactic structures, interference is unlikely to be a major problem. Speakers of South Asian languages, such as Punjabi or Urdu which are based on the subject-object-verb (SOV) clause pattern, rarely encounter persistent difficulties in the early stages of learning English, which is based on the SVO pattern. Research evidence suggests that bilinguals are able to keep the language systems separate from an early age (Cummins, 1979).

Bilingual learner-readers will become more sensitive to syntactic features as their oral fluency in English develops. In the early stages they will find it difficult to make predictions by using syntactic cues and may not self-correct in the same way as their monolingual peers (Gregory, 1996). Teachers will need to take care in selecting texts that have a patterned or repetitive sentence structure. Repeated exposure to the language of core books will be helpful and children should be encouraged to re-visit texts as they progress towards an accurate rendering. This sort of experience can be enriched by using different media including talking books and audio-taped stories.

The grapho-phonemic system

The correspondence between sounds and words and the written symbols that are used to represent them is important for accurate reading and writing. Our understanding of the grapho-phonemic conventions of the English language is used to complement the other aspects of linguistic knowledge we use in the act of reading. With an alphabet of twenty-six letters representing about forty-four phonemes and comparatively complex spelling patterns, phoneme-grapheme correspondence in English is challenging. Bilingual children who are already familiar with the script of another language may observe some interesting contrasts. Some bilinguals may have well-developed phonological awareness through their first language or language of literacy or even a knowledge of an alphabetic script.

The languages we encounter in multilingual Britain do in fact use a range of different writing systems. So, for example, Somali uses an alphabetic system, whereas Urdu uses a consonantal Arabic script. Gujerati use syllabic representation and Cantonese a logographic system of writing. In some of these languages the correspondence between sound and symbol is fairly consistent whereas in others it is more variable – or even non-existent, as in Cantonese where characters represent whole words. There are other areas of variation as well. For instance in Urdu letter shapes vary when in initial, medial or final positions in a word. All this variation adds to the fascination of working in multilingual contexts. The potential for learning about language is considerable and at the same time, there is no evidence to suggest that children from the different language groups experience specific difficulties in getting to grip with the grapho-phonemic system of written English.

Bilingual learners who already have some experience of literacy will need to know about the similarities and differences between their own writing system and that of English. They will need to build on their familiarity with the alphabetic system and they may need to learn about the importance of phoneme-grapheme correspondence in English, the extent of variation (particularly noticeable with English vowels) and the consistency of common letter strings.

Towards a reading policy for bilingual learners

Through this brief discussion of the knowledge of cultural context and cue systems, I have looked at the strategies that bilingual children use to make sense of their reading. I have suggested that these strategies will be used by both monolingual and bilingual readers. I have also tried to show how the home or community language and children's oral proficiency in English may influence how they read. These factors do not suggest that the school reading experience of bilingual children should be substantially different in character. There is no evidence to suggest that specially designed language and reading programmes are any more effective than good primary practice in the teaching of reading. I conclude by looking at aspects of current practice that seem to be particularly appropriate to bilingual learners. These aspects are subdivided into four categories: the reader; reading resources; reader response; and the reading environment. It is intended that these points will be useful in developing school policy for bilingual children.

The reader

- By identifying and using languages other than English, the school is able to give positive value to bilingual pupils;
- Children's experience of literacy in home or community languages can be discussed and used in school;
- Children who are already literate in a language other than English will have an advantage in knowing about the reading process;
- Bilingual children may have different experiences of what reading behaviour is like and how reading is taught and learnt;
- The motivation to read, to make meaning and to enjoy English language texts is important for bilingual learners;
- Reading and listening to stories in both English and community languages will help to develop children's oral fluency in English;
- Careful profiling of children's literacy development should include information about all their languages.

Resources

- Bilingual children can be encouraged to listen, to retell and to read stories in their own language (or languages);
- Good quality dual language texts and books set in a range of contexts are important to use;
- Experience of a wide range of texts, both fiction and non-fiction, is essential;

- The enjoyment of listening to stories told by adults and other children should be developed – commercially produced tapes can be used to extend the experience;
- Interesting stories that are lively and rhythmical can be read and re-read;
- Repetitive and patterned texts will support English language development as well as early reading;
- Re-telling stories using drama, puppets or story maps will help children to build meaning, understand story structure, and develop vocabulary;
- Children can compose their own texts, which can be saved as class books or anthologies that can be re-visited. These texts can use different languages.

The reading environment

- Children should have open access to good and enjoyable reading material;
- The reading environment should include a variety of texts which feature different languages;
- Children should be encouraged to choose what they read as well as when and where they read it;
- An attractive and comfortable reading area is likely to encourage frequent use;
- Opportunities should be created for extended, independent reading.

Reading response

- Children should be encouraged to talk both formally and informally about texts they have enjoyed – this will be particularly beneficial for children in the early stages of learning English;
- Texts can be used as a starting point for other classroom activities – this will help to deepen children's understanding of text structure and specific sentence and word level features;
- Reading and comparing texts as well as re-reading extracts will provide bilingual children with repetition that is supportive.

Learning to read English fluently and accurately is of key importance to bilingual children. In order to achieve this they will need strong experiences of literacy and support that goes beyond the daily regime of the literacy hour. Schools need to develop strong partnerships with parents in order to stimulate a richer discussion of literacy in a multilingual society and teachers need to carry the debate forward. Supporting readers for whom English is an additional language must include careful consideration of biliteracy, since it is the experience of bilingual communities throughout the world that the majority language excerpts a powerful and dominating influence. The following extract illustrates an oft-repeated theme:

> Ty's parents are no longer worried about their son's English. Their biggest concern today is his written Chinese. His Chinese literacy development reached its highest level in first grade: he was able to write fairly long letters in Chinese, and his diary entries were getting longer. Then it began to decline. He is now hardly able to write a letter in Chinese. His diary, which began in Chinese and then became bilingual for a period of time, is now exclusively in English. English has become his preferred language in both its oral and written forms.
>
> (Jiang, 1997, p 66)

Notes

1 Thanks to Graham Morgan of the Equal Opportunities Unit, Walsall for case study material and the language biography of Azizul.
2 I use the term 'biliteracy' throughout to refer to familiarity with the written form of two languages without entering any of the complex debates over comparative levels of proficiency.
3 The language of the home may be different to the language of the community. By 'religious language' I mean the languages of sacred texts. This may mean that children have three or more languages and in some cases it may be difficult to identify which is the first language. For the sake of simplicity I have tended to use 'bilingual' as a broad term to describe children growing up in more than one language community and I have used the term 'community language' to describe the languages used.
4 Thanks to Sue McDonagh, Mary Green and the children from Abbeydale Primary School for their reflections on the Real Book Project.
5 Thanks to the work of St. Giles Primary School, Walsall for their work on bilingual stories.

Questions for personal reflection or group discussion

1 What are your children's experiences of literacy in community languages and how can you find out more?
2 What sort of relationships can be established between the school and voluntary providers of community language teaching?
3 How can you improve the dialogue with parents about the importance of reading in school and in other contexts?
4 How can you involve ethnic minority parents in the school's reading programme?
5 How can your school create an environment in which children's reading and writing skills in community languages are valued and used?

6   How can you give bilingual children access to influential texts in English without de-valuing their own culture and traditions?

7   What are the specific difficulties that your bilingual children experience in reading English and what support do they require to overcome these?

8   What sort of reading materials and resources are appropriate to your school setting and how can you devise a programme of resource purchase?

9   How can more experienced bilingual readers be encouraged to support beginning readers?

10   How can the school's reading policy and practices reflect the linguistic diversity of contemporary society?

Recommended readings

The Other Languages – a guide to the multilingual classroom (Edwards, 1996). This booklet provides useful information on some of the common languages and scripts used by British schoolchildren. It also includes advice and recording sheets for conducting your own language survey. There is also a useful two-page summary of ways of promoting different languages in your classroom.

The Power of Babel – teaching and learning in multilingual classrooms (Edwards, 1998). A comprehensive view of different ways of promoting linguistic and cultural diversity based on case studies of classroom work. Two chapters are devoted to ways of promoting biliteracy. Plenty of useful information on resources and practical approaches.

Making Sense of a New World – learning to read in a second language (Gregory, 1996) A detailed analysis of learning and teaching reading in multilingual classrooms which draws extensively on data gathered by the author in this country and elsewhere.

Read it to Me Now! – learning at home and school (Minns, 1990) This very readable account of the literacy development of a group of primary schoolchildren In the Midlands gives us insight into the varied experiences of children growing up in a multicultural and multilingual setting. Descriptions of learning to read in English and other languages are used in order to make practical recommend-ations for whole-school language policies.

Bibliography

Barrs. M., Ellis, S., Hester, H. and Thomas, A. (1988) *The Primary Language Record – Handbook for Teachers*. London: Centre for Language in Primary Education (CLPE).

Brightmore, R. and Ross, M. (1990) 'Bilingual children and their infant schooling' in Levine, J. (ed) *Bilingual Learners in the Mainstream Curriculum*. London: Taylor and Francis.

Cummins, J. (1979) 'Linguistic interdependence and the education development of bilingual children' in *Review of Education Research*, 4, 9, 2, pp 221–51.

DfEE (1985) *Education for All* (The Swann Report). London: HMSO.

DfEE (1988) *National Curriculum Proposals for English for ages 5–11* London: HMSO.

DfEE (1998) *The National Literacy Strategy – A framework for teaching* London: HMSO.

Dodwell, E. (1999) "'I Can Tell Lots of Punjabi": Developing Language and Literacy with Bilingual Children' in Marsh, J. and Hallet, E. (eds) *Desirable Literacies* London: Paul Chapman.

Edwards, V. (1996) *The Other Languages – A guide to the multilingual classroom* Reading: Reading and Language Information Centre.

Edwards, V. (1998) *The Power of Babel – Teaching and learning in multilingual classrooms* Stoke-on-Trent: Trentham.

Goodman, K.S. (1964) 'A linguistic study of cues and miscues in reading' in Gloasch, F. (ed) *Language and Literacy; the collected writings of Kenneth S. Goodman*, Vol 1. London: Routledge.

Gregory, E. (1996) *Making Sense of a New World – Learning to read in a second language* London: Paul Chapman.

Halliday, M.A.K. and Hasan, R. (1985) *Language, Context and Text*, Oxford: Oxford University Press.

Houlton, D. (1985) *All Our Languages; a handbook for teachers.* London: Edward Arnold.

Jiang, N. (1997) 'Biliteracy Development of a Chinese/English-Speaking Child' in Taylor, D. (ed) *Many Families, Many Literacies.* Portsmouth NH: Heinemann.

Levine, J. (1990) *Bilingual Learners in the Mainstream Curriculum.* London: Taylor and Francis.

Linguistic Minorities Project (1985) *The Other Languages of England.* London: Routledge.

Merchant, G. (1990) 'Teachers' perceptions of linguistic diversity' in James, C. and Garrett, J. (eds) *Language Awareness in the Classroom.* London: Longman.

Merchant, G. and Marsh, J.(1998) *Co-ordinating Primary Language and Literacy: the subject leaders' handbook.* London: Paul Chapman.

Minns, H. (1990) *Read It To Me Now!* London: Virago.

Savva, H. (1990) 'The multi-lingual classroom' in Harris, J. and Wilkinson, J. (eds) *In the Know.* Cheltenham: Stanley Thornes.

Smith, F. (1988) *Joining the Literacy Club.* London: Heinemann.

Verma, M. (1981) *Papers on Biliteracy and Bilingualism.* London: National Council for Mother Tongue Teaching.

Wallace, C. (1988) *Learning to Read in a Multicultural Community.* Hemel Hempstead: Prentice Hall.

Walsall Metropolitan Borough Education Committee (WMBEC) (1989/90) *Linguistic Diversity Project 1987–88, 1989–90.* Education Development Centre, Walsall.

11 Struggling readers

Tony Martin

The optimal state for learning: 'High Challenge and Low Stress' (Smith A. 1996)

Too many children leave primary schools in the UK still struggling with reading and writing. It is not a new phenomenon. Discussing national surveys, Greg Brooks refers to: 'a survey of adults of different ages in 1992–3 which found a low attaining minority among 72–74 year olds, who were born around 1920 and entered school around 1925'. (NFER News, 1998)

Another survey by NFER (Brooks, 1998) found that reading standards had remained stable from 1948 to 1996 but referred to 'the long tail of underachievement' – a substantial minority in each generation who struggle with reading (international comparisons seem to show other countries with much lower rates of reading failure). The current government has translated this problem into percentages of children in England and Wales who attain national curriculum level 4 at the end of their primary schooling, setting these countries the task of raising the percentage of children who achieve this level from 63 per cent to 80 per cent in 2002. The aim is a major cut in the numbers of struggling readers in a short period of time – and a clear strategy to achieve this: The National Literacy Strategy. Will it work? Some clues are to be found in the evaluation of the National Literacy Project that preceded it (Ofsted, 1998). While this was very positive it did not paint a totally clear picture. In general:

> Pupils showed a significant rise in their average standardised reading scores … Although their reading test scores were well below the national average at the start of the Project, their scores were much closer to the national average at the end of five terms.

However:

Statemented pupils and those at stages 3 to 5 of the Code of Practice made less progress than pupils with no defined special educational needs (SEN) or those at stages 1 and 2 .... The picture of improvement in the NLP schools indicates that progress for a significant minority of pupils is likely to be very uneven.

What then will happen to this 'significant minority' over the months and years ahead? Will they become the 20 per cent for whom the Strategy has not worked? It is salutary to realise that 80 per cent level 4s still means an average of six children in a class of thirty who do not succeed in 'making the grade'. Within this six, of course, will be children with severe and complex learning difficulties but there will also be many children for whom the Strategy was intended. The burning question is what can be done to help them achieve levels of literacy which will enable them to have access to the secondary school curriculum and, as adults, power and control over their own lives. Initially the Strategy did not appear to be considering the needs of struggling readers, since it was introduced without reference to children with SEN. Section Four of *The Framework for Teaching* (with advice on 'Children with Special Educational Needs') was added some time after the original three sectioned document had been sent to schools. However an Additional Literacy Support (ALS) initiative, aimed at the 'significant minority' in years three and four (£22 million for materials, training and extra classroom helpers) demonstrates a recognition of the problem by those responsible for the strategy. ALS is the Strategy's way of addressing a seemingly intractable problem. But will it work? At the time of writing, there are no public reports of its impact. However there is an increasing body of knowledge regarding approaches and programmes that are effective in terms of raising the reading attainment of struggling readers. Recently the National Foundation for Education Research (NFER) examined as many of them as could be found with data indicating quantitative gains in reading attainment. The report (*What Works For Slow Readers? The Effectiveness of Early Intervention Schemes*, 1998, Brooks, Flanagan, Henkhuzens, Hutchinson) suggests that there are a number of interesting issues which are important for teachers working in classrooms with struggling readers.

Complexity or simplicity?

Successful approaches varied between those which highlight the complexity of the reading process and invest heavily in long term training of teachers (for example *Reading Recovery*) and 'partnership approaches' which provide a simple, clear model for adult/child or child/child pairs to read together.

'Paired Reading' has such a long, successful track record and is so simple to introduce and manage (and therefore very cheap) that I am surprised that it is not formally recommended as a key element in tackling underachievement in the National Literacy Strategy. The latest development *Read On*, at the University of Dundee, involves 'tutors' (10/11 year olds) reading with 'tutees' (7/8 year olds) and an initial evaluation (Topping, 1999) shows significant reading gains by both tutors and tutees. It is particularly interesting as an approach because the phonological elements of reading are not explicitly addressed at all.

An earlier study of the effectiveness of paired reading stated:

> The general pattern is of Paired Reading being associated with fewer refusals (greater confidence), greater use of the context and a greater likelihood of self-correction, as well as fewer errors (greater accuracy) and better use of phonic skills.
>
> (Topping and Lindsay, 1992)

It is interesting to consider this statement in terms of the searchlight model of the reading cues, which lies at the heart of the National Literacy Strategy. The phonic and context cues are mentioned explicitly in the above quotation and the word recognition/graphic cue is implied in terms of self-correction and greater accuracy. The fourth cue, syntactic, is a key element of paired reading given the intonation patterns for different sentence structures which are stressed as the two readers read together. So, paired reading seems to work in terms of the searchlights model recommended by the National Literacy Strategy and one wonders why such a simple scheme has been largely ignored in the current national developments.

The earlier the better

Within the programmes reviewed by the NFER study was *Reading Recovery*, perhaps the most researched educational programme for struggling readers of all time. This early intervention scheme was developed by Marie Clay in New Zealand and has since been 'exported' all over the world. In the UK, evaluations of it have included a very complimentary OFSTED report:

> The great majority of pupils who undergo the programme reach its objective of matching the average band of reading attainment in the classes from which they are drawn; and most maintain the gains they have made.
>
> (HMSO, 1993)

Two of the most recent evaluations, in New Zealand and Australia, looked at the long term impact of *Reading Recovery* (Moore M., Wade B., 1998) and the NFER as part of the *What Works For Slow Readers?* survey (1998) also considered this aspect. In both reports *Reading Recovery* is seen to be effective. In Britain the principles and practices of *Reading Recovery* have been adapted, for example in The Cumbria/York Reading with Phonology Project in which an element focusing explicitly on phonology is added to sessions based on *Reading Recovery*. Within Cumbria it is now widely used and known as Reading Intervention. The major problem with these intensive one-to-one programmes is the cost of implementation; both in terms of training for teachers and the subsequent work they do with individual children. However they are both early intervention schemes and the NFER report argues that 'though expensive' they 'can give good value for money' in the sense that later remediation costs even more.

In addition to the financial, there is also a powerful professional reason for deciding on early intervention, which is important for teachers working in classes containing struggling readers. As Marie Clay says, in discussing the first two years at school:

> At this time we begin to produce our reading failures by allowing some children to build ineffective processing strategies which limit what they can do throughout their school careers. As older readers they are difficult to help because they are habituated in their inefficiency and because their processing behaviours are hidden from view. In the terms of the computer age they have been poorly programmed. They wrote the programme and we do not know how to get into it.
>
> (Clay, 1991)

The longer a child struggles the more difficult it will be for that child to 'catch up'. To understand why, imagine what it must be like to be a child in a classroom surrounded by others who are learning to read. You watch them beginning to read to the teacher, to read to each other in the book corner, to take books home and return with a successful tick on a card to show the book has been read. In shared reading sessions these other children read along with the teacher – they actually seem to know how to read those marks on the page. We can imagine our initial response would be to try and work out how they are doing it. To come up with the rules so we can join in the game. I once heard a deputy headteacher speak movingly to a large group of colleagues about her memories of being a struggling reader. She remembered watching the other children as they read aloud to the teacher and trying to work out how they were doing it. At one point she thought she had cracked it. The other children did not have 'gaps' between the words, like she did when she read. So the key seemed to be to get rid of the gaps. She recalled the disaster of her next attempt to read aloud without any gaps! The longer we leave children developing the processing strategies they think must lie behind reading, the harder it is to teach them the correct ones. Before too long the questions asked by a teacher are met by a blank look. The reason is not the question itself but what lies behind it – teacher and child are playing different games with different rules. A teacher of struggling readers needs to understand what strategies the children are using and think hold the key, in order to help those children make sense of the reading strategies which *will* bring about improvement.

Focusing on phonics ... and what about vocabulary?

The NFER report *What Works For Slow Readers* is clear that a key lesson from approaches that appear to work is that 'work on phonological skills should be embedded within a broad approach'. Those programmes which focused heavily on phonological aspects of reading showed 'little impact'. The Additional Literacy Support programme focuses a great deal on phonics but pupils are also experiencing the broader picture through their inclusion in the literacy hour each week. The focus on phonics is based on the evidence that one of (arguably the most) important element of learning which beginning readers have to understand is the way spoken words can be segmented into phonemes and the connection these have to the letters of the alphabet (the 'alphabetic principle'). It is likely that struggling readers are insecure in this knowledge and its application. They need to be taught it, but there are other vitally important pieces of the jigsaw.

For an example, we need to keep in mind 'The Matthew Effect', a term coined by Keith Stanovich (1986). It derives from a quotation in the Gospel according to Matthew: '*To he who has, will be given; to he who has not, will be taken away*'. Once children learn to read they are able to read more. They encounter words and sentence structures that enable them to read even more. The gap between them and those who struggle grows exponentially. If we consider only one aspect of this phenomenon, vocabulary, we can see the scale of the problem for the struggling reader. A child once told me as he looked back at his experiences earlier in his school life:

> and she'd say the word – I didn't know what it meant ... and if you never knew the meaning you couldn't get the story could you – so it'd be really boring, the story, if you didn't know what it meant.
>
> (Martin, 1989)

The need to 'catch up' with vocabulary (and this means the vocabulary needed for reading rather than that which is sufficient for everyday, informal conversation) is obviously vital and the longer the reading vocabulary of some children grows away from that of others the harder will be the challenge. The use of powerful computer technology in reading research means we now know that readers do in fact look at every word. But they fixate on some words longer than others. The longest fixations are on the longest words, which may seem obvious but is not simply a result of the length of the word. The longest words are also those which carry the meaning of texts – nouns, adjectives, verbs, adverbs (where readers do miss words out these are prepositions or conjunctions which contain little 'meaning'). The longer pauses made by readers on these words are because the brain has to take account of and provide connections to this meaning. So, for instance, if a sentence begins with the word 'soldiers' the reader, realising this is what the sentence will be about has to provide a concept of a soldier. The reader has to bring background knowledge to bear on the text. There is rarely mention of vocabulary when the problems of struggling readers are discussed. There should be, if not in curriculum materials, then in the planning and reflection jointly undertaken by classroom teachers and assistants.

The National Literacy Strategy – inclusion

The issues above need to be considered whenever classrooms contain struggling readers, which will be the experience of the majority of teachers. Advice on Special Educational Needs pupils in Section 4 of the NLS *Framework for Teaching* shows that a key element of the underlying rationale for the strategy is 'inclusion':

> All pupils should be able to join in at least some of the hour…Where children need to work to different objectives, they should nevertheless be taught with their own class and year group.

These children may need extra support 'to enable them to play a full part in the hour' and teachers 'will need to ask different pupils questions of different levels of complexity …. not simply teach to the middle range of all pupils' needs', but the teaching strategies outlined are seen to be crucial for *all* children.

While this notion of 'inclusion' is vital if expectations are to be raised, especially of children who simply have lower literacy levels than those expected for their ages, the challenge for the teacher cannot be understated. If the aim is to enable these pupils to 'catch up' and work at a comparable level to the rest of their year group simply through lots of whole class teaching with children whose literacy levels are far higher, then the challenge becomes enormous. This is not to say we should not support it, just that the delivery of it will be an incredible achievement. My own anecdotal evidence suggests many schools are ignoring the 'official' recommendations and have begun dividing pupils by ability for the literacy hour so that, in fact, struggling readers will not be taught with their own class and year group. Literacy hour training materials for SEN children illustrate how a teacher might cater for a wide range of ability. Interestingly they also have a short section on the pros and cons of setting.

If struggling readers are to 'catch up' they will require more than can be provided by a teacher in the Literacy Hour. Once additional support had been agreed it crucial that it be targeted at the youngest age groups. The overwhelming message of research and experience shows that earlier intervention has the greater the chance of success. As discussed above, *Reading Recovery* is aimed at children who have been in school for one year, identifying those felt to be at risk and then looking to bring them up in two terms to the level required for classroom work. Again the literacy strategy is moving in this direction, with the new 'Quality First Teaching' programme for year one pupils in which teacher assistants work with the whole class in the literacy hour as well as with targeted children.

Prevention rather than cure

We need to prevent reading difficulties rather than act once they have occurred. It is useful to look outside the UK, at a major report in the USA, *Preventing Reading Difficulties in Young Children* (Snow et al., 1998) which takes this stance. In a key note address to the 1999 International Conference of the United Kingdom Reading Association (UKRA), Marilyn Jaeger Adams one of the authors of the report saw the three main 'stumbling blocks' to children developing as fluent readers being: not fully understanding the 'alphabetic principle', not actively using comprehension strategies, and not having any real motivation to engage with their learning. The report outlines the principles underpinning a reading curriculum for first to third grade children in order to 'prevent' reading difficulties. These principles are:

- a focus on sounds within spoken words and their connection to letters and spelling;
- the importance of teaching children to use letter–sound relationships when they read and therefore to developing the word recognition accuracy necessary for fluent reading;
- explicit teaching of comprehension strategies;

- children being encouraged to use their developing knowledge in their writing, being encouraged for instance to use invented spellings;
- explicit teaching of spelling and the expectation of increasing accuracy;
- daily independent reading of 'texts selected to be of particular interest for the individual student, and beneath the student's frustration level';
- daily 'assisted or supported reading and re-reading' of slightly more difficult texts;
- the promotion of independent reading outside school.

Considering these principles in the light of the British National Literacy Strategy makes interesting reading. They do appear to confirm the rationale that underpins the teaching strategies and objectives now being implemented in our primary schools.

Struggling readers in the literacy hour

So, within The National Literacy Strategy programme, struggling readers get daily literacy hours with the rest of the class, some 'Additional Literacy Support' if they are in years 3 and 4, perhaps further individual work with a classroom assistant (who may or may not be a special needs assistant), and perhaps extra time from the class teacher. How best to provide for them can be discussed under three headings:

- Watching, Listening, Assessing
- Generic Teaching and Learning
- Teaching Strategies For Literacy

Watching, listening, assessing

Watching and listening to children with reading difficulties involves trying to get beneath their surface behaviours and inability to answer our questions. It means trying to work out what children think and feel about themselves as not very successful learner readers. If we simply plough on with more teaching it is unlikely these children will really engage with it as their feelings and confusions will get in the way of them making the necessary connections. And learning is all about making connections. We can learn a lot just from watching. Regularly, during the whole class elements of the Hour, instead of the classroom assistant sitting with the children (perhaps supporting a child), she can sit at the front and observe the behaviour of targeted children. Are they joining in the shared reading? Do they put their hands up to try and answer questions? Do they ask questions? Do they contribute to the word/sentence level work? In the plenary do they appear to know what they have learned? Do they shuffle a lot, gaze around the room and appear to be on a different planet?

Listening to children means giving them the chance to ask questions and comment on their own work and learning. They may require a great deal of time and help. One key element of learning is meta-cognition – reflecting on one's own thinking and learning. Struggling readers are often children who do not do this. They do not think this is the game they need to play in the classroom. They just try and do the work that has been set, regardless of whether it makes any sense to them.

Reading tests can help us understand what a child can and cannot do as a reader. This information is obviously vital. However assessment needs to be enriched with what we learn about this child from watching and the encouragement to articulate what they think and feel.

Generic teaching and learning

The National Literacy Strategy contains a great deal of advice about teaching and learning that has nothing to do with the teaching of reading and writing. It is about strategies that are applicable in any lesson. An example is the recommendation that lessons should end with a plenary – a chance to reflect on what has been learned. This is as important in a Literacy Hour as it is in an art or a PE lesson.

So, in addition to being encouraged to reflect on their own learning (or lack of learning!) what are the key aspects of teaching and learning for struggling readers? Perhaps the most important issues centre on the notion of learners being clear what it is they are expected to learn. They should have explicit short- and long-term targets which have been 'agreed' with the teacher, and the belief that they can achieve them. Children with reading difficulties, more than other learners, need to know where they are going, how to get there and be motivated to succeed. So the Individual Education Plans must be clear to both teacher and child and contain short-term targets that are explicitly reviewed, as well as longer-term targets for, say, termly review. These reviews are not just about words learnt or books finished or worksheets completed but about what the child sees as major areas of progress in learning as well as the problems, so that the learner begins to take control of their own learning and think about it. The best motivation does not come from external incentives but from within – the learner's own drive to succeed. So often I have found myself observing such children working individually or in a small group with a teacher or classroom assistant. Posing the question to either the child or the teacher, 'When is all this going to work in terms of catching up with peers and becoming a fluent reader?' often seems to be a slap in the face for dedicated people. Yet if the work is simply 'to be done' with no aim of eventual success what is the point of doing it? Both teachers and children need to be clear about what success will look like and believe that it is attainable within a given time frame.

A second, connected issue is the need for children to be aware of the teaching/learning objectives for the lesson and week. Many teachers now write these up at the beginning of a lesson and discuss them with the class on the basis that lots of things happen in complex lessons and it is handy for learners to know which bits are important and need to be understood and learnt. Plenaries are then conducted which reflect the original objectives.

Also important is a clear understanding of how whole class teaching needs to be varied so that literacy hours do not end up becoming rituals. A child experiencing their first 'full blown' literacy hour in, say, the summer term of the Reception year will experience over 1,000 literacy hours by the time they leave primary school six years later. If schools are not clear about development as children get older then the danger is that literacy hours will simply become rituals, especially for those 'on the edge' of them – and the thinking will stop. This means that whole class teaching needs to be more than just children sat 'as individuals'. For whole class teaching children can sit as individuals, in pairs or (as they get older) in threes or even fours. Now, regularly, questions are posed to the pair or group and no 'hands up' are expected for, say, twenty seconds while an answer is agreed. Similarly plenaries need to be more than just going from group to group with each group reporting on their own work. There are many variations for plenaries, for example groups sending envoys to other groups who explain what has been done and report back on what another group has achieved. All children require such variations in order to keep them thinking, but for children with reading difficulties these teaching formats maximise the chance of them remaining involved and feeling part of the many literacy hours in which they will (hopefully) participate.

Teaching strategies for literacy

Finally we need to remember that the key teaching strategies recommended in the National Literacy Strategy are powerful strategies for struggling readers. There is Shared Reading, with its emphasis on both the sight and the sound of texts – the latter being the modelling of the 'tunes in the head' which readers need for different text types – so that struggling readers see and hear fluent reading. A key strategy here for older children is the teacher picking out particular sentences, reading them aloud with children listening to the pace and intonation and then have the children practising in pairs the same intonation patterns before some read the sentences to the rest of the class. Shared writing enables us to focus on specific sentence and word level objectives while constructing a text with children – perhaps pointing out, in passing, particular spelling ideas e.g. suffixes, or turning suggestions from children into particular sentence structures which we want them to develop in their writing. For struggling readers 'interactive writing' is a powerful variation, in which the teacher constructs the text with a class or group but children volunteer to do the writing itself. In both shared reading and writing we are working above the level of the children and therefore well above the level of struggling readers in a mixed ability class. If the gulf is too wide in the whole class setting, some thought must be given to children with reading difficulties accessing such teaching as members of smaller groups. Guided and Supported Reading as recommended in the Additional Literacy Support Programme are useful ways of approaching small group reading.

The need for explicit word and sentence level work to clarify and extend knowledge of the writing system itself is a key feature of literacy hours and of great importance to struggling readers. There has been much debate concerning the ways in which such sessions should taught. Should we teach within a context (e.g. finding words beginning with 'ch' in a big book) or focus just on the language itself (a list of 'ch' words on the blackboard)? Of course the debate should not be about an either/or approach but about an important teaching pattern which makes sense to all children but which struggling readers require more than most. So, for instance

- Begin in context: look for 'ch' words in a text which has been read, enjoyed and understood
- Decontextualise: write the 'ch' words on a flip chart, play with them, add to them
- Look for other contexts: who can find a 'ch' word somewhere else. In the classroom, the street, the shops, at home, on television etc.

Decontextualising ensures that children really do focus on the language feature itself. If 'ch' words are being considered in the context of a 'big book' we cannot be sure all children will be focused on them. Some may well be. But others will perhaps be trying to read the rest of the page or recalling the story or noticing the happy ant in the bottom left corner of the illustration or whatever.

This teaching pattern noted above has been used with struggling readers in other ways, for instance:

- read a sentence in a book
- write the sentence on a card and compare it with the original

- take away the book (the context), cut the sentence into words, mix up the words and try to reform the sentence
- cut up the words in the sentence and examine their parts.

Texts for struggling readers

Finally we must be on our guard against providing all children, but especially struggling readers, with a curriculum in which everything which is read is 'on the edge' of their reading ability. A 'difficult' text for shared reading is fine because the teacher is in charge of the reading; a 'just right' text (not too easy, not too difficult) is fine for guided reading with the teacher introducing it and being available for support. But what about the 'easy' text? If the 'reading book' for independent reading has also been selected to be 'just right' then where will children get the reading volume which lies at the heart of overcoming the negative aspect of The Matthew Effect? Keen readers read lots – and most of it is 'easy' (adults are none too pleased if their holiday read turns out to be on the edge of their own reading ability!). So, a good pattern for reading books is a 'just right' book followed by a few easy books that provide both volume and the chance to relax with reading. In the Literacy Hour we can provide opportunities for children to read both levels of text together, in properly structured paired reading sessions. The guidance in the NLS states that in the 'independent time' children should be engaged in either independent reading (i.e. reading independent of the teacher), independent writing (i.e. writing independent of the teacher) or word/sentence level activities. Given the good track record of paired reading discussed earlier, it (and its counterpart, paired writing) should form a key part of literacy hours from the early years onwards.

The optimal state for learning

This chapter began with a quotation concerning the optimum state for learning as 'High Challenge, Low Stress'. For children who have experienced years of failure in an aspect of school life that they know is so important, providing this optimum state is not easy. How struggling readers feel about learning to read and about themselves as 'reading failures' is as important as how they think about texts and sentences and words. This will determine their motivation to engage with teaching and their own learning. Establishing high challenge but low stress for these children is a major challenge facing teachers in the National Literacy Strategy.

Questions for personal reflection or group discussion

1 Do you believe all children in mainstream classrooms can be taught to read?
2 What expectations do you have for struggling readers in Key Stage Two?
3 If motivation is a key to getting struggling readers to engage with teaching, how can we go about motivating them?
4 In what ways can we ensure struggling readers are aware of their short-term and long-term targets?
5 How should parents of struggling readers be involved in the support?
6 What are the dangers of a national target which still leaves 20 per cent of children on low levels of attainment at the end of Key Stage Two?

Recommended readings

Bentley D. and Reid D. (1995) *Supporting Struggling Readers*. United Kingdom Reading Association Minibook 6, Royston: UKRA. One of the very successful books in the UKRA series, this contains clear theoretical underpinning and practical ways forward for the class teacher.

Calver J., Ranson S., Smith D. (1999) *Key Stage 2: Helping Children With Reading Difficulties*, Tamworth: National Association for Special Education Needs (NASEN). Contains a clear review of current thinking together with explicit links to the National Literacy Strategy.

Clay M. (1993) *Reading Recovery: A Guidebook for Teachers in Training*, London: Heinemann. This handbook for reading recovery teachers gives the opportunity to engage with Marie Clay's theory and practice. Lots of food for thought especially in terms of how we can view struggling readers and their often confused ideas about the reading process.

Leeds LEA (1997) *Sustained Reading Intervention: Handbook For Primary, Secondary and Special Schools*. The result of an initiative within one LEA, this loose-leaf handbook contains sections on assessment, a training programme, and parental involvement. In addition there are many practical activities and photocopiable pro forma for monitoring, assessment and teaching.

Bibliography

Brooks, G. (1998) 'What's Happening In Literacy?' *NFER News Autumn/Winter*.

Brooks, G., Flanagan, N., Henkhuzens, Z. and Hutchinson, D. (1998) *What Works for Slow Readers? The Effectiveness of Early Intervention Schemes*. Slough: National Foundation for Educational Research.

Clay, M. (1991) *Becoming Literate*. London: Heinemann.

Clipson-Boyles, S., Bentley, D. and Reid, D. (1998) *The Catch Up Project*. Oxford: Oxford Brooks University.

Department for Education and Employment (1998) *The National Literacy Strategy: Framework for Teaching*. London: HMSO.

Department for Education and Employment (1999) *The National Literacy Strategy: Additional Literacy Support*. London: HMSO.

Martin, T. (1989) *The Strugglers*. Milton Keynes: Open University Press.

Moore. M. and Wade, B. (1998) 'Reading Recovery: Its Effectiveness In the Long Term' in *Support For Learning*, Vol. 13 (3) August, 123–8.

OFSTED (1993) *Reading Recovery in New Zealand*. London: HMSO.

OFSTED (1998) *The National Literacy Project: An HMI Evaluation*. London: HMSO.

Smith, A. (1996) *Accelerated Learning In The Classroom*, Dunstable: Framework Educational Press.

Snow, C.E, Burns, M.S and Griffin, P. (eds) (1998) *Preventing Reading Difficulties in Young Children*. Washington DC: National Academy Press.

Stanovich, K. (1986) 'Matthew Effects In Reading: Some Consequences Of Individual Differences In The Acquisition Of Literacy' *Reading Research Quarterly*, Vol. 21, 360-407.

Topping, K. J. and Lindsay, G.A. (1992) 'The Structure And Development Of The Paired Reading Technique', *Journal Of Research In Reading* , Vol 15 (2), 120–136.

Topping, K. *et al.* (1999) *Read On*. Dundee: University of Dundee.

Index